On the Ruins of My Home; The Destruction of Siedlce (Siedlce, Poland)

Translation of
Oyf di khurves fun mayn heym (khurbn Shedlets)

Original Book Edited by: Melech Fainzilber

Originally published in Tel Aviv 1952

JewishGen
מרכז עולמי לגנאלוגיה יהודית
The Global Home for Jewish Genealogy

A Publication of JewishGen, INC
Edmond J. Safra Plaza, 36 Battery Place, New York, NY 10280
646.494.5972 | info@JewishGen.org | www.jewishgen.org

MUSEUM OF
JEWISH HERITAGE
A LIVING MEMORIAL
TO THE HOLOCAUST

On the Ruins of My Home; The Destruction of Siedlce (Siedlce, Poland)

Translation of *Oyf di khurves fun mayn heym (khurbn Shedlets)*

Copyright © 2022 by JewishGen, INC All rights reserved.
First Printing: January 2022, Shevat 5782

Editor of Original Yizkor Book: Melech Fainzilber
Project Coordinator: David Aron Mink
Layout and Name Indexing: Jonathan Wind
Reproduction of Photographs: Sondra Ettlinger
Cover Design: Rachel Kolokoff Hopper

Printed in the United States of America by Lightning Source, Inc.

Library of Congress Control Number (LCCN): 2021952276

ISBN: 978-1-954176-30-0 (hard cover: 190 pages, alk. paper)

About JewishGen.org

JewishGen, an affiliate of the Museum of Jewish Heritage - A Living Memorial to the Holocaust, serves as the global home for Jewish genealogy.

Featuring unparalleled access to 30+ million records, it offers unique search tools, along with opportunities for researchers to connect with others who share similar interests. Award winning resources such as the Family Finder, Discussion Groups, and ViewMate, are relied upon by thousands each day.

In addition, JewishGen's extensive informational, educational and historical offerings, such as the Jewish Communities Database, Yizkor Book translations, InfoFiles, Family Tree of the Jewish People, and KehilaLinks, provide critical insights, first-hand accounts, and context about Jewish communal and familial life throughout the world.

Offered as a free resource, JewishGen.org has facilitated thousands of family connections and success stories, and is currently engaged in an intensive expansion effort that will bring many more records, tools, and resources to its collections.

Please visit https://www.jewishgen.org/ to learn more.

Executive Director: Avraham Groll

About the JewishGen Yizkor Book Project

Yizkor Books (Memorial Books) were traditionally written to memorialize the names of departed family and martyrs during holiday services in the synagogue (a practice that still exists in many synagogues today).

Over the centuries, as a result of countless persecutions and horrific atrocities committed against the Jews, Yizkor Books (Sefer Zikaron in Hebrew) were expanded to include more historical information, such as biographical sketches of famous personalities and descriptions of daily town life.

Following the Holocaust, the idea of remembrance and learning took on an urgent and crucial importance. Survivors of the Holocaust sought out other surviving residents of their former towns to memorialize and document the names and way of life of those who were ruthlessly murdered by the Nazis. These remembrances were documented in Yizkor Books, hundreds of which were published in the first decades after the Holocaust.

Most of these books were published privately, or through landsmanshaftn (social organizations comprised of members originating from the same European town or region) that still existed, and were often distributed free of charge. Sadly, the languages used to document these crucial histories and links to our past, Yiddish and Hebrew, are no longer commonly understood by a significant percentage of Jews today. As a result, JewishGen has undertaken the sacred responsibility of translating these books into English so that the culture and way of life of these communities will be preserved and transmitted to future generations.

In 1986, a group of farsighted JewishGenners started a project to pool their efforts together in groups based upon their ancestors from each town and donate money to get the Yizkor books of their ancestral towns translated into English. As the translated material became available, it was made accessible for free at www.JewishGen.org/Yizkor. Hardcover copies can be purchased by visiting www.JewishGen.org/Press (see below).

It is our hope that the translation of these books into English (and other languages) will assist the countless Jewish family researchers who are so desperately seeking to forge a connection with their heritage.

Director of JewishGen Yizkor Book Project: Lance Ackerfeld

About the JewishGen Press

JewishGen Press (formerly the Yizkor Books-in-Print Project) is the publishing division of JewishGen.org, and provides a venue for the publication of non-fiction books pertaining to Jewish genealogy, history, culture, and heritage.

In addition to the Yizkor Book category, publications in the Other Non-Fiction category include Shoah memoirs and research, genealogical research, collections of genealogical and historical materials, biographies, diaries and letters, studies of Jewish experience and cultural life in the past, academic theses, and other books of interest to the Jewish community.

Please visit https://www.jewishgen.org/press/ to learn more.

Director of JewishGen Press: Joel Alpert
Managing Editor - Jessica Feinstein
Publications Manager - Susan Rosin

Notes to the Reader

The images in the original book were reproduced from photographs from the time of the first edition. These reproductions were already of poor quality, being pre-war and at least 30 or more years old. As a result the images in the book are not very good and the best achievable.

A reader can view the original scans of the book on the websites listed below.

The original book can be seen online at the New York Public Library site:

https://digitalcollections.nypl.org/items/d0cabd20-3ebc-0133-9fdd-00505686a51c#/?uuid=d10db520-3ebc-0133-b48d-00505686a51c

or

at the Yiddish Book Center web site:

https://www.yiddishbookcenter.org/collections/yizkor-books/yzk-nybc314398/oyf-di-hurves-fun-mayn-heym-hurbn-shedlets

To obtain a list of all Shoah victims from Shedlets (Siedlce) the reader should access the Yad Vashem web site listed below; one can also search for specific family names using family name option. These lists are continually updated by Yad Vashem, so it is worthwhile to periodically search these lists.

There is more valuable information (including the Pages of Testimony, etc.) available on this website: http://yvng.yadvashem.org

A list of all books available from JewishGen Press along with prices is available at: https://www.jewishgen.org/press/

Acknowledgements

I owe enormous gratitude and thanks to Ted Steinberg, who took on the translation of this Yiskor book more as a mitzvah than as an assignment. This was an emotional and spiritual experience and I am grateful for Ted's dedication.

I also want to acknowledge Michael Haber, the last Jewish resident of Siedlce, who explained to me why this book, of the three books about the Jewish community in Siedlce, was the most important.

Thanks also to Lance Ackerfeld, director of the Yiskor Book Project for JewishGen , who kept us on track.

And most of all, thanks to JewishGen which has taken on this immense project of facilitating the translation of over 1000 books of the memory of European Jewish communities. Through JewishGen's efforts, the world will have these eye-witness accounts of the Shoah for the world to see.

David Mink

Credits for Book Cover

Front Cover:

Front Cover Illustration: *The Great Shul in Siedlce. Burned by the Nazis on the night of December 24, 1939.* Page 19.

Front Cover Background Photo: *Fall Grass* by Rachel Kolokoff Hopper

Back Cover:

Back Cover Poem: Excerpt from *In the City of Slaughter* by Hayim Nahman Bialik. Page 6.

Back Cover Photographs:
Top Right: *The 80-year-old community and Zionist leader Moyshe Eisenstadt and his wife Itta. They were taken in the first aktion to Treblinka.* Page 47.

Bottom Right: *People begin taken to the Treblinka death train.* Page 48 (original page 80).

Left Middle: *Founders of Ezras Y'somim in 1903. Sitting, from right to left: Simcha Rubinstein, Moses Greenfarb, Yitzchak Eli Zucker, Dr. Moyshe Temkin Second row: Shia Zilbergleyt, Vulf Tuchklapper, Minia Weintraub, Madszia Cahana, Libba Zeidentzeig, Berl Mintz.* Page 135.

Back Cover Background Images:
Street Map. Page 169.

Part of the Original Cover. Page 2.

GeoPolitical Information

Siedlce, Poland is located at 52°10' N 22°18' E and 55 miles E of Warszawa

	Town	District	Province	Country
Before WWI (c. 1900):	Siedlce	Siedlce	Siedlce	Russian Empire
Between the wars (c. 1930):	Siedlce	Siedlce	Lublin	Poland
After WWII (c. 1950):	Siedlce			Poland
Today (c. 2000):	Siedlce			Poland

Alternate Names for the Town:

Siedlce [Pol], Shedlitz [Yid], Sedlets [Rus], Shedlits, Shedlets, Sedl'tse, Sedlce

Nearby Jewish Communities:

Zbuczyn 8 miles SE
Mordy 10 miles ENE
Mokobody 11 miles NW
Sokołów Podlaski 16 miles N
Łuków 18 miles SSE
Łosice 18 miles ENE
Seroczyn 19 miles SW
Węgrów 20 miles NW
Liw 21 miles NW
Stoczek Łukowski 21 miles SW
Kałuszyn 21 miles W
Drohiczyn 22 miles NE
Miedzna 22 miles NNW
Stok 24 miles SSE
Międzyrzec Podlaski 24 miles ESE
Sarnaki 27 miles ENE
Dobre 29 miles WNW
Sterdyń 29 miles N
Siennica 29 miles W
Żelechów 30 miles SW
Parysów 30 miles WSW
Radzyń Podlaski 30 miles SSE
Adamów 30 miles S

Jewish Population: 11,440 (in 1897), 14,793 (in 1931)

BALTIC SEA

LITHUANIA

RUSSIA

Vilnius

POLAND

GERMANY

BELARUS

Berlin

Poznan

Warsaw

Siedlce

Lodz

Prague

CZECH REPUBLIC

Krakow

UKRAINE

SLOVAKIA

unich

AUSTRIA

250 miles

250 Km   500 Km

POLAND – CURRENT BORDERS

Map of Poland with **Siedlce** indicated

TABLE OF CONTENTS

On the Ruins of My Home;
The Destruction of Siedlce
(Siedlce, Poland)

54°06' / 22°56'

Translation of
Oyf di khurves fun mayn heym (khurbn Shedlets)

Editor: Melech Fainzilber

Published in Tel Aviv, 1952

Acknowledgments

Project Coordinator:

David Aron Mink

Emeritus Coordinator Michael Halber

Translated by:

Theodore Steinberg

This is a translation of: *Oyf di khurves fun mayn heym (khurbn Shedlets)*
(On the ruins of my home; the destruction of Siedlce),
Editor: Melech Fainzilber, Tel Aviv, 1952 (Y 260 pages).

Note: The original book can be seen online at the NY Public Library site: Siedlce (1952)

אלימלך פיינזילבער

אויף די חורבות פון מיין היים

(חורבן שעדלעץ)

תל־אביב   1952

Elymelakh Faynzilber

On the Ruins of my Home
(The Destruction of Siedlce)

This is book has been published by the organizational committee of former residents and friends:

**Monish Ridel (chairman). Leon Gliksberg (treasurer),
Itzchak Arzshel, Abrahm Moisheh Zilbershtayn, Aryeh Liberman, Israel Tabakman,
Yehudeh Mayer Finkelshtayn, B.N. Shlifkeh, Dovid Lustik, Dov Levin, Shmuel Lev, Mendl Burshtin and the writers:
Yuel Mantboym, Dr. M. Dvarzhetsky, Gavril Vaisman, Mordche Yubdyhu (God's servant),
K. Shavtai, Eliezer Rubinshtayn, Layb Rabman and theatrical director, film maker Yakov Mansdorf.**

Illustrated By: **Itschak Margolis**

[Page 3]

This remembrance is dedicated (sanctified) to my beloved mother Tobeh, my brothers: Motl, Yakov, Shlomeh, Dovid and sister Esther along with their families, who were murdered in the death camp Majdanek; my wife, Chana–Rivkeh (of the heat: during the holiday), died on the road while wandering – in far off Uzbekistan and – my community that was cut short. The 25,000 victims of Siedlce and surrounding towns, who were murdered as martyrs at the hands of the German unclean (impure, contaminated) men.

[Page 4]

A Few Words

by Yoel Mastboym

Translated by Rita Ratson

Elymelech Fainzilber's book, "The Destruction of Siedlce" has, understandably, not been able to embrace and draw out all the precious fabric of the city of Siedlce. But it is a significant (important) and earnest work about the past and the present, where the precious threads of life are braided together after generations of people, who have fought stubbornly for a better and more beautiful life.

With great perfection (completion) this writer describes the ideas and people, who lived and fought in this particular city, which considers itself as one of the avenged cities in Jewish Poland. With enthusiasm and that fire of life of youth, the Jews of Siedlce threw themselves into the rows of the Zionist builders and fighters, exactly as the Jewish workers of Siedlce threw themselves with all of their fire of enthusiasm, into the Revolutionary lines in 1905, which had a very strong effect on the general environment.

In distinct colors it was successful for Feinzilber to show the character of people and personalities. We see people with peculiar characteristics, quite different from other cities. With this, Feinzilber successfully shows us the character (personality) and peculiarity (originality) of generations of Jews, who lived in Siedlce.

Understandably, it was possible to add to this book even more interesting episodes of Siedlce of the past. Feinzilber only heard about the past, and described it in a proper tone, but most importantly A. Feinzilber brings out the terrible Hitler years of destruction and devastation.

It is understandable that in this book, there are also merely – some descriptions which are simply long and some have been taken from people who do not say very much. But in general, this book has an important value, not only just for people who lived in the city, but also for the entire world, who will learn a great deal from the past of the spirited city Siedlce.

[Page 5]

A word from the author

Translated by Rita Ratson

It is difficult to write about the Holocaust (The Destruction) of one's own city, about one's own beloved people, families, friends, and neighbors, and those who are now gone, like a bit of scattered ash, thrown about, bones not having been burned up, grave stones broken into pieces, crumbled into small pieces in the streets, and with grass covered hills, like tombs (graves) in the places of their homes.

It is difficult to touch upon and immerse oneself (look into, investigate) into materials, which expose, how our own, close ones, beloved and dear ones, were tortured by hunger and crowdedness, by dirt and epidemics, how they choked in the gas chambers, were shot or were chopped up by dull blades, were buried alive: materials which tell the story of, how children were quartered or received bullets into their opened up mouths, in their eyes, or in the arms of their mothers.

But, when I wandered through the destruction of our destroyed home, on the grave diggers of our Jewish community which has been cut short, having seen and heard everything, which the very few survivors tell about, I thought and I came to the conclusion: if by blind chance, coincidence was the cause, that the sad lots did not divide the community and one survived accidentally, then this is obligated to something. We must pay a great and holy debt (duty), that we owe to our tragic, cut short community: to mark by virtue of proving and by this, which the survivors tell about, and with this to carry out, realize, fulfill, the law of memory and, from the Haggadah, narrating the tale: "the day you have a child you will tell him the story of what happened" – to tell the story to the generations to be delivered (yet unborn), the story of their struggle to survive and suffering as well as learning something from this.

I have begun to mark down, collect, to write, and in addition to this I was forced to fight various interruptions and difficulties: difficult illness, which interrupted my work for a long time: homelessness and the wonderful road to Israel, as well as to fight with the indifferent ice – cold respect, regard from our people who come from our own towns (landsmen), in the country and in other countries, who do not, did not only show any sort of aide to appear in the book, but were not even willing to respond to any letters, which were written in connection to this work. It seems that people want to forget…

Aiding in the appearance of this book, the organization committee, which was organized for this purpose, is extended a hearty thank you, as well as for their encouragement and deep thankfulness to the writers:

Yual Mastboym, Dr. M. Dvorzshetsky, Gavril Vaisman, Mordkheh Yubdyu, K. Shafty, Alyur Rubinshtayn, Layb Robman, Yakov Mansdorf, from Rezshis.

A great job well done is extended to my friend, the writer Gavril Vaisman for his substantial and practical aide with helping to prepare this book to print, as well as to my cousin, Yehuda Mayer Finkleshtayn for his help with copying the manuscript on the typewriter – they all now say that the author is to receive a public and heartfelt thank you.

This book does not pretend to be the complete monument to our destroyed (devastated) home city and the destroyed, castrated community. Too great is the destruction, that a sole person, an individual, should be able to draw out, gather everything that is to be told. This particular book is a modest explanation, interpretation, contribution to a monument such as this.

I have just about touched upon this tragic chapter, which is called: Jewish council and Jewish police, but – having avoided to pass judgement, while keeping with the rule of: "do not judge until you walk in his shoes"…and I was not in their position.

Due to various reasons, a significant part of my noted work was not included in this edition, most importantly about various institutions, fraternal organizations, parties and figures of Siedlce. Only a few of them are included here. The others will be included in a second edition.

[Page 7]

---

1. Returning Home

Translated by Rita Ratson

Edited by Theodore Steinberg

During those bleak days of horror and terror, when the bloody exterminator spread his black wings across the greatest part of Europe, the bitter news came to us in distant middle Asia where that war-storm had carried us—that our that our beloved homes had been utterly destroyed and the lives of our dearest ones, our closest ones, had been cut off.

This terrible news disturbed our distressed souls and filled us with a terrifying sadness.

We clung to the smallest shadow of a hope, which each of us took pains to maintain. This was expressed in the unspoken: maybe I will, at any rate, meet someone there yet? Even more strengthened did the hope become during those long, grey days and nights, which we found ourselves in, in the cars of that long transport train that snaked itself, carrying us over the broad steppes of Kazakhstan and the wide Russian fields and carried us to the direction of our abandoned home. That rocking of the train cars, accompanied by that rhythmic music of the wheels, which for several weeks caressed our broken spirit, was like a remedy calling out in our sleep and in half-awake slumber beautiful, sweet hallucinations and dreams about hot tears, which flow down the face about an old mother, whom we have left behind there; about emotional kisses, which cling to a discovered brother; and about the aroma of warm arms, when you find yourself embraced by a rescued sister.

But dreams, even beautiful, sweet ones, cannot be held onto for long. They melted right away, as the train brought us to the ground of our tragic reality.

Our sober mood was reinforced by the "welcome reception" that a gang of scoundrels gave us immediately at the border: as soon as the train reached Polish soil, they pelted the cars of the freight trains with a hail of stones, and joyfully called out:

[Page 8]

"Away with the Jews!"
And there was something symbolic to this, that our train cars were led to the "worked over soil" and showed us, before we become acquainted with our own ruins, the ruins of the German cities: those large piles of stones, brick and scrap – iron, under which there are buried many of those murderers of our destroyed, murdered people. Our lips quietly murmured a prayer: "May those hand be blessed which took revenge for our needlessly cut short lives…"

Anywhere we were able to find a roof over our heads and throw off from our tired backs those poor bundles that have accompanied our road of wandering for thousands of years already, our first thought was: to travel to visit our parents' graves, to shed a tear for our destroyed, devastated home, and to tear our clothes as a sign of mourning over that scattered ash of our dear beloved ones, and also to seek—maybe? maybe?…

We carried with us Ch. N. Bialik's lines:

> Of steel and iron, cold and hard and silent,
> forge a heart for yourself, you human being – and come!
> Come, go to the city of slaughter, massacre, you should see with your eyes
> you should touch with your own hands,
> on fences, posts, gates and walls,
> on stones in the street, on all the blocks of wood,
> that blood that has dried to black with the brains
> of your brother's heads and throats.
> So I took to the road, to go to the city of slaughter.

Entering the wagon car in the train station of the large city, we received that proper "reception," as it was proper for guests who have not been seen for a long time: a wild laughter accompanied by whispering at my expense and those of my two companion. That whispering was accompanied by a fresh winking of the eyes of the well-known Polish non–righteous, who recall at every word that emerges from their observant lips the holy young lady Maria and her son Jesus; and soon there follows a clear commentary:
"To the devil! People say that Hitler murdered all those dirty Jews, so now—where did so many come from again?"The preacher of these words was a middle–aged blonde man, with a satisfied, happy, satiated face, a pointy mustache and watery eyes, constantly in motion, for whom the presence of the three Jews on the train car (a thing,that he had not seen for several years already), was an irritation, like a hungry wolf, who just catches the whiff of fresh roasted meat…

[Page 9]

A long conversation ensued about familiar themes. We were forced to listen all night long to the forever old–new songs, which we have hear "from Egypt until here," and the principally how we have sinned, for which there I can be no repentance. For instance: for killing the creator of Christendom: for killing Christian children for ritual purposes; for poisoning wells; for spreading epidemics, communism, socialism, heresy, and whatever more? And he concluded that Hitler was right, that the Jews should have been exterminated long ago already.

Understandably, we, the three Jews in the car, were not able to take part in such conversations, we only thought to ourselves: (a thing that no one can prevent-) it is a shame that God had sworn that He would bring no floods to the world any longer. How useful would such a bath be now, like that in the time of Noah, which should wash away this dirt that has collected, in our dear world…

A hoarse proclamation by a sleepy train–watchman, "Warsaw Main," interrupted the conversations of our righteous train neighbors and the thoughts of three Jewish wandering souls, who seek the ashes of their destroyed homes…

At the "Warsaw East–Station," where we arrived several hours before our train's departure for Siedlce, we buried our eyes, in vain, into every passerby's face, looking at everyone who hurried by, searching for a familiar face, an acquaintance. There are none. On this cool, mild spring evening, a wind blows from everyone's eyes and from the entire train station's surroundings, a cold strangeness. If any passerby had slowed his pace and fixed his gaze at us, as if at an exotic wonder, we read this question in his eyes: "What, there are Jews here again?"

Gone are the Jews who lived outside of the towns and cities, with their baskets and tins belonging to their poverty–stricken trade. Gone are the daily travelers of the past, those shipping agents and the commissioners of Minsk, Kalushzin, Siedlce – the Zlatowskys, the Eizenbergs and Gutgolds,with their specifically Jewish haste, laden with variously colored and all sorts of stuffed packages with which they used to honor every one of their acquainted fellow travelers, asking for help in carrying their packages through the baggage check.

[Page 10]

If we had ever carried a grudge against these Jews, who on never rested and did not allow another to rest, with their annoying insistence and mobility, with their long, black caftans and bearded faces—we now walk in the evening's darkness, in the tight, narrow train car in which our gnawing hearts pine away for them.

And not only does one's own heart shrink from pining and from sorrow, but all around there is dark sadness; the outside seeps through the small train windows: all the houses, everything is shattered: all those country homes outside of the towns and cities: in the whistle of the locomotive it seems as if one hears the sound of a crying child. One sees that mourning particularly in that small train station: Rembertow–Milosneh–Minsk–Morozy. It seems that they got shorter, grew closer to the ground, sitting in mourning for their disappeared Jewish passengers, who brought ease and comfort to the stations and without them there reigns an air of hardened emptiness and silence, which becomes disturbed, only at times, by a long yawn of a sleepy passenger. Also, that small shimmering light, which falls lonely and embarrassed from the tall station lamps – it seems, like a NerTamid that burned in memory of the disappeared Jewish passengers.

After four hours of tiresomely dragging oneself from Warsaw to Siedlce – instead of the hour and a half of the past – the train comes to a stop at eleven at night at the collapsed ruins and heaps of grass of the once-beautiful train station. The heart beats more heavily: with heat, the blood pounds to the brain as we tread the threshold of our home town, which that bloody destroyer, forced us to leave seven years ago, certainly half destroyed already, but still with twenty thousand living people, our own people, loving sisters and brothers. And now one thinks, worries: will I find a Jewish home, to go to, to spend the night? And a wonder! While watching pensively the very few passengers getting off the train, by the soft, embarrassed light of the station lamp (one wants to say "from the New Tamid)) I happened to meet a familiar Jewish face: Miss Sukenik, a member of the Pioneer Youth Organization from the past. She was also searching for the same, among the passengers, as I was.

[Page 11]

Quietly she expressed her satisfaction that she would not need to go on her own to that destroyed city in the darkness, at such a late hour.

We go together. I walk automatically behind my guide. Everything in our surroundings k stubbornly holds its breath and we try to hold our breath as well. The silence of a cemetery. We hear nothing except for our own steps, which we try to keep treading more quietly as well. Everything is wrapped in a thick uncommon darkness, which takes a hold of us and impedes our gait. The meaning of the old biblical expression runs through our thoughts, that there in Egypt, of course, there must also have been such bleakness. "But in that darkness in Egypt, Jews went from slavery to freedom and He bestowed upon us wealth" and we came back to life. And the darkness that remained after the present bloody deluge tells the story of something different…and when this thick darkness becomes disturbed by an orphaned band of light, which tears itself away somewhere in embarrassment, out through a window, it falls against us on a smoky skeleton of a former house, whose intestines were wildly engulfed in fire, and is standing now, naked and embarrassed and loudly shouts its silent pain to the deaf world: or onto piles of grass, stones, bricks and iron, which dream in the black night about their noble descendants of the past, when they were still prosperous, dignified, well regarded homes, and complain about their present loneliness and desolate formlessness.

And remarkably! The air is also different. Instead of the Siedlce air of the past, with its specifically delicate moist aroma, which used to softly caress like velvety gentle mother's hands, today it is so hard, dry and heavy that it burns the eyes, chokes the throat, and fills.the entire body with lead; and instead of the natural air of perfume of the past, from the fresh blooming of old, tall chestnut trees, broad, dignified linden trees, and young, slim acacia, which filled the streets of Siedlce on spring evenings – there is the nauseating smell of cemetery air mixed with sour mold and tiny smoke filled drops, which the angel of death left behind after the wild orgy that he performed here.

And when the eyes rise to see how a spring evening looks in the sky above Siedlce, one is annoyed at those small twinkling stars, which still wink down so arrogantly, sweetly – youthfully, exactly like those good times of the past.

[Page 12]

2. In the Ruins

Translated by Theodore Steinberg

I find myself in a home, in my home town of Siedlce, in a Jewish home. I look at the people, at the things in the room; the walls tell everything that has happened. The moving, restless eyes of my hosts, which dart from place to place, also tell. The broken voices with their quiet speech to which they had become accustomed in their underground lives in hiding. The poor broken-up sticks of furniture with their protruding, broken limbs are the few silent witnesses who mutely relate what happened there. Heavy and fearful lies the dark grey gloom that looks out of the despairing damaged walls and from the torn up ceiling that tell of the bitter fate that befell the people who lived there. And when, at my request, my hosts tell a little bit about what he lived through in "those days," one would recall that Italian, Dante, who, with his rich imagination, would give us a picture of how Hell must have looked—or also recall our beloved "Sheet Musar" [*a book by Eliyahu Ha-Cohen*] —who with such innocence depicted the well-known seven levels of Hell—one might say to him: "Come here, dear describer of Hell, and speak with a Jew who went through the Hitler era, and you would change the names of your works to—-pictures of Paradise…

There followed a long sleepless night.

The previous night, our traveling companions had made sure—with their frightening stories—that we could not sleep. And so the next night was also sleepless—thanks to the inner shocks and traumas of returning to the ruined city after seven years.

My host was occupied with finding me a place to sleep that was more comfortable. My body was strained and tired out, but I could not sleep. More powerful than my physical weariness was my frenzied imagination, that would not allow me to forget that there was no more Jewish life, that we would no longer have those whom we had left seven years earlier, and my mind formed one picture after another:

…Now I was on a Shabbos morning in the city park among the strollers who filled all the paths, who occupied all the benches.

[Page 13]

People met friends whom they had not seen all week. People greeted each other and were. Happy. The committees of political parties met there, and representatives of cultural and charitable institutions held meetings.

On a bench in the main path, in the shadow of an old chestnut tree, sat the directors of "Ha-Zamir"; Yosef Rosenzumen, Aaron Shpielfidel, Berl, Czarenebrode, Chaim Schleifer, Moyshe Grabia, Hersh Mendel Shapiro, Menashe Czarnebrode, and for many years—Moyshe Mandelman, and they considered many questions about Ha-Zamir and about the library.

A bit further on, on another bench, at the foot of an old poplar sat Asher Orszel, Levi and Yosef Gutgeld, Yehoshua Akerman, Avraham Shlomo Englander, Shalom Salzman, Henoch Ribak, Moyshe Yudengloyben, and for many years—Fishl Popowski, and they conferred on different Zionist and Tarbus issues.

And there, in front of the summer theater, on the half-open porch, were the proletarian activists: Avraham, Weinapple, Avraham Sluszne, Meir Rzanczaszeva, Yidl Friedrich, who discussed various political and professional matters.

And there, on the grandstand, where the military orchestra played at entertainments in the park, sat Siedlce's literary group: Yakov Tenenbaum, Yehoshua Goldberg, David Greenfarb, Y.Ch. Eisenberg, before whom the young writer Y.F. Greenberg read his newly written story.

And there, a walking meeting: Avraham Bressler, Esther Levenstein, Gutshe Ferster, Leibush Weinstein, Yakov Yom-Tov, Chayah Tenenbaum, Hershel Rosengarten—the directors of Ezras-Y'somim. As they walked, they discussed ways to improve the material and educational conditions of the orphans.

And there again, on a dark side pathway, a Chassidic young man in a long caftan and a small hat walks in an embarrassed manner with intended. And there, in that secluded corner, where no one is walking, an old householder looks around, and when he is sure that there is no "evil eye," he smokes a cigarette with pleasure. And there, between the hill and the shadowed earthen wall, among the thick bushes and young lilac trees, are gathered the young workers for a secret Shabbos "mass meeting."

[Page 14]

They sit there free from their work, on their own time. And on the half-cabin, half-veranda that stands on the hill near the water, a young man stands on guard, looking in all directions in case an unwanted spy approaches.

And there, on the left side of the water, Jewish children are gathered—boys and girls, dressed in their pretty Shabbos clothing. They carry on with ringing voices, clap their little hands, call to the wild geese that swim in the water and feed them the Shabbos challah and cookies that their mothers age them for their Shabbos walk. The park is totally Jewish. Everyone there is Jewish. They all speak Yiddish, sing Yiddish songs, tell Jewish jokes and laugh in Yiddish. And when the breeze blows over the green fields of flowers and trees, they echo it back in Yiddish…

In the evening, before Shabbos ends, Jewish Siedlce has gone strolling on the two main streets: Warsaw and Kilingskieve, on the so-called "promenade," which now has a Shabbos look thanks to the closed shops and workshops. Whom does one not meet there? Pious chassidic Jews, students, who go for their Shabbos "lessons" or to study Pirke-Avos, with their velvet hats and yarmulkes on their learned heads—or they sit down for the third Shabbos meal, singing to the departing Shabbos queen; and there the merchants walk slowly and proudly, their hands clasped behind them, with quiet steps. They do not think about their businesses; they focus, this once in the week, on God's world. And there walk also the craftsmen with their wives and children, all cleaned up, nicely dressed, and agreeable after a week of hard work. Their faces are serene. You can see the pleasure they have derived from their Shabbos rest. And there a group of wives are walking, dressed in their best seasonal clothing and hats, made specially for their Shabbos walks. Each one wanted to outdo the other in elegance and chic; it made an impression as if one were at a traveling fashion show. In addition, older, prosperous ladies, who from Friday on wore well-tended wigs on their shorn heads, dressed in their wedding-clothes that they aired out from Shabbos to Shabbos. They sighed and shook their heads over the modern styles with décolletage and the short, sleeveless clothes worn by the young women and girls.

[Page 15]

There, walking in large packs, were hearty young people—men and women, playing, laughing, with resounding happiness that broke through to even the gloomiest and sourest passersby.

It seemed like a parade. Jewish Siedlce marched on the streets as if it were a holiday, with their Shabbos souls—as Y.L. Peretz had described—before her majesty, the Sabbath queen. As the weekday night approached, the streets emptied. Some people returned to their daily jobs and reopened the stores and workshops.

Some—the younger ones—who wanted to seem like intellectuals with contemporary attitudes went to the films, theaters, and concert halls. Those who were more observant and older sat in their unlighted "prayer houses," from whose open windows came devout songs, and from the observant women one could hear the common womanly tune of "God of Abraham, of Isaac, and of Jacob," until late into the night.

* * *

And thus through the whole night pass these images that are engraved in my memory, molded in blood and marrow, images of everything I experienced and and in which I was a living participant. And while these images burn with fiery heat in my mind and through my whole body, robbing me of sleep, which would be a cure—when it comes—even so the procession of these domestic images lasts for a long time, and I peer at them, as one clings to the monument that stands at the head of a beloved relative's grave.

Blue streaks of light come through the window and announce the arrival of a fresh, new spring day, My weariness disappears; the images dissolve. I am moved to get up and leave the house. I want to see the devastation in the light of day.

Like a religious cantor who approaches the High Holiday Amidah with a quiet prayer of "Hineni he'ani mima'ash," I, with a similar feeling, mixed with fear and discomfort, allow myself to go to the city of slaughter on the ruins of my destroyed home. I look around and recognize in a small remnant of a street that by a miracle was not obliterated that I was on the former Sholem Asch Street. The half-ruined city is still sunk in its early morning nap.

[Page 16]

I begin to walk but…a circle of speakers, multihued, mostly in fiery colors, dance before my eyes and drive the blood through my arteries, sending it forcefully and heatedly Tony heart, to my brain. My feet are immobilized and cannot move. They find themselves among smoothly blasted, black stones with hollowed out white and gold colored letters—recognizable Jewish letters. I look at them with horror and read: [in Hebrew]. "Here lies the upright, righteous, and generous R. Chaim Yakov ben R. Shlomo, who lived all his days righteously, may his memory be a blessing"…I feel pain in my feet, as if a snake bit them or as if there were a fire beneath them. I move from that spot and go on a bit and find myself at a second similar stone with similar letters, and I read: "Here lies the modest woman…Chayah Gittel bas Avraham who went to her reward on…". I cast my gaze further on the blasted sidewalk and see many similar stones lying around and bearing similar inscriptions, with other names. I stand anad wonder: am I dreaming or am I in the cemetery? I feel certain that I am awake. It is no dream, and I am not in the cemetery, because here and there I clearly sees indications of a city. The old water carrier, Joseph, goes by, sees my confusion, sets aside his two pitchers of water, crosses himself, and says: "Do you wonder what this is? The accursed Swabians [an insulting term for the Germans] ordered the monuments to be taken from your cemetery and used for the city sidewalks. That is why I walk in the middle of the street. A righteous Christian would not tread on them.

It all becomes clear to me, and with great sorrow I cry out to myself: "Master of the universe! Is our shame so great?"

---

3. Pienkne Street

Translated by Theodore Steinberg

As if from fire I spring up to an area that is not paved and not plastered. I look around: a plain field, long and wide, is spread out as far as the eye can see, with a mournful, desert-like appearance, overgrown with wild, prickly grasses. Only the tossed about piles of stones and mounds of rubble indicate that houses once stood there and that it was an inhabited street. On the left side stand several abandoned houses, embarrassed, damaged, defaced by bullets. One recognized there the former Pienkne Street – the heart of Jewish Siedlce.

[Page 17]

Generations dwelled there, created and maintained a special kind of Jewish life. No non-Jews lived there, as if not wanting to disturb the specifically Jewish appearance of the street. Jews multiplied there, married off their children, and when a house became too small, they built on a wing or a little building in the courtyard for children, grandchildren, and great-grandchildren. And thus grew the famous Pinkie alleyways that were a symbol of Jewish Siedlce.

There one could see – once – four generations in a single home: an old, gray-haired grandfather with a broad long white beard, with a broad yellow stateliness, the color of parchment, with a forehead full of creases. A grandfather who awakens at midnight, at the first cry of the rooster, and says the midnight prayers, cries over the exile of the Shechinah and the destruction of the Beis-Hamikdash; he fills his days with Torah and prayer, and when anyone will listen to him – he tells stories about the old Kotzker rebbe. Nearby lives his son, already old himself, who runs a business with his children. Early each morning he goes with his overstuffed talis bag and two pairs of tefillin to pray in the prayer house. By day they are involved somewhat in the needs of the community, somewhat in the Talmud Torah. In the evening, between the afternoon and evening prayers, he learns in a study group with other Jews, and when the High Holidays come, he leaves his wife and children and his business and he goes to his rabbi.

Separately, in the built-on wing, lives the grandson, an up-to-date young man, a maskil, who is active in a political party. A member of "Ha-Zamir," still, after fifteen years of marriage, he eats at his in-laws and helps his father in the business, sends his young son to a high school, accompanies him to a football match, at which the grandfather and great-grandfather shake their heads in disapproval.

And if someone has a difficult question about Tosafos and cannot find an answer, or he wants to discuss Chassidus, he comes to the scholarly family on Pienkne Street, to R. Chaim Shmerl Goldzak and his two sons, who live not the income from the bakery that is run by the old mother Toibe and her two daughters; they earn so that the men can sit and study, and the women are prepared to be their footstools after a hundred and twenty years. There the questions will be easily answered, and thus is provided a new insight into the weekly portion according to the teachings of the Chiddushei HaRim [the teachings of the rabbi of Ger].

[Page 18]

And if a person wanted to hear some curious stories about the Polish uprising of 1863, he would go to the elderly Yisroelkele Schlosser (whose name among the people was – "Yeled"), who could always be found at his locksmith's workshop, which he had established some eighty years back and where he worked with his sons grandchildren, and great-grandchildren. One had to shake the hand of old Yisroelke Yeled, who would not let go until the handshaker had to give up because of the pressure. Yisroelke would ask: "What do you say about my hundred and seven years?" The more one allowed him to shake one's hand, the more exciting stories one heard from him. And if one wanted to know the secret of how he had lived to such a healthy old age, he would reply immediately that it was because every day he had drunk early in the morning, on an empty stomach, a glass of pure spirits.

If one wanted to discuss current Zionist or Tarbus matters – which needed immediate attention – one would go to Yehoshua Ackerman on Pienkne Street. He greeted everyone with a friendly, open face and shining eyes, abandoned his business matters and with great respect fielded all questions.

If a small merchant was disgruntled, vexed about his taxes or some other nuisance, he went to his union on Pienkne Street, where he could speak from his heart to the good-natured, always welcoming secretary, Yechiel Meir Zeidenzeig, and he would leave happily, fortified with good advice.

And if someone had to pay for a bit of merchandise that had spent several days at the train station or had to pay off an IOU, take out a patent, or fulfill a vow, he would go to his credit bank on Pienkne Street. He would be apologetic to the bank director and founder R. Monish Ridel, and he would leave happily, having been aided.

And not far away, in the home of the popular workers aid Meir Radzanczadszewe (Shimon Vechter's son), things were always happening. People dealt with serious questions: about declaring a strike of the shoemakers, about calling for a meeting over political detainees, and so on.

[Page 19]

And if one went through Pienkne Street on market days, one would see a crowd of hundreds with heads raised, standing and staring up at the sky. In the middle of this crowd, one would see the most popular man on Pienkne Street, the greatest jokester in Siedlce, R. Feivel Greenspan, who also stood with his head raised, pointing with his forefinger toward the sky. To the questions of why this crowd is there and what they see in the sky, no one can answer, and then Greenspan laughs and calls out: "Animals, why have you gathered here in the marketplace and what are you looking for in the sky?" – Embarrassed, all lower their heads and depart with chagrin that they have allowed themselves to be made fools of.

Going to any home in the Pienkne alleyways, one hears the rasping of a saw or the scraping of a wood plane accompanying the song "The Worker Makes his Goods for Someone" – indicating that there is a carpenter's workshop. And a few steps further on comes the tick-tock of a sewing machine accompanied by Yossele Rosenblatt's "Rachem-na" or Sirota's "K'vakaras" – showing that in that place lives a tailor of the older generation who prays at the Tailor's Shul "Parkhei Shoshanim," which is at 25 Pienkne Street. From a second window emerges another tick-tock from a tailor's machine, this one a bit more desolate, beating in time to Y.L. Peretz' "The Eyes Red, the Lips Blue," sung by a solitary, pale woman at her work; and if one goes a few steps further, one hears the quick pounding of a shoemaker's hammer that beats on the sole of a boot in time to Morris Rosenfeld's "I Have a Young Son."

I see the solemnity that takes over Pienkne Street after half the day on Friday: the street is filled with the aroma of freshly cooked fish and freshly baked challahs. No one walks on Pienkne Street now. They run. The women run with their Erev Shabbos treasures, with their Shabbos baked goods from the bakeries. Tailors run with newly sewn clothes over their arms, and shoemakers run with newly finished boots, shoes"carrying them to the householders who ordered them. Jews run to the mikveh with packs of clean clothing under their arms, and Jews run back from the mikveh, half-dressed, disheveled, sweaty, with drops of mikveh water dripping from their beards. Members of the association "Shomrei Shabbos" [Guardians of Shabbos] run through the streets crying out, "Shabbos! Shabbos!" Soon all the stores and workshops will be closed. Through the windows on Pienkne Street one can see the Shabbos lights, the twinkling of the Shabbos candles.

[Page 20]

kindled with softly whispered prayers and with hand-covered eyes by the Jewish women of Pienkne Street.

Most members of "Ha-Zamir" and readers of Yiddish books have described Pienkne Street and its surrounding alleys that cultivated a specifically Jewish kind of poverty. They have described participants in various pioneer and revolutionary youth organizations. In 1905, throughout the country resounded the contribution that Siedlce made to the revolution. And Siedlce itself knew that this was the greatest service of Pienkne Street and its surroundings. And if one at that time had to clear out of the way czarist official, a worker for the Okhrana, a follower of the Jewish revolutionary youth did Pienkne Street offer up as a voluntary hero, like Moyshe Radzinski (Moshe Gabbai), who carried out such work. And when the czarist dogs engaged in a ferocious pogrom against Siedlce's Jews, they unleashed their greatest fury against Pienkne Street and its surroundings.

The greatest number of Jewish organizations in the city were found on Pienkne Street: the first Jewish people's bank, the so-called Loan Association, the small merchant's bank, the merchant's union, the small merchant's union, all kinds of illegal political organizations and stores, several souls, especially those belonging to certain professions, such as the shoemaker's soul "Parchei Shoshanim," Sheflan's shul, a traveler's home, and others, where everyday, ordinary Jews could study every evening from "Ein Yakov" and a chapter of Mishneh, and there were also many Chasidic prayer houses and charitable fellowships.

But such a disaster? That was all in the past. I see it all in my imagination, in a fantasy. The reality is that I am standing in the cemetery of Jewish Siedlce, near the stones and remnants that remain, a reminder of the destruction, like monuments to an extinct life.

It is now early morning. Once at this hour Pienkne Street would have been full of Jewish children rushing to the Talmud Torah, to the Tarbus, or to the Folk School with their schoolbags on their backs and under their little arms. Where are you, pale Jewish children? It has already been several hours that I have wandered through these ruins, and I have not encountered a single child, nor a single Jew. I walk through an empty field among stones and stinging grass.

[Page 21]

I know that once there was a whole stretch of Jewish streets between Pienkne and Warsaw Streets – Kasze, Pszeyozd, Proste, Szpitalne. I know that I am treading upon the graves of an extinct Jewish life, but will future generations also know when they walk here? Or will no Jewish foot walk here at all?

* * *

Three structures adorned Pienkne Street, not specifically Jewish but of a general city character: on the eastern side stands the old city hall with its specifically Old Polish architectural style, which there founder of Siedlce, Countess Oginska, ordered built for the needs of the city. Then there are the surrounding shops, as a business center. From the city council hall, an underground cavern led to her palace, the old Oginski Palace near the city park. And the last historic building was the city library.

On the lofty tower of the old city council hall stands the naked, gold-colored "Jacek," who has held on his poor shoulders for many generations the heavy burden of the globe, within which could be found, written on parchment, the story of how five hundred years earlier the foundation for the capital city of Podlasie was laid.

On the other side, at the second street corner on the western side, at the exit from the street stands a tall, gray fortress wall with small, barred windows. This is the famous Siedlce prison, an inheritance from the former czarist times that was built opposite the Jewish center "Pienkne Street" as if to throw fear over the Jewish residents, who were not considered "nobility" by those who had God's grace.

At the end of the street, in an honored spot, stood the city hall, a simple unadorned building without great architectural or historical pretensions. But it occupied a prominent spot on the streets. Principally, it graced Pienkne Street with its high tower, which held a massive, round clock that showed the time on all four sides and communicated it through its bells to those who could not see it. On the tip-top there was always walking a watchman from the fire patrol on the lookout in case there was work for his crew.

[Page 22]

The city hall with its surroundings was the center, the heart of Siedlce. Every resident of Siedlce had to pass at least once every day through one of the four streets – if you wanted to meet someone, it was sufficient to stand for a while by the city hall and that person would come by. Aside from the many passersby, there were in the area always groups of people standing or sitting by the city hall. In summertime one often saw on the Pienkne Street side, close to the wall, at the foot of the high clock tower, resting in the shadow of the huge walls of the city hall a group of transport workers, coachmen and porters with ropes at their hips, some with whips in their hands, some sitting on the ground with their booted feet stretched out as free as anything; those who were standing there with their broad shoulders were always ready to carry burdens. Leaning against that huge city hall wall, they were ready with their strong backs, and right in the middle of this world of porters sat Avraham Weinapple, the head of the transport union, with his hat down on his forehead and his large glasses settled on his nose, reading to the group the "Folks-tzeitung" and instructing them about the world's political situation.

On the other side "by the entrance to Warsaw Street" there appeared, like a stock exchange of loafers, a combination of Jews and non-Jews who were unemployed and waiting for the monthly payment from the unemployment fund. They passed the time engaged in fervent discussions.

Groups of older Jews were there, too, propped up on canes; ruined businessmen told about the great businesses they once had and about the noble customers they had; they chewed the ends of their beards and looked out for the postman who might bring a letter with a check from a rich relative in America.

In the midst of this deserted field that lies far and wide around me, I stand now by a new plaza full of greenery and flowers. They are covered with glistening drops of dew that the morning sun has not yet made disappear. It is like an oasis in a wasteland. I sit down on one of the benches that are placed around as if I found myself in the domain of the former city hall, which I had seen in the first days of the bloody flood half destroyed, with its fallen clock tower.

[Page 23]

How from its ruins did such a beautiful plaza with benches arise? I look all around. There is nothing wrong with my eyes. One sees far and wide. There is nothing blocking the way.

Then I see the long prison building. The czarist bequest was lucky – nothing happened to it. It outlived Pienkne Street and all its inhabitants and stands and dominates its ruins. One sees the old city council hall, but little more than its bare skeleton. On its burned out high tower there remains standing only the shameful lower section of naked Jacek, poor thing, without his head and without the globe that was cut off with his shoulders. Poor Jacek. He shared the heavy fate of his Jewish fellow citizens.

---

4. Kilinske Street

Translated by Theodore Steinberg

It was good to sit a bit among the greenery and flowers, breathing in the fresh early-morning air. It helped me to forget just a little my tragic surroundings. That thought gives me momentary relief from the images of destruction. And that thought was helped by the appearance of the opposite cozy little street, which, with a few exceptions, had not suffered the same fate as its near sister, Pienkne Street. There it stood, with a line of upright houses on both sides and before, like soldiers – standing upright as if for roll call, two rows of growing trees with broad tops of green leaves that threw thick shadows over the gardens in which they stood.

But I could not sit and rest for long. The desire to see all at one time, as quickly as a breath, the whole scope of the destruction – raised me from the place. Now appear Moyshe Rotbein, the Halberstam brothers, Goldman, Kravietz, and others who had been stuck deep in the wolfish maw, ripped apart, away in underground holes, bunkers, woods – and survived. Survived in order to tell what had happened. They, and others who returned from the distant East where they had wandered, like myself, sought the bones of a father, a mother, a sister, a brother – the remains of the Siedlce Jewish community. We walk around in a group, casting shadows, and we move in silence, as if at a funeral.

[Page 24]

On the right side we see the shoe businesses that stood one after the other, and on the left – the sewing goods store, the haberdashery, stationery and bookstores. Then, just as I did in earlier times I look at the writing on the signs and read new names, unknowns. And then, those unknown proprietors peer out of the open doors of their businesses that they opened with a clatter, like old, established residents.

My eyes devour all of the remaining houses on the once sparkling little branch of Kilinske Street and they search: perhaps I will see something from that earlier time. There are the windows from a house on the left side that for long time housed the Zionist organization – the "Merkaz." The same windows from which the notes of "od lo avdah tikvateynu" [words from "Hatikvah"]. There are the walls on which were written out in large blue and white letters the whole Basle program: "Zionism intends to fashion for the Jewish people a legal, secure home in Eretz Israel." For many years, people discussed and clarified what it meant to be a people without a home and warned about the tragic consequences of eternal homelessness. And there was the office of the "Keren Kayamet L'Yisrael" where Jews brought their saved up groschen to purchase land in Israel for Jews to live on; and there was the editorial office of the "Siedlcer Vochenblat," the popular Jewish weekly in Podlosie.

And there, opposite, on the right side stands the building that housed there professional union of Jewish leather workers. On its walls were written the slogans, "Workers of the world, unite," "Fight against fascism and reaction," and others. There people spoke about the brotherhood of nations, about a better future that had to come. From its windows, the notes of the "International" and other songs of hope and freedom could be heard.

There are windows of the premises of the former merchants bank, the institution that played such an important role for the Jewish merchants in the times when all credit and business concerns in the city were closed to Jews. For them the merchants bank was like a mother, where, besides a loan or a discount, one could receive a nice greeting from the always friendly and talkative chairman, R. Asher Orszel, and good advice from the always taciturn director, R. Avraham-Asher Kwiatek.

[Page 25]

And there, in that building, set in on the side, were the premises of the artisans union. After a hard day of work, each evening the Jewish worker found here a place to relax. He came to read the newspaper, play chess or dominoes, and seek protection from the decrees and repressions of the health inspectors with their boycott politics that shadowed his poor existence.

A vast gloom emanates from the windows of these premises that once had been so pleasant, heimish, familiar, and dear. An ice-cold strangeness comes out of those remaining buildings on the bit of Kilinske Street, and although a radiant springtime sun shines in the sky – all my bones are frozen.

I sneak over to Sienkiewicz (formerly Ogrodowa Street) and – again a wilderness: on both sides, right and left, wherever I look, I see nothing but ruins, heaps of stones, goats, little hills overgrown with grass. On one such plot of grass, where the beautiful house of R. Yisroel Gutgelt once stood, horses pasture with chains on their front feet.

And in the middle of the street, amidst the ruins and destruction, there stands, as it did before, the great Russian Orthodox Church that was later converted into a military facility, with a high, ruined roof surrounded by a forest of growing green trees, like guardians who would protect it from attacks. It seemed as if the high, four-cornered tower with a cross at the top proclaimed proudly: "You see, the corruption has no power over me. I remain intact." Instinctively I turn my glance to the exit from Pienkne, by Florianske Street, and on the side of Dluge, opposite from Sokolower Street. And from there, as the metal crosses shine in the early morning sun holding fast to their metal towers, they proclaim that in the struggle with the bloody destroyers, they emerged unscathed…

---

5. On the Sacred Area

Translated by Theodore Steinberg

We found ourselves on the area that lies like a four-cornered box where the four streets meet: Warsaw, Dluge, Stari-Rinek, Yiddishe, the sacred area of Jewish Siedlce. It recalls the old biblical call, "Remove your shoes from your feet, because the place where you are standing is holy ground…" As they did once for the tabernacle [in the wilderness], our forefathers and foremothers brought their gifts and constructed on this spot a Temple complex, with a shul, and over the entrance, as in old Chumashim, pictured the Two Tablets with Ten Commandments, with their eternal warning, "Thou shalt not murder." They also constructed a room for a rabbinical court, an apartment for the rabbi, a room for the community council and all other community needs.

In order to have a secure place for the community's belongings and sacred objects, which might be subject to theft or fire, our forefathers built from stone and iron under the floor of the great synagogue a genizah. There could be found a great many sacred objects, such as: Torah scrolls, megillot, manuscripts, ark covers, silver candlesticks, menorahs, shofars, and many other things of historical and artistic value. The genizah was closed behind three doors of iron and wood, disguised, and closed with seven locks. The keys were held by the gabbai of the beis-hamedresh, who trusted no one else with them but opened and shut the room with his own hands when anything needed to be removed for a holiday or for a special occasion.

Early every morning, while it was still so dark that one could not distinguish between a dog and a wolf or between blue and green, the believing Jews of Siedlce would stream there to pour out their beleaguered hearts before the Creator of the world. It was too early for the official prayers, so in the meantime people said Psalms and called out from their overflowing spirits, "From the depths I call to you, O Lord."

As soon as it was day, people said their prayers devotedly as a congregation. Early on, the simple Jews, workmen, small merchants, who had rushed in before going to their workshops and stores in order to pay the Master of the World his due. Later on the "finer" Jewish scholars, who had more time, who were not rushed, said their prayers slowly, drawing out their words for half the day. After prayers and before going home, still wearing their tallis and tefillin, they learned a page of Gemara.

[Page 27]

And even before they left, the tables in the beis-medresh were filled withother learners, young men and old Jews who learned some by themselves and some in groups, reciting aloud, with the special niggun, the special melody that Bialik had given eternal life in his "The Constant One." The melody wafted out through the windows and into the street, informing all passersby that the people of Israel will not pass away.

In the evening, the shul and the beis-medresh were filled from corner to corner with people who were there for minchah and maariv. And there was no lack of children, who cried out with their youthful voices, standing on a bench, lamenting with great sorrow the injustice of having lost a father or a mother – reciting the ancient words "Yisgadal v'yiskadash."

Between minchah and maariv, people would listen to a preacher, an emissary from a yeshivah who stood all excited on the dais and emotionally described what awaited in Gehenna with such detail as if he had just returned from there: how evil people were fried in huge frying pans, how they were hung on hooks and burnt in barrels of pitch, and he concluded that to forestall such things one had to give tzedakah and support Talmud students, and he ended with, "May the redeemer come to Zion in our time, amen…"

After maariv, all the tables were completely filled and the sound of Torah again rang out.

Now R. Shlomo-Shmuel Abarbanel studies the Eye Yaakov with a group of everyday Jewish workers. At another table, R. Paltiel Rubinstein studies a chapter of Mishnah with a different group. And – quiet. Be polite!! There at the eastern wall, near the aron-kodesh, at a table surrounded by the scholars of the city, one of the greatest scholars in Siedlce gives a lesson, the prodigy R. Nechamkeh Lev. And at another table, also at the eastern wall, surrounded by fine Jews, well-to-do scholars, half-maskislim, the old Havurah scholar and mask, the silver-haired, stately R. Yitzchak Nahum Weintraub teaches the daf-yomi.

Thus it is, day in and day out, until deep into the night.

But even deep into the night the beis-medresh is never deserted. After the departure of all the worshippers and the students, there always remain, throughout the night, tucked away in a corner among the stoves, some of the eternal poor, by the small light from a tallow candle with the whisper of a strangely sad melody that lasts through the night.

[Page 28]

My mind runs through images of how the shul and the beis-medresh appeared on Shabbos and holidays and at other special moments, like, for example, on Tisha B'Av: in the evening, the sky in the west is wrapped in flames that recall the fire of Nebuchadnezzar's time that consumed the First Temple, as well as the fire from the time of Titus that consumed the Second Temple, just as the shul and the beis-medresh now appear as ruins. The tables and the benches are turned over, the Holy Ark with its Torah scrolls stands as if embarrassed, stripped of its cover in near darkness, with the light of a small candle. The whole congregations sits on the ground, like mourners, in their socks. The chazan recites the book of Lamentations with a mournful melody, as if lamenting the dead, while everyone, with tears and sadness, cries quietly to themselves, "Look and see whether there is any pain like my pain" and sheds bitter tears over the fate of a people who for thousands of years have wandered in the wilderness. And year after year, generation after generation, the earth on which we stand has absorbed the warm well of our tears.

Or: this picture, how the shul appeared and the beis-medresh, on the night of Yom Kippur for Kol Nidrei – how in sacred, silent ecstasy the people cried out their powerless protest against the evils of the world in tones enmeshed with the melody of Kol Nidrei; and at Ne'ilah, when the congregation was pale, wearied from the long fast, wearing kitties and talisim, pounding their sapped hearts at the "Al Cheit" forcing they had not committed, while in the twilight cutting through the hushed, sacred air came the cry of generations: "When I see every city built on its site" [a line from one of the piyyutim recited on Yom Kippur]…Their hearts are full of sorrow that every city and country of every people stands fast while ours lies in ruins – like our whole lives.

There were also moments of light and joy that the congregation experienced in this spot. For example, Purim, when the old Megillah was unrolled and they read about the defeat of an old enemy of the Jews who once thought he could wipe out the people of Israel. In the lusty tune of "Shoshanas Yakov," and in a joyful dance, the elders let loose; and with wooden graggers and clapping of the hands and stomping with the feet, the children carried on, the young ones. And everything reflected joy that once, though very, very long ago, we did not lack the justice that so often renders us like a stepchild.

[Page 29]

Or Simchas Torah: the shul and the beis-medresh swim in a sea of light. Everyone, dressed in their finest clothes, beams with joy. It is no trifle, Simchas Torah for Jews! On the reader's platform stands the chazan, beaming, in his holiday cantorial garb, with the permanent gabbai of the shul, the distinguished R. Eliezer Shlifke, with his silver beard and his golden glasses on his nose, with his volunteer helper, the ever-moving R. Avigdor Kartoflia. They give out the honors – they call those who will come up to carry the Torah. First come the "fine" upper-crust, those who come to the shul regularly to pray – those at the Eastern Wall. They are called up with honor, with a melody and with their full titles, like this: "Our teacher, the great scholar of a fine pedigree, the descendant of Avraham, Yitzchak, and Yakov, R. So-and-so is honored with the procession of Abraham." Later on come the simpler Jews from the Western Wall and those who come less often for prayers. They are called up without titles, simply as "Reb So-and-so is honored with the procession of Yakov." The congregation dances in a circle with the Torah scrolls clasped to their hearts around the reader's platform, rejoices in the Torah, dances and sings: Happy are you, O Israel, that God has chosen you as His beloved people and thought you worthy of the Torah. The children, boys and girls, who on Simchas Torah are not chided for coming among the adults, shine with happiness, looking around, mingling with the crowd, holding the lower part of the wooden pole on which the Torah is wrapped, which their fathers hold while dancing. The children stomp their feet and sing with the adults, worthy stand on the tables and benches with Simchas Torah flags in their hands. On the tops of the flags are red apples that reflect the light. With their flaming red cheeks and burning brown eyes, they provide a wonderful picture of the holiday.

* * *

The bloody destroyer understood how there people were bound up with their shul and beis-medresh. Therefore, before he killed the people, in order to cause even more pain and suffering – first he destroyed the sacred place so that no trace of it remains where it once stood. A sad, empty place is spread out before my eyes, and in the middle is a broad common grave of marble and concrete, topped with a high tower – a reminder adorned with a hammer and sickle, under which one reads the inscription: "Praise and honor for the heroes of the Soviet Union who fell in the battle with the wild fascist beasts to liberate the city."

[Page 30]

There follows a long list with the names of the fallen heroes whose bones rest at the bottom of the memorial in this community burial place.

A holy shudder runs through my heart and my whole body at reading the names, which, though they sound strange and unknown, are still heimish, familiar, and dear.

I want to fall to my knees, to lay my hot forehead on the cold marble and call out: Who else, like myself, the cluster or surviving Jews, captives, persecuted by the wild fascists, returned from bunkers and underground holes, woods and taiga, could appreciate what you did to liberate us and to liberate the world.

An eternal light of love and gratitude will always burn in the pantheon of our hearts in praise of your young lives that you sacrificed to cleanse the world of that dark plague.

In the most beautiful and most important places of our destroyed city, people should erect such remembrances to serve as monuments to the heroic fighters – and as a warning for coming generations against the rebirth of fascism.

But is it not a mistake or a misunderstanding? Is this really the right spot for a communal grave and for a memorial for fallen heroes?

Consider – that on this bit of earth for hundreds of years stood a shul with a beis-medresh and that the earth absorbed so many tears and prayers from many generations – and it is a shameful dishonor to the last tragedy – the destruction of its congregation. They should erect a different monument, a monument of the Eternal Jew who sits Shiva on the ground, shoeless, with along gray beard and deep creases in his forehead,, with large eyes turned toward the heavens, cloaked in a tallis and kittle, a sack with ashes over his gray head. In one bony hand he should hold the number "six million" and in the other – the symbol of the eternal falsehood, with the inscription: "When you receive a slap on the cheek–turn the other one…" – Such a monument I have envisioned for this dishonored sacred spot to tell coming generations about the disgrace of the years 1939-1945. And perhaps in the future a passerby will stand and consider and – strike his heart with an "al chet" for the sins of his grandfathers.

[Page 31]

Survivors recount:

…Late one cold, dark winter night – on Christmas of the first year of the bloody Hitler lordship in Poland (in 1939) Siedlce shuddered with alarm, for the beis-medresh with the shul were burning! The vandals spared no amount of benzine and naphtha so that the wild spectacle would create a more imposing effect. The flames reached miles high and lit up the dark night sky. Around the auto-da-fe stood the wild beasts carrying machine guns and handguns and they made sure that no Jew, God forbid, could try to extinguish the flames or bring out a burning Sefer Torah. In the shul and the beis-medresh were quartered several hundred homeless Jews from Kalisz, Wloclawek, and other cities of western Poland. The fire in the middle of the night found them sleeping. They jumped through the burning doors and windows, some with children and some with the elderly or the ailing in their hands, receiving burns and cuts, rifle and bayonet wounds from the frenzied man-eaters. The screams of the victims were mixed with and drowned out by the joyful cries of the villains who celebrated the wild conflagration that they had caused in the Christmas celebration to honor the birth of the savior of the world, who built his teaching on "You shall love your neighbor…"

During this wild orgy of flames, nearby on Warsaw Street near the Pilsudski Monument, representatives of the Murder-Race sat around tables "SS men, Gestapo, gendarmes, and other big Nazis, stuffing themselves like pigs, swilling, and singing in their loud, drunken voices the Horst Wessel Lied, while they "immortalized" on film the results of their wildness: the burning shul and beis-medresh with the burning and beaten Jews…

When the vandals were good and roused up, heated up by the flames and the alcohol, they realized that one thing was lacking in their spectacle – having a band of them descend on the despairing Jews who stood on the side and in their great helplessness wrung their hands and lamented their dishonored and destroyed holy site

[Page 32]

. The beasts in human form grabbed their first victim who came into their paws – it was Pinchas from 7 Florianska Street (Pincze Czach) – they dragged him to the burning shul and ordered him to bring out Torah scrolls from the Aron Kodesh and dance with them around the reader's stand. As the flames spread through the entire shul, the murderers slammed shut the doors and the unfortunate Pincze was incinerated along with the Torah scrolls that he held close.

On the morning after the fire, the vandals came to the Jewish community and collected signatures on a document testifying that the shul and the beis-medresh were burned through unknown circumstances.

Happy with their accomplishment, later on in a similar way they destroyed all the other souls and beis-medreshes in the city. Later on, the Jews were taken from the locked up ghetto and the murderers forced them, with terrible beatings, to take apart the remaining walls of the soul. The stones, concrete, and iron the Germans took for their "Lebensraum" purposes.

And again my glance went to three points in the city: Kilinske–Florianske–Dluge, to the tips of the high towers from whence dance the reflections of the crosses that play like carefree children with the beams of the springtime sun…

6. At the Old Cemetery

Translated by Theodore Steinberg

We take a few steps further from the destroyed holy place on this sacred ground and find ourselves in the old cemetery on the side of the shul…

There was once in Siedlce an old cemetery, the first of three in the city…

One generation related to the next that: once—once, hundreds of years ago, when all of Podlasie was a huge forest, a rich old lord, who owned the whole area, ordered that in the woods, which extended a great distance, an area should be carved out for a city. Because of the beauty of the area, which in Polish was known as "Pienkne-Shedlisko, the city was called Siedlce [in Yiddish, "Shedletz"].

The Great Shul in Siedlce. Burned by the Nazis on the night of December 24, 1939.

**Ghetto gate at Stari-Rinek reading,
"Entrance forbidden to Germans and Poles due to danger
of an epidemic"**

Ghetto wagon transporting the dead

[Page 33]

Desiring that the city would be built and developed quickly, the lord summoned Jews from other cities, descendants of those Jews who once for the Egyptians built Pithom and Ramses; for the old Babylonians—cities on their shores; for the Greeks and Romans—circuses and theaters; for the Spaniards—Cordova and Toledo; for the German barons—Mainz, Worms, and Frankfurt; for the Ukrainian hetmen—Uman, Proskurov, Kishinev, and other cities, where they were later robbed, deafened, or burned in autos-da-fe. They were given certain privileges, among which was the piece of earth on which we now stand. On one side they built a shul with a beis-medresh, and the other they set aside for a cemetery—surrounded with a thick, strong wall, built to last generations. There rested the bones of the first Jews of Siedlce. The people called it "The Sacred Spot." With great solemnity the Jews walked the surrounding streets, Jewish Street, Dluge, and Stari-Rinek. Good Christians doffed their hats before the old "czmentasz" [Polish for "cemetery"] of the "staro-zakonnik" ["the old monk"]. Time has done its work and flung the old monuments onto the earth. Only a few remain, covered over with green moss. The engraved lettering on them is no longer legible. The earth that once was heavy with human bodies is now covered with plants, tall grasses typical of cemeteries and wild flowers that hold the secrets of hundreds of years. Their holy rest has not been disturbed. The surrounding wall has held them all, like a holy thing, closed to the surrounding hubbub, preserving it as a holy place.

Old people used to say that in their childhood years this was "outside the city," where cemeteries were traditionally located. Later, as the city spread out, people built building after building, street after street, until this spot became the center of the city. With the growth of the city, the old cemetery became more heimish and familiar, so that no one, even the oldest inhabitants of the city, knew when it could no longer accept burials. It reminded all its neighbors that "man comes from the dust and returns to the dust." But it did not frighten or throw fear on passersby. In the shadows of its walls, Jewish children played ball and jumped rope.

[Page 34]

And anyone who passed by in the twilight and stood on tiptoes and looked over the wall would see the thick woods with the high grasses full of their secrets, rocking back and forth as if they were sending to heaven a silent prayer from the first generations of Siedlce's Jews, who rested under this sacred earth.

No one dared to tread upon this sacred place and to disturb the quiet sleep of Siedlce's first Jews, who had slept there for hundreds of years, until the earth of Poland was shaken by the bloody hordes of Hitler, who carried out the last act of this holy place before the destruction of Siedlce's Jewish congregation.

---

7. The Last Hours in the Large Ghetto

Translated by Theodore Steinberg

Several witnesses who miraculously survived that mass execution recount:

…It was a frightfully hot day. Aside from the daily suffering and pain that the imprisoned inhabitants had to endure from their torturers, with their wild, sadistic innovations—horrible ideas spread in the. Ghetto and further embittered their already embittered lives.

The Jewish Council had received a strict order from the labor office to send several score works to unload a train car in the train station, which, thanks to a fire in the axles, could proceed no further.

Rumors spread through the ghetto that in the train car there were Jews from Radom. Consequently, together with the workers went Heniek Adler, who was from Radom and who now lived in the Siedlce ghetto.

The sight that the workers encountered was horrible: the car was part of a death train that was taking the Jews of Radom to Treblinka. Because of a fire in the axle, the car could not continue and was held up in Siedlce. When the opened the car, they found packed together a hundred corpses.

[Page 35]

They were horribly stuck together from the crowding, the heat, and the gas that the lime that was spread on the floor gave out. Adler recognized inhabitants of Radom. The SS convoy that guarded the Jewish workers, urged them with clubs to unload the clumped bodies quickly. They were taken to the cemetery and there buried in a make-shift communal grave.

Many of the workers thought, in view of the horrible scene with the Radomers in the car: Is not a similar fate awaiting the Jews of Siedlce?

Then a Jewish woman came who had escaped from Minsk-Mazowiec and she related how all the Jews there had been taken to one spot. Many of them were shot right there and the rest were taken in an unknown direction. Dr. Lebel, the head of the Jewish Council, tried to telephone the Jewish Council in Minsk, but no one answered.

Then we heard that a special band of Gestapo and Ukrainians were in the city with a special secret mission.

Christians who encountered Jews during the day related that they had heard from the train workers and others in the depot that people were preparing train cars for the Jews.

And then there came to the ghetto, to the seamstress Mathil Greenberg, a gendarme with his wife, who had ordered clothing from her and now demanded back the material, as that…they were leaving Siedlce.

Also the commander of the Polish police, Graf, came to the watchmaker in the ghetto and demanded back the watch that he had left for repairs.

It also became apparent that in the evening there arrived in the ghetto many Polish police—many who had never been seen before. And when the downtrodden and worried ghetto dwellers asked the police what had happened in Minsk Mazowiec, they sought to calm them and said that near Warsaw there had been a train accident and two thousand Jews were taken there as workers.

These, as well as other facts, showed that something was in store, that something would happen. And though no one knew where or when, people instinctively felt that something horrible, frightful, was coming.

[Page 36]

* * *

…It was dark night in spring—erev Shabbos, the ninth of Elul, 1942, after three years of Hitler's bloody domination in the country, when the Jews of Siedlce, beaten down and bedraggled by the hard labor which they were forced to do every day, swollen with the hunger that the Nazis imposed, brought down and weighed down by the terrible craziness of the wild sadists, robbed of faith in God, man and the world, lying cramped in their small, dirty ghetto cots, dreamed—some of how to get a few potatoes the next day for the wife and children; and some of how to escape from their cramped, larked ghetto prison, to go the woods to the partisans and to help defeat the bloody enemy; some lamented quietly with their broken hearts by saying a chapter of Psalms and waited for a miracle; and some, with the greatest despair, resigned themselves to a longing that death should come as the only thing that could free them from these terrible conditions, while some who came under the reign of typhus in the ghetto or of starvation writhed in their last agonies, pronouncing their last despairing curse in the darkness of the dark world.

During this dark night, the ghetto was surrounded by a black, bloodthirsty international rabble: by Ukrainian brigands, who got their thieving pedigrees from their bloody grandfathers, those who served Chmielnicki, Gotta, and the Fetluras {Ukrainians who at various times led attacks against the Jews], who from time immemorial bathed in Jewish blood; by Latvian criminal young people, for whom robbery and murder were genetic inheritances, were entertainments, sport, like chasing in a mob after rabbits or ducks; by Lithuanian ne'er-do-wells who voluntary joined up with the German murder bands so that they could freely murder and steal Jewish clothing; and by home-grown"grenadiers" and other scoundrels who were as faithful as dogs to the bloodthirsty German occupiers, as they had earlier faithfully served the fascist Sanatzia rulers in the country and even earlier served loyally as the handle of the czarist whips.

[Page 37]

The leaders of this bloodthirsty family were, you understand, the most refined murderers of all times and generations: the German SS.

This siege was like iron, with hand grenades, machine guns and other instruments of destruction, as they wanted to conquer a strong, powerful enemy and not—the worn out and tortured skeleton-like Jews who lives, for the past three years, had been as worthless as dust.

Getting out of the ghetto "immediately" was impossible. The tragic hours of that dark night seemed to last forever. The half-dead people of the ghetto felt as the end was approaching, and the skeleton-like bodies pressed together, the swollen mother clasping more tightly to her breast her withered child, a sister holding more tightly to her sister, a brother to a brother, one to the other, all huddled together like the trees in a forest when the woodsmen come and—waited for morning.

And then morning arrived with its horror and terror.—— —— —— ——

When the first blue traces of light broke through the dark sky over the Siedlce ghetto, everyone knew about the terrible order that was worse than all previous wild orders that the Nai murderers had issued during the three years of their bloody lordship over the unfortunate Jews:

"All Jews must immediately abandon the ghetto, taking along only the smallest handbag. They must appear at the square of the old cemetery.—— —— —— ——

When the sun arose in the east that morning, as it did every day, fresh and beaming, it encountered in the emptying ghetto a wild mob of bloodthirsty raptors, like hungry locusts on an abandoned field of grain. The nearest thing to this wild pillaging was, you understand, the knights in their steel helms who came to get tokens for their "beloved ladies," whom they had obtained for a big lunch or a stolen Jewish watch, and now they were coming to get a whole wardrobe. The Ukrainian brigands, the Latvians, and the Lithuanian robbers worked assiduously for the "holy cause" that had brought them into the war.

[Page 38]

Like the vilest reptiles in a horrible place on a hot summer day, they swarmed through the emptied ghetto, by the side of the uniformed thieves, all sorts of awful people:

Professional bandits, whom the Germans had recently released from prison; unemployed prostitutes who were not successful at their "craft" because of their advanced age; former assistants in Jewish businesses in better times; religious women with crosses who had heard from their priests on the holy altar in church that Jews were a sinful people and therefore God punished them; there were many from the "golden youth", educated by the "Orendownik" and "Sturmer" and by the most recent bible—"Mein Kampf"—they came to see the fulfillment of a great ideal that they had heard about for years—a "Poland without Jews." There were also Roma—the future victims of the Treblinka gas chambers—to seize a few pieces of Jewish bedding.

The happy news that the ghetto had been emptied spread quickly throughout the neighboring villages, and bands of thieving peasants came with horses and wagons, bringing their wives and children to help pack their loot in large bags. They dug in the cellars and the courtyards, seeking Jewish gold; they tore apart chimneys and ovens, ripped up floors and ceilings, ransacked attics, made holes everywhere; they stuffed sacks, baskets, and suitcases, dragged out pots, pieces of furniture, sewing machines, whole and ripped up Torah scrolls, whatever might be useful—and if it was not useful, American Jews would pay well for it. And everyone, everyone—the bloodthirsty thieving mob of international zealots disappeared, beaming with joy and thanking God, although the wait had been long, but now the great, joyful day had arrived…

———————————————————

8. At the Umschlagplatz

Translated by Theodore Steinberg

And the old cemetery—the quiet, holy spot where for hundreds of years the bones of the first Siedlce Jews had lain in quiet—received a new name, in accord with the terminology of the murderers: Umschlagplatz.

[Page 39]

Through the wide opening that had been created at the cemetery at that time, where the shul with its beis-medresh had stood, which the Nazi vandals had burned down for the spectacle—in honor of the first Christmas celebration in Siedlce—through this opening there entered the fifteen thousand Jews of Siedlce, together with the Jews from surrounding cities who had been found in the ghetto. They were herded in like persecuted creatures into a cage, like a helpless herd of oxen into the slaughterhouse courtyard before slaughter.

Beyond the surrounding walls of the cemetery—the Umschlagplatz—which had long stood there, was another steel-like wall of armed Ukrainians, Lithuanians, Latvians, and many armed police, and there were several local people, even children and young people, who voluntarily participated in this "sacred labor," especially because they would be rewarded: the Germans had promised to take from the dead, or from living Jews, their clothing and shoes, and all those volunteers were worried that someone, God forbid, might escape from that encircled Gehenna.

The executioners did not quickly finish with their victims. Slowly—calculated according to a thought-out and prepared plan that was intended to satisfy and delight the wild beasts's instincts—the work was carried out according to all their rules and precepts that their people had learned in the Kazarma schools and in the literature for the hangmen.

The work was divided up in a systematic way according to the groups. Each group had to carry out its mission in a designated area.

One group of armed murderers set out in a wild mob through the ghetto to force the unfortunate into the Umschlagplatz and to organize the theft of their remaining possessions. With bizarre wild voices and unceasing shooting, they caused a terrible uproar and panic. They went from house to house, looking in every hiding place, in every cellar, attic and covered hole, shooting every Jew that they found and brought out of the hiding places. They murdered and plundered, stole and destroyed everything that came into their hands. Thus were the streets of the ghetto transformed into a slaughterhouse. Every courtyard, pavement, and sidewalk was covered with corpses that were tossed there like formless piles of rags upon which the murderers' hard boots had stomped.

[Page 40]

The drunken cries of victory and calls of joy from the frenzied cannibals mingled with the cries of the helpless victims, with the lamenting cries of the terrified and hunger-tortured children and deafened and maddened those who had come from the ghetto.

A second group of killers went to that part of the ghetto that was shaped like a triangle, where Sokolow, Aslonowicz, and Okopowa Streets came together to prepare a spot for the able-bodied men who were to be selected at the Umschlagplatz. This was a very simple matter: everyone who was within the triangle was gathered together and shot.

At the same time, another group of killers, armed with all sorts of killing devices, was already waiting and "greeting" the unfortunate victims right by the entrance to the shul- courtyard-Umschlagplatz. The frenzied human-animals had arranged themselves in two rows—a kind of road—through which the victims had to pass. Their murderous propensities were delivered to the heads and backs of the people, who were considered as absolutely worthless and—that sacred area of the synagogue courtyard ran with blood and was covered with corpses.

Another group of killers—entirely Ukrainian—sat on the surrounding old cemetery walls with handguns and machine guns and never ceased shooting at the mass of half-dead, piled up people.

They also had the duty to pay attention that this order was carried out: everyone had to sit with their heads down to the ground and be silent; for getting up or raising one's head, one would be shot. This gave them the opportunity, those heirs of Chmielnicki and Petluro, to shoot Jews for the slightest movement. Every Jew was a target, and every shot hit the bullseye.

Certain groups were selected to conduct the decorative aspects of the program, as, for instance: taking away their lunches from the Jewish crowd, who were in the presence of their executioners.

A special group was assembled in various spots around the Umschlagplatz with photographic and film equipment in order to memorialize in film all the details of the extraordinary "adventure"—the bloody spectacle.

[Page 41]

Also the metropolitan Polish fire brigade was mobilized to take part in the "exceptional impression." Their job was: from time to time to spray the beleaguered community with water—so ordered the executioners—and they did so with enthusiasm and pleasure.

Nor were the Polish police left behind: they had known their former neighbors, the Jews, for a long time, and they knew that the Jews could hide or escape from the Umschlagplatz [trans. note: probably this should read "the Jews could *not* hide or escape"], and they knew everywhere that the Jews might have hidden their possessions—the gold and jewelry that the Zhids owned in such quantity. So these important police were everywhere: in the ghetto, where they could find a few Jews in hiding and kill them at leisure; because they were local, they knew all the hiding places, all the holes, and they knew where to look…And there, in the Umschlagplatz and around the square they were present. There they encountered well-known Jews who, in the last hours of their lives, surrendered their watches or some last few hidden zlotys in the naive belief that their hometown police would save them or at least give them a little water to quench their terrible thirst. But the Polish police did not stand apart from their German or Ukrainian colleagues: they beat, robbed, and murdered along with them, those who for generations had hated the Zhids, from whom they would finally be free.

A special time in this program was the executioners' mealtime. Near Pilsudski Street, there where the beis-medresh stood, the serving tables were set up, around which sat the executioners and began to eat and guzzle, while, lying in their own blood, hundreds of Jews who had been whipped and shot, and others who had been tortured, with pale yellow faces, were forced to come to the meal site and were forced, by blows, to sing and dance for the drunken villains. They toasted each other with glasses of wine and with chins red with wine they sang in chorus, "When Jewish blood spurts out from the knife" [lyrics from the "Horst Wessel Lied"].

One of the executioners stood up at the table, an Obergruppenfuhrer from the SS, all inflamed, a drunken guzzler. He waved his hands to show he had something to say.

[Page 42]

His subordinate Germans and Ukrainians perked up and with the help of their whips and rifle butts they quieted down the dazed crowd. The coarse, hoarse voice of the killer in his white gloves thundered over the Umschlagplatz: he must have two pairs of silk stockings for his girlfriend, who sat next to him; he gave fifteen minutes for the socks to be brought to him.

Finished with the meal, they approached the climax of the program—to the selection from among the young, healthy, able-bodied men of 16 to 40 years of age, whose working skills could still be useful to the devilish German war machine. A selection—that is what the killers called it in their murderous language.

It was clear immediately that all women, all children up to 16, and men older than 40 were all consigned to death.

At the selection table were seated the leaders of the different killing groups, extermination and destruction companies, Gestapo and work leaders—ed by the chief executioner, Fabish.

Everyone was forced to go along that "highway," from the selection table all the way to Dluge Street—between the two rows of frenzied murderers, who lashed and killed the Jews who passed through with their specially prepared tools of death.

The whole community of people was forced along this hellish road ibefore the wild hordes in a parade of death. Drunk and aroused by the their successful undertaking, they called out in one breath: "Left, left," which meant—to the Treblinka gas chambers. Their place was on the left side of the shul and the cemetery square, on the side of Stary Rynek. Seldom did the executioners call out, "Right," and that only for the young men, who could demonstrate with their healthy muscles and work-hardened hands that they could still be useful for the wild machinations of the bloody sadists. "Right" meant: survive for a bit. Their spot was in the right sight of the square by Ber-Yoselewicz Street (formerly Jewish).

They amused themselves well, those wild sadists, at the selection table after their lunch of chicken and wine among the tortured and dead Jews.

There ran the Jews with heads split open, eyes gouged out, knocked-out teeth, and all, all—bathed in blood. There a woman carried off her dying child; there crawled on the earth a gray-haired old man with pierced side; and everyone made such wild grimaces and hoarse cries, making such bizarre sounds, and—the killers rolled with laughter.

[Page 43]

Some of the Jews would not go to their assigned spots, right or left, and remained lying in the midst of the "highway" being flogged and hacked at on the ground. This mass of bodies was trampled on by the stiff boots of the murderers and also by their own unfortunate brothers, who ran over them in order more quickly to pass through the "highway" and all the more quickly to arrive at the—left, left, left…

There were also some chosen "lucky ones" who had the. Luck to take a shortcut on the last road: unnoticed by the executioners, they snuck around those being flogged on the left of the killing ground and thus avoided the bloody course. One such successful person was pale, ailing Yisroeltsche Yom-Tov.

After a half a day, the selection ended, and the executioners' helpers had counted and registered those young men on the right side. They were counted like horses, oxen, or like some other beast of burden. There were five hundred and seventy of them.

Under guard and with blows they were led to the triangle of the ghetto: Aslonowicz—Sokolower-Okopowa, which was thereafter called the small ghetto.

Those there on the left, the greater majority, were not counted—it would be a waste of effort. Soon they would be sent to Treblinka and to the gas chambers. What would the difference be of a few Jews more or less? What need to be formal? But they could be further degraded, abased, tortured, beaten, killed. They knew, those practiced killers, that by tomorrow those Jews would no longer exist, and so today they could be afflicted with pain and suffering.

With the arrival of night, the frenzied killers redoubled their devilish labors against their defenseless victims. The more the victims writhed in their agonies, the greater grew the bestial ecstasy and the more the bacchanalia grew. They became more inventive, seeking new means of torture and death, smashing heads, aiming and shooting in eyes and ears, ripping little children out of their mothers' arms, cutting them in half, bashing children's heads on the stone monuments that were there or against the walls of the old cemetery.

[Page 44]

A crude, overstuffed German offered a piece of chocolate to a pale, emaciated child. The starving child opened his little mouth, but…instead of chocolate. He received a bullet in his open mouth. And as his grieving mother, who was pulling her hair out of her head, pleaded for a buillet of her own, the German complied. Her riddled body fell and covered the splayed out body of her dying child.

A second killer stuffed into the mouth of a Jew a piece of solid sugar. When the starving Jew had the piece of sugar in his mouth, he received on his cheek, which was bulging from the sugar, such a blow that his cheek was punctured and his teeth fell to the ground in a pool of blood.

On the cheek of Shalke Felsenstein, a maddened German saw a mole. The German aimed at it. Three times his revolver jammed, but the fourth time it shot and he fell to the ground, dead.

Leibl Mandelbaum got lucky—for a large sum, a policeman brought him a flask of water. Nearby lay Freyda Barchowski with her small children, who writhed and suffered from the fiery heat. Mandelzweig [called "Mandelbaum" earlier] gave her a bit of water for the children. For this sin, an SS man shot him.

Young Pesach Rosenberg could not withstand the suffering from the heat and the anguish. He began to move his head in order to straighten his stiff back, and he sought a bit of water. Immediately a hail of bullets struck him in the head. Rosenberg was left lying dead in a pool of blood.

Yisroelke Teller, the "rabbi" of Siedlce's underworld, raised his head a little way off the ground. A Ukrainian saw him and—struck his head with an axe.

Those who were sitting on the walls surrounding the cemetery increased their devilish efforts, Chmielnicki and Petlura's grandchildren, who called themselves by the name of their new "hero": "Wlasowces"—they did not hesitate to shoot into the clustered,, beaten mass. Others took stones, bricks, from the old cemetery walls, as well as bottles, pieces of iron or of wood and—everything that could kill was thrown from that height onto the unfortunate victims.

[Page 45]

Every new "accomplishment," every new "brainstorm" of theirs was met with joy and wild encouragement from their German comrades and commanders.

This wild bacchanalia and bloody orgy lasted through the whole night, from Saturday to Sunday, and for several days after that.

* * *

And the great beaten-down mass lay pressed together on the ground with their heads bent, as if sitting shiva for themselves, whose lives would soon be cut short; still, the community that would be cut off huddled close together. And in order not to give the killers any pleasure, they held in their woe and protest that the horrible beatings and indignities called forth. So their tortured limbs they held still. Their only goal was: to be a worm, an ant, whose life no one sought and who could crawl freely and hide in the ground.

The mass was ruled by a dull, hardened despair. From a passive resignation, that came through necessity, that the world was worthless, without law and without a judge, after losing a belief in God, man, and the world, not hoping for a miracle, not making any plans for escape, for running away, Run where? The bloody rule had spread it dark government over the whole country and in almost all the countries of Europe. A full three years had led to this day and had prepared the masses through hunger and pain; isolated in the dark ghettos; with tears day in and day out for human feelings; knocked down and stole the human "I" and led people to the level that they regarded death as the only liberator from all sorrows. So the mass did not cry out, did not complain, did not protest, and accepted all with a resigned indifference that things were as they had to be.

It was as if the whole huddled mass became one congealed misfortune. Its consciousness was dulled and atrophied by the wild three-year labors of the people-devourers. Their great woe, sorrow, and suffering could not call forth the feeling of "Let me die with the Philistines" (Judges 16:30), or other stories of revenge and rebellion. They strove to be silent, the great mass. Only their eyes wandered around.

[Page 46]

There, the heavens, today, no more than any other day, remained self-contained and stubbornly quiet, sent forth no rain of fire, sulphur and stones like that hail that once avenged such tortures in Egypt; here—the sun, that burns hotter than ever, stings with its hot rays, as if with glowing spears, in the exhausted eyes, mixing with the hot, dry dust. It creeps into the nose, onto the neck, goes deeply into the empty, emaciated bowels, as if sent expressly to incinerate the unhappy victims, who yearn for a sip of water that they cannot get; and the same sun is too stingy to send out such a fire that it would ignite and burn everything—the whole world, along with those who are suffering.

And here the exhausted eyes look to the ground, which lies there quietly, dumb, sees everything and keeps silent. Under the surface of the execution grounds rest the bones of the victims' ancestors. They have no will that the earth should open, tear open in a terrible earthquake and swallow up everything, as once happened in the sinful city of Pompey.

Only the high grass of the cemetery and its multicolored flowers, which the late summer sun had brought forth in that spot, stood until yesterday proud and playful but not lie trodden down, mixed with dirt and blood, crushed under the feet and the boots, sharing the fate of their unfortunate neighbors, the trampled community.

* * *

However, there were also cases of individual heroism, outburst, and protest that were expressed in various forms in those tragic moments at the Umschlagplatz.

There were some who understood what was to come and did not wait to be killed at the hands of the murderers. They had prepared for themselves potassium cyanide—the dearest merchandise in the ghetto—and ended their lives there in the square, like Mrs. Dr. Papho and others, whose names I do not know. Others cut their veins with razor blades and bled to death.

An older gray-haired man arrived at the Umschlagplatz in his tallis and kittel, occupied himself for all of Shabbos and the whole night with heartrending prayers and selichos, said his confession [vidui] and concluded with "Shema Yisroel"!

[Page 47]

Elsewhere, a Jew sat in a corner, wrung his hands, and argued with the Riboyno shel Oylam. He asked: "Is it possible? Who will maintain your holy Torah if you have decided to annihilate your people Israel? Remember that today is the holy Shabbos, in the month of Elul, near to the Yamim Nora'im, and that should protect your hoy community. A miracle should happen. Why should the Gentiles say…Father in heaven???"

In another corner an observant mother laments over the dead body of her tortured child. She groans aloud, this unlucky mother, her great woe and sorrow and sharp words against Heaven. She asks bitterly: "Where is the Father who pities His sons?" She tells her neighbors, who lie fainting around her, that she herself had read in an old holy book in Yiddish

That once, in an evil time for Jews, there were great righteous people who called the Creator of the World to a judicial hearing. Now, in our great sinfulness, we are so guilty that there is no one to call them to justice.

And there, hidden under the wall of a house near the corner of Stari Rinke and Dluge, among all the bullet-riddled half-dead, are young couples. On their round, pale, almost childlike faces and big, open, blue eyes, which are turned to the far distance, is frozen—together with youthful fire, which kindles love in its first springtime, is the whole sorrow, hatred, and scorn for the accursed world that can destroy such young lives along with their newly awakened love. They have known each other since childhood. They went to school together. The pain and sorrows of the ghetto brought them closer together. They sit pressed together, bound together by their hands and glances, unafraid of being lost in the wild chaos on the threshold of death.

They will not be allowed to live together—but they prepare themselves to die together: "In their lives and in their deaths they were not divided" (2 Samuel 1: 23).

* * *

As I have already related, the killers had ordered their victims to sit with heads bowed to the earth and to keep silent.

[Page 48]

Suddenly the quiet was broken by one of the condemned—the always calm, thoughtful, teacher of religion Avraham Wasserzug, who used to teach the Jewish children history, how a small group of persecuted and oppressed Jews called the Maccabees stood up to battle their tormentors, who were great in number, and defeated them. He sprang up like a bound. Lion who had broken his fetters, stood on a rock and fire shone from his eyes. His voice thundered like the noise from a volcano with words of consolation for the suffering about the eternal Jewish tragedy that produces in every generation a Pharaoh, a Haman, a Torquemada, a Hitler, who wants to destroy us; and he spoke about the triumph of Israel that burns eternally that bush in the wilderness and will never be burned out. He called out to the killers: "Today you are strong, armed, and you can demonstrate your 'bravery' to us, killing those who are defenseless. But the day is near when you will have to pay a reckoning for your bloody deeds! You are drunk and blind on blood and evil and you cannot see the hand that writes on your killing walls, "Mene! Mene!... [a reference to the handwriting on the wall in the book of Daniel]. Count the days of your bloody rule, you mass murderers!..."

Like a tree that has been chopped down, Wasserzug fell from a rain of bullets that pierced his abused body and interrupted his words of consolation and vengeance.

The interrupted speech of the fallen Wasserzug was completed by young Nahman Rogowikamien (son of Paltiel), who was also one of those destined for Treblinka. He sprang up and with all the fury of youth his infuriated spirit called out: "You are not a people of thinkers and writers, only of thieves and murderers! The strong hand that comes from the east will take vengeance on you for our innocent blood and for your bloody deeds erase you from the face of the earth...!"

Like Wasserzug, so Rogowikamien ended his young life on the Umschlagplatz.

* * *

The unfortunates were not soon taken to the train station, as had appeared to be the intention. Although everything had gone according to schedule, they had not prepared enough cars for the trip to Treblinka. Was this done intentionally in order to for the victims to be tormented in their last days before death or was it a mistake? Who can know the intentions and plans of mass murderers?

[Page 49]

Early on the next day, Sunday, the first group was taken to the station. They were lined up in rows of five, holding each other's hands. Whoever could, tried to be among the first-desiring to be more quickly killed, annihilated—to put an end to things! Whoever from hunger or beatings or shame could not stand up and go on the death march was left behind, thanks to a murderer's bullet. Many of those who were weak were helped along by the healthy.

This last shameful march of the great community to the death wagons took a long time, until daytime on Monday.

The sacrificial victims were packed in the barred freight cars like dead objects. They were stuffed in and crowded together with the help of rifle butts, axes, and other weapons, causing horrible, Dantesque scenes: Here a woman was packed into one car and her child, whom she had kept by her side the entire time, was torn from her grasp and put into a second wagon on top of those who were already there. As the terrified mother and the child yelled and cried, there were two shots and—they were quieted forever.

Here a man was shoved into a packed wagon. He could not get in. But the hangmen shut the doors with all their might and the man was crushed hanging between the wall and the door—half his body in the wagon and half outside.

Shmuel Levita did not get into the wagon as quickly as the murderers wanted, so he was hacked to pieces by a will Ukrainian with his beloved national weapon—an axe.

The wagons, treated with fresh lime, thanks to the terrible crowding and burning heat, were filled with poisonous air and many of the victims lost consciousness or lost their minds and suffered terrible torments.

The way from Siedlce to Treblinka was not long—about thirty kilometers—but it was enough that half of the victims could not survive the short trip and arrived at their last station already dead.

It took two days to load and send the transport—

[Page 50]

Monday and Tuesday—the last transport left early Wednesday. A long, terror-filled whistle from the locomotive of the death train gave notice that it was bringing fresh fuel for the most recent invention of the twentieth century—for the gas chambers of Treblinka.

* * *

Throughout the time of this never before seen extraordinary "spectacle"—the action, the selection, and the death march, the streets where all this was happening were filled with curious citizens. The former neighbors with whom they had lived, worked, and done business came in unfriendly wonder. They watched this excellent picture, and in the sweet smiles on their pious Christian faces and the sparkling fire in their bright eyes, they showed their happiness and thankfulness to the organizers of this interesting undertaking. More than one rubbed his hands with great pleasure and called aloud so that the both the victims and the killers could hear, "Finally we're free of the bedbugs! Now we can live in Poland…"

[Page 50]

9. Bloody Statistics

Translated by Theodore Steinberg

What people called "the first aktion" lasted for four days. Four hopeless days and nights lasted the "liquidation" of an old Jewish community that with hundreds of years of effort and industry had grown to be a city and a mother in Israel; to be one of the most creative communities in Poland with about twenty thousand Jews. There remained in your ruins—aside from the five hundred seven young men whom the executioners had preserved for their liquidation work—yet a thousand living shadows who, during the aktion had hidden in bunkers, caves, covered-up holes and who now converged in the small ghetto. The killers "solemnly" assured them that they would not be harmed.

And this remained: an open cemetery with scattered bodies that lay on all the streets of the liquidated ghetto, in all the courtyards, in the attics and in the garbage heaps.

The old cemetery-Umschlagplatz and the surrounding streets—Stari Rinek, Zhidowska, and First of May—looked horrible.

[Page 51]

Hundreds of dead people, killed by various instruments of death, lay all around—trampled, stiffened bodies soaked in pools of black blood.

Most of the dead had had their clothing, their shoes, and even their underwear ripped off of them. Thus did the hometown robbers worry over them.

During the whole four days of the wild bacchanalia, the murderers did not allow the dead to be cleaned up or buried. As the sun did its work and heated the corpses, the air was filled with a nauseating odor from the unburied bodies.

Only on Wednesday morning were the Jewish police allowed to move the dead.

With the aid of some of the selected Jewish workers from the small ghetto, some people were harnessed to wagons and dragged them through the streets of the liquidated large ghetto, while others threw the bodies into the wagons, like slaughtered calves or pieces of wood, dragged them to the walls of the closed off ghetto, where, on the Aryan side, Christian workers waited. They took the loads of dead to the cemetery and buried them in common graves.

How many Jews were killed in those terrifying four days cannot be accurately determined. At a time when Jewish lives were considered worthless, no one cared to count them systematically. Consequently, the numbers given by surviving witnesses differ and contradict each other.

In those dark, hellish days, the Jewish section of the magistrate's office was led by councilman Gluchowski. As told by Leibl Mandelbaum (one of the chosen 507 who later hid in the woods and the villages), the last report was that the number of murdered Jews on those days was 3,200. According to an eyewitness who then served in the Jewish police and helped to gather the dead, the number was 2,000.

There is also no precise knowledge of the number of Jews who were transported to Treblinka. A number of eyewitnesses say 12,000, others 15,000, and still others, 8,000.

[Page 52]

No one will ever know the bloody statistics. The actual eyewitnesses, the streets of the ghetto and the earth of the old cemetery, which absorbed the spilled blood of that portion f the community, and the accursed field and woods of Treblinka, where the ashes of the cremated martyrs were scattered, are stubbornly silent and say nothing about their tragic secret.

No more the centuries-old community—Siedlce! No longer its twenty thousand Jewish inhabitants!

Now, when we note what we have encountered in the ruins of our destroyed home, we have the tragic total of the remaining statistic: about forty pale shadow-men with deeply burrowed foreheads, dull eyes, and almost all with old, gray heads on their young bodies, men who for years felt like worms under the ground, between life and death; and several score broken migrants, returned from Siberia and the taigas of Kazakhstan, sole survivors of their large families. Altogether—an unhappy small group of lonely orphans, who roam about on the roads and fields, digging and seeking a sign, a bit of ash from their nearest and dearest and from their destroyed homes.

---

10. The Large Ghetto

Translated by Theodore Steinberg

A. Stary Rynek

We wander further over the ruins of our destroyed home and find ourselves at Start Rinek.

The street is an old one. One of the first Jewish streets in Siedlce. The name Stary Rynek—Old Market—remains from the time when it, together with the neighboring cemetery, were beyond the city limits and were the site of a market for cows, oxen, sheep, and horses. This was also the source of another name, used by older folk—Konski Rynek (Horse Market).

Although the place has a genuine Polish name, it was a thoroughly Jewish street, like Pinkie. Actually, it was not as wide nor as long as Pienkne.

[Page 53]

It had fewer inhabitants, did not provide as many revolutionary fighters is the days of the czar as Pienkne Street, and also did not have as many Maskilim, community activists, and pure Jewish scholars as Pienkne Street—but it had its own special distinctiveness.

First of all Stary Rynek was proud of its old, distinguished, substantial homeowners, with their long-established grocery, flour, and tobacco businesses, which lined the left side of the street, one after the other—from Warsaw Street too Dluge—and marked the real business center of the city.

On Stary Rynek lived the patriarchal Jews, distinguished, virtuous before God and before people, like the 95-year-old baker and Old Gradzisker Chasid R. Leibl Prives; there R. Chaim Shloymo Yablon and his sons conducted the oldest grocery business in the city; there lived and conducted his many-branched business such an old, established resident as R. Avigdor Ridel with his large family; his son, the most prominent mohel in Siedlce, R. Shimon Ridel, who made his living from the flour business on Stary Rynek, although his major concern was by his hand the Jewish boys of Siedlice became Jews, and to a poor man he would give several rubles after conducting the bris; there, too, lived his learned sons-in-law: R. Nachman Lev, the Tiktiner prodigy, R. Dov Berish Yom-Tov, the distinguished only son of the Szelekover rabbi; R. Eliezer Lippe Yom Tov, who boasted that he was a descendant of the Tosafist Yom-Tov; and R. Yosef Rosenbaum the astute student and scholar of the Ger rabbi. On Stary Rynek lived the respected arbitrator of business affairs, R. Sander Kantor, the Szelekover rabbi R. Yehoshualeh and many other Jews of the city.

Furthermore, Stary Rynek merited having within its borders the great city shul. On the right side of the street, right next to the old cemetery, it stood, a high, proud place, behind a white fence, with fine, twisted iron towers; with its painted image of the Ten Commandments, it reminded passersby that there is a God in the world…

The many businesses that were found on Stary Rynek attracted the smaller merchants of the city. Many small merchants from neighboring shtetls who came there to buy goods, many business agents, travelers, brokers, shady characters, carriage drivers, and porters with their horses, wagons, and handcarts, in addition to random Jewish loafers who came to observe how other Jews went about their business—all together carried on, made a racket, and went around, creating the impression that a constant fair was in progress.

[Page 54]

But when Shabbos arrived, and even more a Yom Tov or a Shabbos of the new moon blessing, when there state chazan led the prayers with his choir and people streamed into the shul from all sections of the city both for prayers and from the love of music, Jews all dressed up in their Shabbos garb, with their solemn Shabbos gait, with their taleisim under their arms, and women all arrayed in silk and velvet, in atlas and Georgette [types of fabric]. Their Shabbos necks were hung with strands of pearls and golden necklaces. With sparkling rings and bracelets on their white Shabbos hands, with their fancy shoes and their prayerbooks, with little silver locks, under their arms. Then the fuss and tumult disappeared completely. The street lost its weekday nature and put on a cloak of Shabbos sanctity, and the whole street appeared to be an antechamber to the shul, a foyer where a great many of those who pray and those who love the music stand because, thanks to the crowd, they could not gain entrance in the shul itself. There, through the wide open doors of the shul they can gather fragments of the chazan's performance, which rings through the outdoors.

For non-Jews, too, Stary Rynek was important because opposite, by the exit to Warsaw Street, was the city hall, so that this spot was the central point of the city. After the death of Josef Pilsudski, when the city wanted to erect a memorial to Poland's hero, people decided that the most appropriate spot for such a memorial was the square of Stary Rynek.

Because of the many wholesale businesses that were in Stary Rynek, the mobs from neighboring towns came with their horses and wagons and set up on the streets in order to buy different products. They unharnessed their put-upon horses and tied them to the heavy wagons, leaving them alone there with a bag of oats as they went away on business for half the day. And when they returned, they lay down on the wagons and went to sleep and grubbily snored away as if they were in their own homes...

[Page 55]

Across from the businesses dealing in flour, sugar, herring, and rice that were set out on the ground or on the iron barrier that went around Stary Rynek Square, porters with ropes around their hips waited for a job or rested after a hard bit of work. Some ate their lunch from blackened pots that their wives brought and discussed issues, told stories, or exchanged low, porterish jokes, after which loud laughter filled the street.

For years, Jewish droshky drivers had no place to take a rest. in whatever parts of the city and on the streets where they took their droshkies, they had to put up with their Christian rivals and also from the city powers that gave them troubles until they received a set place in Jewish Stary Rynek, where they could stand in a long line of shiny black droshkies on part of the street across from the wholesalers. The harnessed horses, adorned with badges, stood with raised heads and half-sleepy expressions or flicked away flies with their long tails. The owner sat in the droshky dressed in his driver uniform, and just like his horse, was half-asleep on the soft cushion, until a passenger appeared and awakened him. Others sat in a group in one of the droshkies and talked about how difficult it was to earn a zloty since all of the Christian drivers had, under the slogan "Keep to your own," had inscribed on their hats in red letters on white linen: "Droshky for the baptized," so that the Jewish droshky drivers who lacked that slogan were boycotted by Christian passengers and went hungry, along with their wives and children and their poor horses...

The broad square, the only square in the Jewish area from Warsaw to Dluge Street , made Stary Rynek an important place. This was a square specially for Jews and Jewish children, who were afraid to venture into the city park lest they get hit in the head with a rock thrown by the wonderful Polish children, or lest a fierce dog rip their clothing.

[Page 56]

Jewish children felt secure there that no goyish stone-thrower would come. They had better places...and the dogs who came into the Jewish butcher shops looking for a bone were quiet and calm. They were happy that no one beat them, and they even liked to be petted by the Jewish children.

The fact is that there were no trees or green things in the square. The tiny bit of grass that began to sprout from the dug up earth was soon trampled by the proud young feet, along with the boards on which had been written, "Keep off the grass." The yelling of the city garden overseer did not help, even when he chased after the children with his big broom. He soon grew tired, and the children played hopscotch. They scratched boxes on the ground, and they hopped from one to another. Others pretended to ride horses: one would sit on another's back, and he would gallop around; others played at soldier, in two opposing armies. They played at war, but often their play became too real and adults would have to intervene and make peace...

The girls played at "house," rocking their "babies" in metal or paper cradles, washing clothes and cooking the best meals out of sand for their "babies"...

Many real mothers also came to the square with real strollers, in which real children either lay or sat. They came for a bit of fresh air. They would flirt with a young man whom they had known and while rocking their child, they would gossip with the other mothers...

The square also served as a place to stroll and as a refuge for various categories of Jews from different classes:

One would encounter the most prominent wholesalers, their hands behind them, thinking about their competition with other merchants, about the "refugees," evil customers, and about the difficult tax situation, all of which made life difficult.

There were also those who constantly stood by the city hall who, when they grew tired of long hours standing in the street, would gather in the square, sit on a bench and listen to a bit of wisdom from the old Stary Rynek buffoon R. Shloyme Nisman.

From the nearby beis-medresh, those who always sat and learned often came to the square for a little fresh air and even to learn what was new in the city and what the newspapers were saying about the larger world.

[Page 57]

If people had a conflict and wanted a religious court to make a judgment, they would come to the square of Stary Rinek. They would often take a bench across from the shul, a crowd of Jews arguing, yelling, wrangling, and fighting. In the middle of the bench sat R. Shlomo Shmuel Abarbanel representing one side and R. Sender Kantor representing there other. They listened to the flood of words and yells from both sides and had to decide who was right and deliver a judgment in this merchant's court.

And over there, in the shadow of the broad shoulders of Pilsudski's memorial, Jews conducted various transactions. They tested grains or manufacturing samples; they discounted bills and discussed old times.

Parallel to the great wholesalers, thee was also in Stary Rynek a poor, small business:

Such a business had blind Yudel always conducted among everything else in the square. He would fall in among the children, unpack his goods and wait for the children to interrupt their games and gather around him and his great selection: different colored balloons that waited to be released from their sticks so that they could escape to the clouds; mechanical toys that ran by themselves when they were put on the ground; rubber dogs that barked loudly when given a push under the arm and dressed-up dolls whose eyes closed when they were laid down to sleep. He also had an assortment of sweets: chocolates, mixed with almonds, frozen treats, red sugary candies, and many-colored lollipops on sticks. And even though it was not Simchas Torah or Chanukah or Purim, he also had such seasonal articles: Simchas Torah flags, Chanukah dreidels, and Purim graggers. Children bought, and even if one had no money, that was not so terrible. Yudel gave credit and inscribed it in his memory. He knew that tomorrow he would be paid what he was owed.

A constant competitor for Yudel's business was Naomele. She was exactly the opposite of Yudel. Yudel was tall and thin and moved quickly, while Naomele was tiny, Lilliputian, and fat. She moved slowly with tiny steps and she appeared like a fat child.

[Page 58]

You would not have known that she was thirty-something, a poor orphan, whom the community had married off to Arkel— who was also Lilliputian, as fat as she was, and also a poor orphan. She, Naomele, was the breadwinner. She trudged around holding two large bags of merchandise in her hands. In one bag was a variety of cookies, pieces of honey cake, beans, egg bagels, and other sweets. In the second bag was a great deal of writing material: notebooks, pens, pencils, scissors, rubber bands, and other things that children needed.

From early in the morning, Naomele would go around with her bags of goods to the schools: the Tarbus School, the Folk School, the Talmud Torah, and in the general schools for Jewish children. These places were her business sites. On days when the schools were closed, Naomele would take her moveable goods to the square of Stary Rynek, where there were so many children.

When she appeared with her two big bags by her sides, she seemed so huge that she looked like a portable pyramid. Because she was small and broad and looked funny, the children surrounded her, as soon as she appeared. They laughed at her and bought her goods.

Naturally, Yudel was not overjoyed that Naomele invaded his territory with her goods in the square of Stary Rynek, where he had long reigned. But he never fought with her. Only, when she appeared, he would gesture with his hand and even more with his blind eyes, that thus became totally white—as if to say, "What should I do with her? She also has to live." So once in a while, Yudel would also go with his merchandise to the schools that constituted Naomele's area of business.

Another constant business in the square was conducted by Tzlove the cripple. Both of Tzlove's legs were paralyzed, so that she could not walk. She would sit on a little bench, and she could manipulate the bench so that she move all around, wherever she wanted. In her lap she had a tray of shelled peas and beans, half of the tray with big yellow peas and half with big brown beans, covered with pepper.

[Page 59]

In the middle of the tray was a Shabbos glass for kiddish, that helped her earn a living all during the week. She sold cheap—five groschen for a kiddish-glass of peas and beans. As a bonus, she also gave the purchaser a blessing. The essence of the blessing depended on the buyer's age: for a young child she wished that at his bar mitzvah, people would have such good beans and peas; a teenager, boy or girl, she wished that at their wedding people would have such good food; for a mature man or a young wife her blessing was that they should eat such food, God willing, at a bris. For older people she wished grandchildren and great-grandchildren, and so on.

For the whole day Tzlove went around on her little stool with her large tray of merchandise among the people in the square. In the evening, when everyone began to go to the shul for the afternoon and evening prayers, she situated herself right by the doors of the shul with her tray on her knees. The aroma of hot peas and beans mixed with the sharp odor of pepper invaded the noses of the passersby, who had to give in to their inclinations and buy some. Even in the cold of winter, Tzlove would sit there on her stool with her goods. She had near her a pot with hot coals to keep her warm. She would invite her freezing customers to warm themselves, too.

Thanks to the good "geographic situation" of the square, which was right in the center of the Jewish area, among totally Jewish streets, people could feel free whenever they wanted, thanks to its intimacy; thanks to its Jewish heimishkeit, which allowed people to appear in their everyday clothing without putting on anything special. One could even leave by itself, without any special preparations, a sleeping child in a carriage, and go inside to prepare lunch—the squad and the whole of Stary Rynek was the most popular spot in all of Jewish Siedlce for teenagers and for children.

Yes, there was once such a Jewish street—Stary Rynek.

And when the bloody machine devised its devilish plan to assign Siedlce's Jewish community to a living grave—in the ghetto—Stary Rynek was the threshold to that grave.

The exit from Warsaw Street was shut up by a wall of barbed wire. O n the side, between the Pilsudski monument and the community buildings was placed an entrance to this living grave. Over the entrance was a sign inscribed in big, fat letters:

[Page 60]

"German and Polish citizens are forbidden to enter the Jewish quarter because of the raging epidemic." A policeman was stationed by the entrance to prevent any of the Jews confined in this living grave from going out into the freer world. And no one from outside could enter the confined error and bring help, a little bread or some potatoes.

The second duty of the police at the ghetto gate was early in the morning to open the gate and allow out the enslaved Jews who marched to their daily hard labor, and at night to allow back in the worn out and beleaguered Jews who were returning "home" from their difficult labors.

And the police guard had yet another duty that did not allow him any rest: opening and closing the gate for the black wagon, which, from early morning until late at night, was busy collecting and taking to the cemetery the great number of dead who were served up by the two angels of death in the ghetto—on the one hand by the wild hooligans from the worked up bands of murderers and on the other hand by hunger, crowding, and filth—with the resulting epidemics that such conditions called forth.

By the wall of barbed wire on Stary Rynek, near the ghetto gate, was the favorite spot of the barbaric Germans, who would sit there for entertainment and amusement—this was an everyday occurrence—they would come in groups to the gate like hunters, sit at tables that the Jewish council had been forced to provide, and eat and drink—and fire shots through the holes in the barbed wire at the captive Jews who appeared on the other side. And as the victim shuddered and fell to the cobblestones, wild, loud laughter resounded through the street. They toasted each other and drank in honor of the victory of German arms, which always hit their target.

Soon after, the wagon arrived and took the victims to the cemetery.

By chance it happened that the fire that the vandals had set to burn down the community buildings with the shul and the beis-medresh had spared three buildings that the community had there, near the shul, which had been built for financial reasons: they served as butcher shops where people could buy kosher meat.

[Page 61]

Now those innocent buildings had been converted by the executioners into butcher shops for Jewish lives. They served as the ghetto prison, and woe to him who had the misfortune to go there. The road from there led straight to the cemetery.

Many tragic stories were told about what happened in those three buildings at the time of the ghetto. The tragic chapter "Ghetto-Prison" closed with the confinement there, after the liquidation of the large ghetto, of thirty girls and women, who were tortured for many hours before they were taken to the cemetery and shot. (More will be told about these thirty girls and women in a forthcoming chapter.)

In the early days of the war-bacchanalia, when the city was reduced to nothing by the fire and death from the enemy airplanes, Stary Rynek, like all the other Jewish streets, made its own contribution: a row of houses at the corner of Warsaw Street went up in flames before collapsing, burying a number of their inhabitants.

Later, at the time of the ghetto's liquidation, a group of twenty-some unfortunate Jews in a neighboring street, among the ruins, in a dark cellar, made a subterranean bunker and hid there for a whole year. In the summer of 1943, by accident a car with Germans came upon this bunker. The roof, which was covered with a layer of dirt and grass, broke, and the hidden Jews were discovered.

The unfortunates were shackled in chains and held for several weeks in the cemetery, where they were forced to work at cremating the corpses, which had piled up so much, and to clean up other traces of German crimes and horrors, until they themselves died from the hard work, the hunger, and the torture.

On the dark day of the last judgment of Siedlce's Jews, which the killers called "selection," when the old cemetery was overflowing and could not contain the whole community, the execution grounds were broadened into neighboring Stary Rynek and its square. The once heimish and beloved earth, like that in the old cemetery, drank in the last tears and the blood of the tortured victims.

[Page 62]

Just as there in the cemetery-Umschlagplatz, so also in the square the curse of the time was afoot: The earth grew rich with the blood of the tortured community, but even after many years without the jumping feet of Jewish children, the earth lies dead, naked, ashamed, with even less greenery than earlier.

Now Stary Rynek is as quiet as a cemetery. There are no more scamps claiming the streets with their childish voices while playing hopscotch in the square or playing horses or playing house.

The old city garden watchman has no one to chase with his big broom, no one to disturb his rest, and he sits there lazily, stretches out his arms, and soaks in the sun's warmth.

There are no more shiny black droshkies with their uniformed owners that used to fill Stary Rynek; there are no more big, heavy wagons with their big, broad wagoners; there are no more porters with their ropes wound around their hips sitting on the iron barricade of the square, none of the merchants, homeowners, negotiators, beis-medresh students, nor the random Jews on the street for whom Stary Rynek was a second home.

The street is as quiet as a cemetery. The few remaining houses are decked in mourning, those that were not destroyed by the enemy's dynamite and fire. Black, damaged, strangely cold, even the little signs by their doors speak of their past glory, as we read: heirs of Ch. Sh. Yablon, Reichenbach, Nissan, Ridel—house number 9. It is like having my legs cut out from under me. I stop automatically. A terrible coldness runs through my bones. I stare through the open window on the second floor, where my wife's parents and family lived.

My heart twists from sorrow at looking into the room that twenty-some years ago filled me with so much love and took me in as one of its own. I became a member of the Yom-Tov family, a transplant in this city. How many beautiful recollections arise in my mind, how many wonderful memories of those times sit in my consciousness, mixing in with the endless sea of horrors, sadness, flooded and drowning by them.

Dragged from that room by the German murderers to prison, to the concentration camp, leaving the family behind.

[Page 63]

For a second I feel an urge, a longing to its familiar walls, its heimish furnishings—but my feet do not move. They stand there as if in concrete. In the struggle of conflicting feelings, between yes and no, no wins, because I did not want to see the place from which my nearest and dearest were led to the sacrifice.

Through the open window I see the same armoire, the same bookcase that stood there before. I see the same lamps, even the same plant pots as before. And when in the window there appear unknown faces with angry eyes that stare with cold strangeness, curious and mocking, my glance and my heart can stand no more and I walk away. No, I run away, away from there.

B. Dluge Street

We find ourselves on the second street of the living ghetto grave—Dluge, which, in 1927, when the socialists had a majority in the city council, was renamed "First of May."

Both sides of the street, both the east and the west, were inhabited by non-Jews as well. There were also central institutions of great importance, like the Orthodox cathedral on one side and on the other the chief court, the post office building, the women's gymnasium, and others.

But most of the inhabitants were Jews from various groups. Members of the intelligentsia lived there as well as ordinary Jews: major merchants and poor craftsmen, workers and "upper class" Jews, Chassidim, teachers who gave the street its Jewish character and appearance.

In the bloody early days of the war, before the city was taken by the bands of German murderers, when their aircraft had according to their plan "accidentally" covered with fire, explosives, and death the totally Jewish streets of the city—the non-Jewish part of Dluge Street could not be defended separate from the Jewish part, and the greatest part was divided between bare earth and sheer ruins, including the popular "Yisroel-Yechiel's Beis-Medresh" and the so-called "Petersburg" Beis-Medresh.

[Page 64]

The barbed wire of the ghetto fence closed off both ends of the street: on one side, by Kochanowska, it separated the ghetto from the church. On the other side there was a wall of barbed wire by Sandowa-Posta Street, which separated the ghetto from the area of the court.

There were also barbed wire fences at the cross streets: Berko Joselowicz, Mala, and Oszeshkowa, which closed off the road that led from Dluge out to Warsaw Street.

Here and there we come across remnants of that barbed wire that encircled those enclosed in the ghetto. At spots there is a pole sunk deep into the ground. At spots, pieces of wire litter the ground. And the rusty wires stick not only the feet but also the soul and the heart when one remembers the function they fulfilled in the recent past.

Some houses remain standing on Mala and Sandowa Streets. Among them is the Dluge-Warsaw passage courtyard. This courtyard was the window for the living ghetto-grave to the Aryan side: when a neighborly Christian would remember a Jewish neighbor who had done him favors, he could sneak in a bit of bread through that entranceway.

Ghetto business was also conducted in the courtyard: if someone wanted to trade a couple of potatoes for a pillow, a piece of clothing, or a wedding ring—he did it in the courtyard, and there were many on "the other side" who wanted to make such deals.

When the Germans realized that this "illegal activity" was going on, they built in the courtyard a high concrete wall that made further smuggling of such goods impossible and thereby increased the number of deaths from hunger in the ghetto.

The wall also remains as a "memorial of destruction," and it bears silent witness to the pain, horror, hunger, and death that took place behind it.

And one encounters other remnants from the past that recall what once was. The same butcher shop stands as it once did in the red Rogowin house, hung with different cuts of meat. Across from it stands open the same haberdashery building and the same pharmacy with the same large signs and inscriptions as before.

[Page 65]

Only when one looks more closely, one sees that it is not Yankel Tabakman starting there behind his counter not Moyshe Kruszel in his notions shop and not Yankel Sarnacki in the butcher shop. There are totally new, strange owners who look out, some with open and some with hidden mockery at the sorrowful pair of Jewish passersby.

C. The Jewish Council

Dluge Street "merited" having within it two institutions of central importance in the enclosed ghetto: the Jewish Council and the ghetto hospital.

Like all of Jewish life and all of its institutions, the former Jewish community structure was quickly dismantled when the Germans took the city.

It is understandable that in the flood of utter darkness and terror, of complete confusion that the Germans brought with them, no Jewish institutions could continue their normal work. All of them were abandoned. There were only two undertakings: the Jewish community organization under the new name of "Jewish council" and the hospital.

After an interruption of several weeks in its activities, full of confusion and terror, the community organization was revived by the Germans themselves.

As it soon became apparent, the Germans themselves needed such an organization that indirectly conveyed their thieving and extortionist orders for money and goods, for people to work, and for all their other wild demands.

At the end of October, 1939, the order came out to create a Jewish council of 25 people.

Understandably, as with every order, no one knew how to go about it, but the result of several consultations with community leaders and leaders of the political parties, the following people were decided upon:

[Page 66]

Yitzchak-Nachum Weintraub, Dr. Henryk Loebel, Menashe Czarnobrode, Eisenberg Hersh, Moyshe Rotbeyn, the lawyer Yoysef Landau, Eizik Lipsker, Yoysef Rosenzumen Yehoshua Ackerman, Avraham Altenberg, Yoel Levin, Velvel Barg, Leon Greenberg, Moshe Radzinski, David Altman, Yonasan Eibschutz, Dr. Leon Glazowski, Dr. Belfar, Dr. Shaul Schwartz, Dr. Shlomo Tenenbaum, lawyer Rubinstein, David Liebman, Moshe Greenwald, Avraham Yoysef Kornitzki, Binem Huberman.

The list was submitted to the German governing council and was approved.

Later, when 3 members of the Jewish council died from the epidemics that raged in the ghetto—Menashe Czarnobrode, Yoel Levin, and Yonasan Eibschutz—they were replaced by Mendel Goldblatt, Yissachar Yablon, and Berl Czebutski.

The most senior of Siedlce's Jews, the excellent leader R. Yitzchak Nachum Weintraub, was elected unanimously as the honorary chair of the Jewish council, but this had only a decorative and moral significance. This new Jewish organization that was created in such difficult circumstances before the Jews of Siedlce wanted to demonstrate its love and unity with the old, true servants of the community, who, for half a century, had led most of the community and charitable organizations in the city, and especially with the everyday people and served them heart and soul. But actually to lead such a complex organization as the Jewish council, and to be an intercessor between the community and Hitler's rulers was beyond the abilities of an elderly man like R. Yitzchak Weintraub. So as director of the Jewish council, Dr. Henryk Loebel, director of the Jewish hospital, was elected chair. He was known as a man of great energy, of humanistic and Jewish virtues, and of cultural qualifications reflecting all of greater Europe. In the course of his activities for the Jewish council, and also as director of the hospital, he often showed that he was the right man for the job. (You must understand that I mean under those conditions)

Two circumstances dictated that the Jewish council would grow strong and become a dynamic, many-branched organization that would incorporate everything that was relevant to the current life of the suffering community. On the one hand were the wild demands of the Germans, their insatiable appetite for Jewish possessions, for Jewish lives, for laborers; the flood of discriminatory orders that fell unceasingly on Jewish heads (all through the offices of the Jewish council).

[Page 67]

And on the other hand the needs of the oppressed Jews—material, physical, psychological, hygienic, medicinal requirements and all other sorts of sorrows and pains which overflowed upon our unhappy fellow citizens in times of despair and need caused them to seek help from the Jewish council—these two circumstances were the factors behind the Jewish council's growth in stature, with so many divisions and sections and with so many staff members and clerks.

The work of the Jewish council was assigned to the following managers:

General matters—Personnel: Heschel Eisenberg; Finances: Menashe Czarnobrode; Labor: Moyshe Rotbeyn; Social Aid: lawyer Yoysef Landau; Provisions: Avraham Altenberg; Health: Dr. Loebel; Legal Matters: Leon Greenberg.

All divisions and sections were subdivided and were swamped with work. The most dynamic and active, however, were the divisions whose duties involved serving the wild German appetites. Among those divisions were the work division, which had to provide people for forced labor, and the finance division, which had to extract money from the worn out people in order to pay the constant extortionate demands and other demands that the Germans placed on the Jewish council. Many activities were incumbent on the divisions that served the internal needs of the people, such as social aid, health, and others.

In addition, there were special divisions that required contact between the Jewish council and the German offices. The long-time secretary of the Jewish community, Herschel Tanenbaum, was named as liaison between the Jewish council and the Gestapo. His duty was: every morning he had to go to the Gestapo and receive their wild, sadistic demands, which the Jewish council had to carry out.

The other community employee, Ezriel Friedman, was named as liaison between the Jewish council and the German labor office and police office. His duty was to send forced laborers to all kinds of hard work that the Germans systematically demanded of the Jewish council.

Several score helpless shadow-men—they are what remains from the great old Jewish community of Siedlce!

[Page 68]

D. Extortion

In October of 1939 on the first day of its renewed activities, the Jewish council received and order from the German common to pay 10,000 zlotys in extortion money that was demanded from the Jewish population. This was only the beginning, because soon after this there arrived at the address of the Jewish council extraordinary demands from extortion money. Thus, a few weeks later, in December of that year, there was a demand for 20,000 zlotys; in November of 1940—100,000 zlotys; in March of 1941—100,000 zlotys, and from January of 1942 until the final destruction of the Jews of Siedlce, the extortion became a regular payment of 100,000 zlotys each month.

In addition to extortions of money, there were daily orders of extortion in, for example, furniture, utensils, linens, clothing, furs, jewelry that the Germans could get from Jews.

In December, 1941, the Germans ordered the Jewish council to deliver all furs and fur-making equipment that belonged to Jews.

The entrapped Jews, who for the most part suffered from hunger and need, having been robbed of the most elementary necessities, lost the power to exist and lived only on what they could sell of their possessions. They had to surrender to the Jewish council everything to satisfy the wild desires for extortion and confiscation.

Thus, for example, the vandals came to the Jewish council at the end of December, 1939, on the morning after they had brewed the shul and the beis- medresh and demanded from the council a certification that the shul and the beis-medresh had been burned in unknown circumstances.

[Page 69]

On Purim of 1942, the murderers seized and arrested ten Jews and took them to Stak-Lacki (a village near Siedlce) and shot them there on the orders of the head of the district council of Labor Office—on the pretense that they had refused to work.

The Jewish council was forced to issue a statement that the Germans were right and that the death sentence for the ten Jews was correct.

Among many other wild extortionate schemes, particularly characteristic was the Gestapo's order to the Jewish council to prepare and organize with all its facilities (at their own cost, of course), a brothel for the pure-raced Germans, in the house of Hesche Kaplan at 11 Pienkne.

In the summer of 1942, the Germans ordered the Jewish council to present a variety of craftsmen with their tools. The Jewish council made known that these craftsmen were needed. The chosen Jews, with their tools, were sent away somewhere. Later on it was learned that the chosen craftsmen had been transported to an extermination camp.

On August 22, the black Shabbos, when a band of murderers arrived in the city to conduct the slaughter which became known as "the first aktion," the Gestapo ordered the Jewish council to set out chicken, wine, and pastries for lunch, which the killers devoured at the Umschlagplatz during the selektion.

Later, when the Jewish council had again resumed its activities (in a reduced form) in the small ghetto, it was ordered by the Germans to pay a city fireman for his work in helping to torment the Jews, for spraying them with water, when they were suffering on that Shabbos in the Umschlagplatz.

* * *

For the first two months of its existence, the Jewish council was located in the hall of the Jewish community in the kehillah building. At the end of December, 1939, after the vandals burned the shul, the beis-medresh, and the kehillah building, the Jewish council moved to the premises of the library in "Ha-zamir" (61 Pilsudski Street). By that time the library had already been vandalized, destroyed, and shut up.

[Page 70]

A short time later this locale was taken by the Germans for their own purposes, and they ordered the Jewish council out. The council relocated to Szenkewicza 14. Then later they moved to 34 Pilsudski (Epstein's house) and then again to 14 Pilsudski (Shmerl Greenberg's house).

With the closing of the ghetto, the Jewish council found its resting place in the house of Zelnick's heirs at 36 Dluge. The courtyard there became a vale of tears in the closing ghetto. All of the bitter orders came there, all the bloody decrees and wild demands that the vandals could devise in order to dishonor and steal the lives and possessions of the beleaguered Jews in the ghetto. All of the despairing and broken Jews came there to pour out their troubled hearts to the council members. Some were naive enough to believe that the Jewish council could do something to cut through the evil decrees, and some just wanted to pour out the sorrow and need of their hearts for a few minutes.

The Social Help division of the Jewish council came those who were swollen with hunger. They came seeking a bit of bread and something to allay their hunger.

Every morning hundreds of Jews came to the courtyard of the Jewish council because they had been called up for forced labor for the German killers. In the neighboring cross street from Dluge to Browarna they were arranged in rows, and under the command of the ordnance police, they were led to various places both inside and outside the city for hard labor.

E. The Tragic End of the Jewish Council

On the same day when the large ghetto was liquidated and the Jewish community was forced to the Umschlagplatz, that black Shabbos of August 22, 1942, the Jewish council was also liquidated.

False was that illusion, just as so many illusions were proved false, that many of the Jews in the ghetto had maintained, that belonging to the Jewish council entailed certain privileges, that having a document attesting to one's membership on the council would be a treasure in a difficult moment.

[Page 71]

Many people believed this. They regarded Jewish council members with jealousy, as though their lives were more important, more secure, as if they belonged to an organization that even the Germans needed, so that they would not kill such members. Many would have paid a great deal for such a charm as a Jewish council membership card.

Being a member of the Jewish council also gave the privilege of not having one's goods confiscated day in and day out, of not being extorted. It also provided the possibility of avoiding forced labor.

But when the day came for the final judgment on the whole community, the members of the Jewish council, along with their associates and assistants, even those who had used the opportunity to seek favor with the killers, were just like all the other Jews and suffered the same fate as all their brothers.

After the great slaughter of the first aktion, of the twenty-five council members, only five remained, because they had hidden. They were Yitzchak Nachum Weintraub, Moyshe Radzinski, Moyshe Rotbeyn, Heschel Eisenberg, and Dr. Belfour.

Four members—Dr. Loebel, Glazowski, Schwartz, and Tenenbaum—were killed two days later when the hospital where they worked was liquidated.

All the rest, together with the whole community, were forced to the Umschlagplatz and from there, all together, transported to Treblinka.

Along with the Jewish council, almost all of their associates and assistants were liquidated in the first aktion.

Thus was killed Herschel Tanenbaum, the long-serving secretary of the community and latterly the liaison between the council and the Gestapo. Almost everyone envied him because of this unlucky post, with his acquaintance with the higher levels of the killers and murderers as they ordered whatever their wild fantasies devised. He, along with his whole family, was sent to Treblinka.

[Page 72]

The liaison between the Jewish council and the German labor office, Ezriel Friedman, for his "service" in arranging Jews for forced labor, merited a "special handling": on the day of the selektion, he was allowed to live, along with with his selected assistants, but two days later he was called out of his home at the corner of First of May and Targowa by Gestapo head Duba himself, who, with his own bloody hands, shot him by the wall of his house.

* * *

On that day of destruction, August 22, the premises of the Jewish council remained empty and worthless. A band of killers entered and utterly demolished it, stole the funds that were kept there as well as anything valuable. The whole rich archive with all its documents and minutes, which, in clear words and numbers, conveyed the martyrdom and pain of Siedlce's twenty thousand people, they destroyed.

In the time of the ghetto, the Jews lived in a troubled era and came to the Jewish council seeking advice, a word of consolation, and perhaps a bit of protection.

On that tragic Shabbos, on a day of massive slaughter, when all avenues of rescue closed upon our unfortunate fellow citizens, many Jews sought protection from the Jewish council, and when they could not find such help, they took to the cellar and other hiding places in the building. These unfortunates, about thirty of them, were discovered by the German and Ukrainian murderers, dragged into the courtyard, and shot.

Among them were the family of Ephraim Zelnick, Yakov Levin, and other prominent Jews.

---

11. The Ghetto Hospital and Its Liquidation

Translated by Theodore Steinberg

Opposite the slaughterhouse of the old cemetery-Umschlagplatz, among the other ruins, standing in a little garden, like an old aristocratic woman, behind an iron fence, in the shape of the letter "ches," are the white building of 26 Dluge Street.

[Page 73]

The buildings have always served humane purposes: for a number of years they housed a Polish Folk School for Jewish children, a so-called "Shabbosvokes," where Jewish teachers taught Jewish students Polish history and culture.

Before the outbreak of the war, the Red Cross occupied the buildings and conducted its medical and aid activities for the city.

In October of 1941, when the large ghetto was locked up, the Jewish hospital was brought to the buildings, since it had been outside the borders of the ghetto—on Swietojanska Street.

In those dark days, when the Angel of Death had cut down the inhabitants of the ghetto in such large numbers with his associates—various epidemics that had been called forth by crowding, hunger, and need—the hospital was the only oasis in the valley of tears that could help the sufferers even in a small way, giving some of the ill and pained a bit of medicine and food, a roof over their heads and a clean bed—things that for the majority of ghetto dwellers were fantasies that in their "normal" conditions they could not attain.

The director of the hospital was the energetic and totally dedicated Dr. Loebel, who devoted all his strength and industry in organizing the aid work of the hospital. To this end he also used his position as chair of the Jewish council. He had the ability, whether on his own authority—which he

1. Gynecological, led by Dr. Loebel;
2. Internal medicine, led by Dr. Glazowski;
3. Surgery, led by Dr. Belfour;
4. Infectious diseases, led by Dr. Tanenbaum and Dr. Schwartz

All of the divisions helped, to the extent possible, the ill, the suffering, the hungry, the swollen, and all the unfortunates whose number was so great in the ghetto.

[Page 74]

And when that "black Shabbos" of August 22 arrived, when at the Umschlagplatz, which was only a few score steps from the hospital, there lay so many Jews who had been beaten and shot—then, too, the forceful Dr. Loebel intervened with the German killers and extracted permission for the hospital to come to the aid of the wounded.

The doctors and the nurses, clad in white hospital garb, carried many beaten and wounded Jews into the hospital and cared for them. The injured were celebrated like little children: their lives were saved. Fabish himself declared that the hospital, with its wounded, should be spared. Those who were shot in the hand or the foot were saved. A small number of healthy people also used this opportunity to be saved from the Umschlagplatz: the nurses threw white hospital garb on some people who then helped gather and carry the wounded, and in this way they managed to get into the hospital or onto the street.

But the joy of the rescued did not last long, for the fists of the murderers also reached them.

* * *

How the hospital was liquidated, how there ill, the doctors, the aides, and all the personnel of the Jewish hospital were murdered is told by several survivors of that time, and especially by Mrs. Leonie Halberstam-Greenspan, the only surviving witness of this tragic chapter:

On Shabbos, August 22, the dark day of the great slaughter, there were about a hundred patients in the hospital, men, women, old people and children, among them several ailing Roma who were receiving treatment. In the course of that tragic day, the number was increased by additional ailing people as well as healthy people who had been saved from the Umschlagplatz. For a whole day the hospital personnel, as well as the patients, had the illusion that they were safe. But that same evening, when the small ghetto was created for the working men who had been chosen in the selektion, Fabish ordered the hospital director, Dr. Loebel, to leave his residence in the hospital and go to the small ghetto.

[Page 75]

People saw this as an omen that the hospital would soon be liquidated.

Dr. Loebel proudly responded to the executioner: "I will not abandon the hospital. I will share the fate of my ailing sisters and brothers."

In this way the hospital continued for two full days between life and death, between on one side beautiful illusions that people talked themselves into, that the murderers would not dare to destroy a healing institution full of sick people, and on the other side the shadow of death that loomed on all sides.

On Monday, August 24, during the day, when the last victims from the Umschlagplatz had been taken to the train ramps, to the Treblinka death train, the hospital was invaded by a band of German and Ukrainian murderers under the leadership of Fabish himself.

It appeared that a glance at so many sick people and at the hospital personnel in their white uniforms confused a little the murderous thoughts of the bloody sadist and he issued contradictory orders, each one countering the one that preceded it.

Thus he ordered that all the sick should go out to the hospital courtyard. Then he countermanded this order: No, all the sick should lie in their beds.

In another order he called on the doctors to go each to his department, to his patients, and in the presence of the doctors he ordered his men to open fire on the patients lying in their beds. The short, staccato firing of handguns accomplished their goal—ending lives.

In the gynecological section there were ten young, nursing babies who had the misfortune of entering this murderous world only days, weeks, or months earlier. Their parents had, with great devotion, managed to get them into the hospital before they themselves were transported to Treblinka or had hidden in an underground bunker, thinking that the hospital was a safe place where the children would be rescued. Among them were the children of Sarah Yom Tov-Halberstam, of Chana Piekorsz, Sabke Benkowicz, Bracha Radashinski-Neuman, and others. Each of these infants received a bullet in the heart.

When they were finished with sick, there came another order:

"All doctors, aides, nurses, and all other personnel should go out to the courtyard."

[Page 76]

In the courtyard, arrayed in a line against the wall, were Dr. Henech Loebel with his wife and son, Dr. Leon Lazowski, Dr. Shaul Schwartz, Dr. Shlomo Tenenbaum (Dr. Belfour, sensing the end, had escaped from the ghetto some nights earlier, hidden in a village, and later committed suicide), the two beloved older aides Yosef Olaberg and Yakov Tenenbaum the nurses Feige Friedman, Sarah Robinowicz, Edushe Alberg, Rivkeh Barg, Epstein from Lodz, the laboratory worker of the hospital Lola Saltzman, the young hospital employees Tzeshe Temkin, Dvorak Goldblatt, Branke Shapirman, and others who worked in the hospital.

Fabish the executioner ordered that the first bullets should go to the "head dog"—as he referred to Dr. Loebel—and he fell first, along with his wife, from the quick shots of a handgun with these words on his lips: "Death to you, murderer. The Jewish and Polish people will outlive you!"

All the doctors, aides, nurses, and other workers fell from the short, staccato shots. Along with them died all who believed that the killers would not attack a hospital full of sick people and who sought protection by hiding there over the previous days, pretending to be ill or to be employees. Among them were Ester Saltzman with her young daughter Rahel, Berl Czarnobrode with his wife, Mrs. Levin-Eisenstadt, Ewo Greenspan, and others.

For a long time these people had lived there as an extended family: the doctors, the aides, the nurses, the employees. They worked together as a fellowship, caring for the unfortunate of the ghetto with love. They left the world in fellowship, all together, clutching each other—they fell wearing their white hospital gowns, as if in shrouds, in a single pile, one body having fallen on another, one body lodged up against a second, and this—among the greenery and the flowers, under the bright, clear, blue sky with the beautiful full beams of a late summer afternoon sun.

[Page 77]

Those many sunbeams played in and reflected from the dazzling white kittles of the dying heap of people and in the freshly shining blood that streamed from all sides into a pool and turned into a river, absorbed by the earth of the hospital courtyard and ran further and more quickly, before it cooled and congealed—to sink deeper into the earth and moisten the roots of the many plants and flowers that decorated the hospital garden.

The lead executioner of this murderous group, Fabish, who himself led the slaughter at the hospital, rejoiced—at the sight of so many dead and so much spilled blood he was like a drunkard. His murderous eyes gleamed. He rubbed his dull face, running with blood and happiness, and nudged his nearest comrade and co-worker, the purely evil wolfhound. He led him to the pool of blood and ordered him, "Drink, comrade, from the dogs's blood." And that dog drank the fresh, warm blood.

* * *

From the open doors and windows of the hospital building, the cries and dying confessions of the patients lying in their beds reached out to the street, strangled cries for help that no one heard. The quick revolver shots cut short their terrible cries and transformed them into the quiet wheezing of a death rattle that was heard under the quiet coughing and terrible calls that emanated from the heap of people who had been shot by the hospital wall, and all combined into a single horrible symphony of death, which became quieter and quieter until it was utterly silent and disappeared into the deaf hole of that accursed summer day.

* * *

The Germans' bloody method of murder worked perfectly to destroy the hospital: the shot bodies of the children, of the ill, and of the hospital personnel had cooled off. They had ceased their death convulsions and were quickly thrown into the large wagons, still wearing their hospital garb. The wagons had been prepared earlier and had waited by the ghetto entrance.

The Jewish police were required to carry out this gruesome job of taking the murdered patients from their beds and loading them on the wagons, together with the executed heap of doctors, aides, nurses, and hospital personnel from the courtyard. But not the little children.

[Page 78]

The Germans "played" with them, dragging them by the feet from their beds, several at a time, dragged them with their lolling heads, and threw them on the crowded wagon like slaughtered little dogs. On the open wagon, through the lively streets, they were taken to the cemetery, where graves had already been prepared. They seemed, on the cobblestones of the streets where they were led, to illustrate with their blood, which dripped from the wagons, the story of their murders.

It took a long time for the wind to carry dust and for the rain to wash and for the sun to dry the streams of blood from the cobblestones of Siedlce's streets.

From that slaughter had escaped Lola Saltzman (the daughter of Sholem Saltzman), who worked in the hospital laboratories. She had been shot in the armpit and fallen to the ground, and she was covered by the dead bodies of her mother Esther and her younger sister Rochel, who two days earlier, on that tragic Shabbos, had come to hide with her in the hospital. After the killers left, she crept out from under the pile of corpses and took backroads, through gardens and fences, on all fours, and crept into the small ghetto. After many changes and false starts, she found a hiding place in Opola (a village near Siedlce) with other Jews. Shortly before the liberation, they were denounced and all were killed in their hiding place.

Rusze Landau, the wife of the lawyer Yosef Landau who was rescued on that tragic Shabbos by the hospital personnel, was hidden there as a nurse. Unnoticed by the killers, she made it to the hospital garden. From there, through gardens and fields, she managed to arrive at the small ghetto, where, two days later, along with twenty-eight women, she was shot at the cemetery on Fabish's orders.

Young Vitek Loebel, the son of Dr. Loebel, escaped. In the last minutes before the executions, he managed to run through the hospital garden. He suffered for a long time in different woods and hiding places and finally fell into the hands of the Polish police, who killed him.

[Page 79]

The survivor of that horrific slaughter, Mrs. Leonie Greenspan-Halberstam, told us the bloody story. It seemed as though Providence assured that at least one witness would remain of that terrible slaughter who could tell the world how one people— the Germans—had destroyed another people, large and small, from nursing children to the aged with its invalids and those who cared for them—in order to counter the suspicious deniers, who would not believe and who would maintain that the Jews invented horror stories to besmirch an innocent people.

Mrs. Greenspan-Halberstam, on that that tragic Shabbos, was also rescued by the hospital people. Donning a white hospital gown, she acted like a nurse. On Monday, at the time of the slaughter in the hospital, when she, with the others, was taken to the execution wall to be shot, she, unnoticed by the killers, escaped to the hospital garden hid among the tall plants and by back roads managed to get to the small ghetto. She suffered all the levels of Gehenna at that time in underground bunkers on the "Aryan side" and—she gave us all the horrible details of the tragedy at the hospital, which stands to us as a testament for all the martyrs who suffered there, of the idealistic doctors aides, nurses, and other workers who with love and dedication until the last minutes of their lives did the sacred work of helping their unfortunate brothers and sisters in the ghetto and who, at their deaths, called out, "Death to the killers! The Jewish people will outlive you." The testament of all the tortured patients the broken ones, who were shot in their beds, and death had frozen on their lips their last curse for the murderous world, and the testament of the little babes, the day-old, week-old, month-old tiny ones who, like little angels had committed no sins except that they had the misfortune to be Jews in the bloody era of Hitler and therefore received bullets in their tender, gentle little hearts as they lay in their white cribs with sweet little smiles on their angelic faces, dreamily smiling with their little lips, dreaming that they were sucking at the breasts of their mothers, who had already been transported to Treblinka—the testament of all who had been tortured and made to suffer, who had one final bequest: *Tell it, tell it, tell it! Remember! Never forget!!!*

[Page 80]

Asher Urszel

The 80-year-old community and Zionist leader Moyshe Eisenstadt and his wife Itta. They were taken in the first aktion to Treblinka.

People begin taken to the Treblinka death train

12. Asher Orszel and his Heritage

Translated by Theodore Steinberg

The closest house at 24 Dluge Street, which stands surrounded by a little garden, set off from the workaday street, was built by the aristocratic Orszel-Neugoldberg family several decades ago. Through luck, it stands whole today. It stands as it once did in the shadow of its old chestnut trees and dreams of its past glory.

If houses had mouths and could talk, this house would have a lot of interesting stories to tell. It would tell how under its roof dogmatic Jewish traditions and modern European innovations coexisted in peace like old Jewish twins.

On a summer's afternoon, one would often hear through the open windows the haunting Gemara melody coming from that part of the house where old R. Naftali Neugoldberg or R. Asher Orszel would be sitting. And soon the sounds of Tchaikowsky or Mendelssohn being played by the children on the piano would come out of a second window and fill the street.

Old, religious Jews would stand there and listen: some at the first window, some at the second. Whispering quietly, shrugging their shoulders, waving their hands, as if to say, "Such bizarre ways"—and then move on.

And young, up-to-date people would drink in thirstily the beautiful tones of the piano and look jealously at the open window.

From his father, the outstanding, fine Jew R. Itzel, Asher receded a strictly religious education and was a fine student with a sharp mind. At 18, he became the son-in-law of the brave, notable Chasid of the Parisower rebbe, R. Mendel Beyer. Together with his father-in-law, during the first years of his marriage he would travel to the rebbe to celebrate with the Chasidim, but that did not last long: young Orszel soon connected with the free Haskalah movement, which in those days was making inroads in the learned Chasidic circles.

[Page 81]

The rise of political Zionism had an especially strong influence on Orszel. With youthful enthusiasm he threw himself into the movement and remained an active member for the rest of his life.

Orszel threw off the superstitious covering of his former way of life, but he continued to hold by tradition, to learn Gemara and other sacred volumes, and he even enjoyed looking through a Chasidic book, but at the same time he read modern Hebrew and Yiddish books. He cast off his long caftan and the shtreimel and wore European clothing, and instead of going to the rebbe for Chasidic celebrations—he went to Zionist conferences and celebrated Zionism.

Religious Jews used to whisper quietly that Asher Orszel would study a page of Gemara with his head uncovered, just like a Litvak (Heaven forbid)…

In Asher Orszel's study, on his large, oaken bookshelves, his leather-bound Vilna Talmud volumes stood shoulder to shoulder with the new Hebrew Encyclopedia, like brothers and sisters who had grown up together. Next to the old books like *The Guide for the Perplexed, The Kuzari,* and *The Duties of the Heart* stood the latest issues of "Ha-Te'kufah" and the most recent publications of Bialik and Tchernikowski's poems; the *Kedushat Levi* of R. Levi Yizchak of Berdichev stood next to Herzl's *Old New Land.*

And not only on his bookshelves did the ancient and modern spiritual treasures stand together harmoniously. In his graying head, as well, the old and the new had dwelling rights. One complemented the other. And always, when R. Asher Orszel spoke or explained something, he would throw in a word of Gemara or something from Tanach or a sharp Chasidic story, mixed together with liberal Maskilik ideas.

For explanations, R. Asher Orszel always had time and patience. Even when he was very busy, he would do his work and then explain. At every opportunity, at every event and action—he would tell a story or offer a word that was always right to the point.

[Page 82]

If a Jew came into his iron business or into the merchant's bank where he was the director about some business matter—he first had to hear a word of Torah from R. Asher Orszel; if a Jew was downcast, had a business entanglement, was involved with the tax office, a conflict over an inheritance, or a question about making a marriage, he would come to R. Asher Orszel to ask advice. And the advice that R. Asher Orsel gave was accompanied by a beautiful proverb, with a verse from Tanach, or an encouraging word (that he had for everyone), and people always left him happier than when they arrived.

He had a wonderful disposition.

For his friendly demeanor toward people he was beloved and praised by everyone—he was called "Zeyde"—"Dziadek" [in Polish]—and the city bestowed on him its highest honor in electing him as a councilman on the city council, chair of the Zionist committee, member of the Tarbus committee, managing member of the "Ezras Y'somim," "Moshav-Z'keynim," and what else? There was not a single organization in the city where R. ZAsher Orszel was not among the ten leaders.

At all meetings, gatherings, or random get-togethers that concerned an organization—no matter whether it was about finances, welfare, or cultural-Zionist matters—everywhere Orszel was the central figure, everywhere he had something to say, not as a formal speaker but with a bit of good advice, a word here and there, a story, or a proverb. And when he met with the Zionist, pioneer, or Tarbus young people, he felt right at home—he carried himself not like a man of seventy but like a youngster.

Orszel was beloved and honored also among the Christian population, and many Christians came to him for advice and to hear a story with a proverb or witticism.

It is interesting to characterize R. Asher Orszel by recalling the following fact:

At the city tax office, there was a consulting commission whose members were assigned by different communal organizations. Commissioned by the city council was Orszel. He was chosen unanimously by both Jews and Christians. For his bold and energetic guardianship of the interests of the taxpayers at the commission, Orszel was investigated by the tax officer and the city council was ordered to elect a second delegate to replace Councilman Orszel.

[Page 83]

For a second time the city council unanimously elected him and announced to the tax office that Orszel was their most suitable candidate, and they also made it known that the tax office had to right to question him.

Consequently a quarrel arose between the tax office and the city council, a quarrel that the city council won so that Orszel remained as the representative on the tax commission.

R. Asher Orszel's house served as a salon for the reception of important Zionist leaders. When Yitzchak Greenbaum, Dr. Shiffer, and once Shaul Tchernikowsky came as guests to Siedlce, they were received at R. Asher Orszel's home, where solemn banquets were arranged during which actions were proclaimed for Keren Ha'y'sod, The Jewish National Fund, or for Tarbus. And once when the Grodzisker Rebber came to Siedlce, he was received at the other side of the house, where his brother-in-law, Naftali Neugoldberg, lived, he who had not abandoned the customs of the old way of life (and who used to visit the rebbe).

* * *

I saw R. Asher Orszel, z"l, for the last time after the German hordes tore into the city. The cannonade had ceased, and we came out from our hiding places outside of the city to see the damage to our burned up houses. When I asked where he had been and what he had done during the days when the enemy's airplanes had ceaselessly spread death and destruction, R. Asher Orszel answered with a smile: "Since I had never in all my life seen such a spectacle, I stayed outside, near my home, and put on my glasses so I could better see and wonder at the interesting events…"

In October of 1939, in the first weeks of the dark control over the city, a band of Nazis in their trucks went to his iron warehouse and stole everything, then beat him up. But then—and also later—R. Asher Orszel continued to tell his stories, spread Torah with his comments to the Jews who in those difficult days cameo to the "grandfather", as they had earlier, in his business to forget for just a little while the bitter suffering of everyday reality.

[Page 84]

R. Asher Orszel also died honorably: when he felt what the German murderers had planned to do the Jews, he did not wait for them to sent him to the gas chambers of Treblinka. He lay down in his bed and died a normal death, mourned by his relatives and friends, of whom he had so many. No one envied him: a successful Jew who was worthy to have such a luxurious death.

* * *

Orphaned and alone among the ruins, his little palace stands deep in its garden, holds itself in the shadows of the old chestnut trees, and dreams nostalgically of the old Gemara melody and the newer notes of the piano that have been abandoned and made silent forever. Over the front door, near the street, a sign hands with an inscription from its new heirs: "Evidence Department of the Siedlce Magistrate."

Further on lies an empty field, exactly as if there had never been any life there. In some spots there still remain parts of the wire fencing—vestiges of those dark, hellish days. And since the earth has not been walked upon by human feet, nature has taken over: the earth is thickly covered with grass and wild plants.

We measure with our feet the lots on which houses stood: Weingarten, Marchbein, Oppenheim, Shmerl Greenberg, . I look for the spot where I lived during the last seven years, where I grew up, which was part of my essential self. Over there was the courtyard on whose right side stood the two-story wing of the large building which contained my family's nest. In the first days of the bloody flood, the enemy's fire and dynamite destroyed it all. Later on the Germans, together with home-grown thieves, hungry for abandoned Jewish property, took whatever was left: goats, stones, metals, and anything else that the fire had spared, so that nothing more was left than a flat little burial mound, overgrown with grass.

[Page 85]

Such overgrown burial mounds are found on the whole area, up to the corner of the street, where there is a small shaft that indicates "Yisroel Yechiel's Beis-Medresh," the immaculate little beis-medresh wherethose who prayed and learned often included such patriarchs and aristocrats as R. Yitzchak Nahum Weintraub, R. Hersh Yosef Czarnobrode, R. Noson Dovid Gliksberg, R. Moyshe Abbe Eisenshtadt, R. Yisroel Rubinstein, R. Yishaiah Rabinowicz, and where Kaddish would be said for deceased relatives by modern Maskilim, enlightened Jews who wanted to hide their attendance at shul, like the leader of the Folks Party in Siedlce. Menashe Czarnobrode and the old, aristocratic Shmerl Greenberg. Of the beis-medresh nothing remains but that little flat space, overgrown with grass.

It makes us feel as if we are in an abandoned cemetery. An almost tangible silence rules there. The only living things we encounter there, in what was once a thickly inhabited Jewish area, are two goats. One eagerly devoured the young springtime grass, while the second lay spread out, warming itself in the sunlight and casting tin its animal way a pair of large, wondering eyes on the peculiar visitors.

I dig a little in the mound on the site of my former home. I seek something that will recall my former warm home, something from among my loved ones' possessions. I find a few scraps of burned and mangled house goods that were worth nothing to the thieves. It seems as if they cry out from their rusty open grave and ask dumbly: "Why embarrass us? Why such an empty end?" And they beg, wordlessly, to be put back, so their shame will be hidden.

13. The Old City

Translated by Theodore Steinberg

Further wandering through the ghetto ruins through the former Post Street continues with difficulty. Nothing remains to remind one of the formerly tidy little street with its white houses all built in a similar style. Everything lies broken, crumbled into formless heaps, scattered over the whole breadth of the street, in mounds, in valleys, through which one has to creep and jump until one comes to the other end of the street on Aslanowicza (Prospektowa), Blania, Yatkowa—into the so-called Old City, which was once the center of Jewish poverty.

[Page 86]

There, in the streets of the Old City, lived toiling Jewish laborers, wagon drivers, beggars, itinerant merchants, teachers, and those who lived on the merits of a rich relative in America who would send a few dollars, as well as those who were simply poor, who lived there because their grandfather or their father had left him a little room as an inheritance and who derived a living from a small table of goods in the city bazaar, which he had to carry out early every morning and drag back every evening in a bag on his back, back to his poor little room.

The women of the Old City were active col-workers in their men's businesses and sometimes ran poor little businesses themselves. They had to spend the whole day in the store, in the butcher shop, or by a stand in the bazaar. They left their children alone in God's care to lay in the courtyard with the children of the neighboring butcher who had gone to a nearby village with his partners, who had combined their funds in order collectively to buy a cow. And they, the butchers, had to spend their whole day in their shops and leave their children alone. And as the children played outside on the cobblestones, they hoped that nothing bad would happen to them, God forbid. The streets there—Aslongowicza, Blania, Yatkawa, Browarna— were quiet and still, as quiet and still as their inhabitants. Seldom did a car or a carriage or a wagon pass through, unless— when the wagon driver or the droshky driver who lived there went in or out with his team of horses, at which time he would pay close attention so that he would not hurt any of the children.

When a mother brought out to the street a dish of warm food to feed her playing child, she thought, too, about her neighbor's children, who were on their own, and she gave them the same amount to perk them up. She knew, this ersatz mother, that tomorrow or another day she would have to be away and leave her children alone and another neighbor would feed her children.

Life in these little streets of the Old City passed quietly. The Jews there did not rush about. They moved slowly, at a more leisurely pace than the Jews on Pienkne, Kilinske, Warsaw, or Stary Rynek. Even those who went to work every morning went at a comfortable pace, not running as those others did. It was not because they were lazy or industrious, God forbid. Remember, most of the inhabitants were hardworking people who lived by the sweat of their brows.

[Page 87]

Nor was it that big-city life had not come there to disturb small-town comforts. Because there were more broad open spaces there, people could see more of nature, more of the sky and the ground than in other streets, as well as a bit of greenery, a tree between the small wooden houses—all of this contributed to a quieter and more comfortable way of life for the inhabitants, so that they proceeded in a more leisurely way, like people in a village. Even the four-cornered clocks with their chains and weights the hung on the walls in the small dwellings and were driven by brass pendulums seemed more leisurely, quieter, and peaceful than the modern alarm clocks in the homes on other streets—truly, what was the rush? Everything would work out.

Those who dwelled there were quiet, peaceful folk, unpretentious about living in the city. They led a quiet, peaceful and gray life. Just like the Old City area of Siedlce, so was the lifestyle there old-fashioned, primitive, small town.

At many homes one encountered, behind the doors or windows, a tied-up Jewish animal, a goat, which considered the world while chewing its cud, little more than skin and bones, like its owners. The little milk it provided constituted half of their income. The other half came from teaching, teaching the youngest children, or being a sexton in some shul or beis-medresh, being a broker for apartments, or selling trinkets or shoes or whatever—all those means of earning a living that only Jews have mastered and can live from.

Sometimes there was a little store that resembled the stores that children make when they are playing: a few onions, some carrots, parsley, with a few bags on a shelf—a display of Jewish poverty.

The store was run by the wife of a teacher, a sexton, or a wagon driver with the help of her children. From a man's salary one could go hungry for half a day, so they had to find a second income. One could transform a window on a door into a little money maker [by creating a room to rent]. Raising higher the lower window, one had to bend over to enter, like when one bows during Aleinu in shul, in order not to bang one's head, and thus—a second income.

[Page 88]

Others, the more well-off citizens, did a little business: they cultivated a few hens, ducks, geese, while others even had a milk cow. From the few pails of milk that one got from the said cow, one could take some outside of the city to a big farmer and make a business from the milk. His wife would take it with a dipper into neighboring houses where the women would eagerly buy it—milk from a local cow…

Others had small gardens where they grew some greens for themselves: onions, carrots, some cucumbers, and some had an apple tree or a pear tree.

In one of the modest houses was a home-factory where children's toys were made. It belonged to the proletarian bourgeois [?] Moyshe Grobia. A soup of young men and women sit on small benches and make the toys. It seems as if children are sitting there playing with their own handiwork. They are happy, the children with their pale cheeks and darting eyes. They know that their boss is a socialist, tending toward communism, and he will not trouble them, so they sing happy songs as they work.

* * *

In the quiet streets of the Old City, the greatest movement is that of the pumps that bring water for the inhabitants. There stands a droshky with its owner, the driver with rolled-up sleeves, holding rags, cleaning and washing his droshky before going out to the street. A wagoner passes with a bucket in his hand to water his horse before going on a trip. It appears that he does not lead the horse but the horse leads him, the wagoner, to the pump. A big black-haired Jew in a caftan stands with his white shirtsleeves rolled up like a bagel, cleans and washes his cow that he led there for a drink. A group of pale, black-eyed children stamp their barefoot feet incessantly in the puddles around the pump. There one encountered different people, Jewish men and women, boys and girls, who waited in line with pails or jugs in their hands to get water. As they waited, they became acquainted and exchanged a few words, and fairly often a shidduch [a wedding engagement] would follow, just like at that well in the biblical times of Jacob and Rachel.

* * *

[Page 89]

Among the ordinary inhabitants of the quiet streets in the Old City, one could a few exceptional people who stood out from the surrounding ordinariness, as certain trees stand out in the woods, having grown wider or taller that the whole surrounding mass so that they can be seen more clearly, more distinctly when seen from afar, when they stand at a greater distance…

Such a person, living in his small home at the edge of the Old City on Aslonowicza-Teatralna was the great scholar, the devoted Ger Chasid, R. Shmuel Zeidenzeig. His home, which was filled with a sea of books, served as a kind of parliament for Talmud scholars. Often the scholars of the city would gather in his apartment to discuss Torah matters with old R. Shmuel.

In the summer afternoons his rooms became hot and crowded, so they took a bench outside . There would sit R. Itsche Meir Shochet, R. Leibush Feivel, Rr. Ben-Tzion Zuker, R. Eli Henech and other scholars from the Ger prayer house. They let themselves drift on the waves of the sea of Talmud. They got excited. They raised their voices, as if they were discussing an unclear statement in the Gemara in their own homes.

And nearby, behind the wall, in a poor little house, lived the veteran of the Jewish laborers in Siedlce, Avraham Weinapple. Herschel Oyfgang, Meir Rzanczazszewa, Yudel Friedrich, Moyshe Grabia, Moyshe Kaddish, and other Jews would attend secret meetings in his house, along with non-Jewish labor leaders. They would consider various labor issues and they discussed socialism, communism, as well as political and revolutionary issues.

In the summer afternoons, his rooms became hot and crowded, so they took a bench outside. They sat around and conducted their discussions in loud voices (because in the heat of discussion, people forget to be conspiratorial), as if they were at home. They mixed in and braided together references to Marx, Engels, Kautsky, and Bogdanov with the names of Rambam, Rabbeinu Tam, Maharam, Chidushei Harim, that came heatedly from the speakers in R. Shmuel Zeidenzeig's domain.

A bit further on, in another small dwelling on Prospectower Street, lived the scholar and devoted Koszenitzer Chasid R. Hershel Koszenitzer. Only God knew whether he was called Koszenitzer because he followed the Koszenitzer rebbe or because he came from Koszenitz.

[Page 90]

R. Hershele Koszenitzer had created the Shomrei-Shabbos fellowship in Siedlce, of which he was the gabbai. The members, and particularly R. Hershele himself, would go around late on Friday afternoons to the business district and remind people that it was time to close the shops by crying out: "Shabbos! Shabbos!" In the bakeries they became aware that it was time for the cholents to be put into the ovens because Shabbos was imminent. They reminded the women when they had to light candles, and they fought with the hairdressers who worked on Shabbos.

On Shabbos afternoons, after their naps, and particularly on holidays, the whole membership of the Shomrei Shabbos would gather at R. Hershel's. They would discuss a bit of Torah, but their main business was singing: they sang about Shabbos, or the holiday, with the old Koszenitz melodies. Then they would gather a few groschen, not, God forbid, in actual coins—it was, after all, Shabbos or a holiday, when handling money was forbidden—but they would indicate with a glance or with a motion of the finger, that meant, "I will give such and such, which I will pay tomorrow." They brought some bottles or a cask of liquor and let loose. They drank "L'chaim." Then they put their hands on each other's shoulders and they danced fervently around the table, singing ecstatically, in the old Koszenitz way. It seemed as if the old wooden house danced along with them and creaked as if it would collapse.

Also in that neighborhood was a poor bent over little house in which dwelled the rebellious, revolutionary worker family the Slushnas—the most popular home for Jewish workers in the city. In that home, the two leaders of the revolutionary workers movement in Siedlce grew up—the brothers Yosef and Avraham Slushna. The first was the leader of the leftist "Poalei-Tzion," and the second was the leader of the "Bund" and later of the communist party. Both were gifted with iron wills and strong revolutionary temperaments. They attracted to themselves the working masses, not only with their appearances at organizational gatherings as greatly talented speakers, but also their home was the home for many workers, who found there the latest forbidden newspapers and books, a friendly environment, and a place to socialize.

In an earlier time, when people did not work on Shabbos or a holiday, a group would assemble in the proletarian home of the Slushnas.

[Page 91]

In comfortable, informal conversations but most earnestly, they would discuss literature, political economics, and revolutionary matters, in which the leading voices would be those of the Slushna brothers. When everyone was roused up by the heated discussions and conversations, they would turn to song. They sang enthusiastically a variety of workers songs and revolutionary songs by Avraham Reizen, David Edelstadt, Morris Rosenfeld, and others. The sounds of the songs emerged from the poor, narrow proletarian home into the surrounding streets, mixed in with the fervent singing of "Menuchah v'simchah" and "Yism'chu b'malchuscha" [Shabbos songs] that came from the neighboring home of R. Hershele Koszenitzer.

* * *

Come, my friend, and let us take a walk on Friday afternoon in the poor streets of the Old City and see how the simple, everyday Jewish people, who work so hard for the whole week, preoccupied with seeking a living, how they prepare like princes to receive the Shabbos queen.

The movement on the quiet, peaceful streets becomes more forceful. Women, laden down with baskets and pots, hurry home from the shops, bringing home from the market the goods they have bought for Shabbos. From the houses emerge the rhythmic banging of knives cutting up the poor small fish. By the water pump there is more activity than usual, and the pumps never rest. Today people in need more water than at other times: for cooking, to wash the floors, and to wash the children in honor of Shabbos.

With noise and tumult, the wagoners and droshky drivers return. The horses stamp noisily on the cobblestones and the drivers never cease crying "Whoa! Whoa!" To their overworked horses, who do not understand that it is late, Erev Shabbos, and people must hurry. Porters go about with the handcarts, merchants from the market with their poor assortment of merchandise rush about, and those who have traveled to other villages with their packs on their shoulders move more quickly, push themselves to go faster.

Inside, the houses are crowded—many people try to work outside: people come out with borscht and with grease to fix up the dusty threshold and shoes; the young women rub and polish the brass candlesticks with water and sand; in bright bowls the mothers wash their children's heads in warm water, while the children shriek as if they were being drowned.

[Page 92]

`Jews rush with little packs of clothing under their arms to the mikveh, and then they rush back, scrubbed, damp, ruddy.

-And as the mothers light the Shabbos candles in the shining brass candlesticks, their growing daughters stand outside the door with their shiny, wet braids, dressed in their Shabbos finery in order to watch the well-dressed young men who go together with their fathers to pray in the shul. And when their glances meet, they turn as red as their clothing and run quickly back into their houses.

With weary steps the overworked Jews return home after praying. Some of them have a guest with them for the Shabbos meal. Quite varied are the melodies of their Shabbos songs. The simpler, more overworked and more tired Jews hum strange little sounds under their breath, hard to recognize, whether they are improvising to the difficult words of "Koa M'Kadesh" or trying to capture a tune that they once heard. From those houses where better off young people live, one hears more "modern" melodies taken from theater songs or from popular folksongs; from the few scholarly households, one hears the true Shabbos melodies that were sung in the Ger or Koszenitza prayer houses. From somewhere one also hears a Modszitzer melody. Each does as he can, but all sing about Shabbos. The exhausted working Jews are weary from their week of labor and go early to bed. But from the scholarly Chasidic houses one hears sounds late into the night: at first the Shabbos songs and then later the sound of Torah study.

The young people—boys and girls—stroll around until late in the night, exchanging wisdom, joking, romancing, while their parents have sunk deep into their Friday night slumbers or are engaged in Torah study.

* * *

Shabbos morning Is different from every other day int he streets of the Old City. The early risers have to be out on the street: the wagoners, the droshky drivers, and the dairymen bring out their horses and animals to the pumps to provision them. The old Shabbos goy, Franciska, who waits impatiently all week for the arrival of Shabbos, is up, and as the day dawns, he is already out in the streets with his challah sack hanging from his arm.

[Page 93]

He bangs on the closed shutters: "Yankel, wake up. It's time to light the oven." His wife, called Franciskowa, goes around to the dairymen to milk the cows and goats. All around is the sound of voices praying the early prayers and saying Psalms. Jews in black Shabbos caftans begin to make their way to the souls at a deliberately slow Shabbos pace, with their taleisim and Chumashim under their arms. They make their way back slowly as well. There is no hurry. They have time. On the way they speak of "politics," about the controversies that have gone through the city with the hiring of a new rabbi.

A particular group of Jews, sticking together, speak among themselves in loud voices, so that one cannot hear what the other is saying. Anyone who wants to interrupt another holds his beard or grabs the lapel of his caftan or takes his sleeve. He says quickly and good-naturedly that the Khaderower rabbi and no other is the most appropriate candidate for the Siedlce rabbinical chair.

And there, on the cobblestones in the middle of the street, goes a tight group— someone from a shul or a prayer house had invited them to a kiddush for some occasion—a yahrzeit, a bar mitzvah, or because today he had said a thanksgiving prayer for not having died from a rock that a ruffian threw at him in a village. And if there is no such occasion, the men go in together on a bottle and some pastries—it is, after all, Shabbos—and together they make a kiddush.

Women, girls, and young men hurry through the streets carrying cholent pots from the baker. The aromas of cholent and kugel arise out of the different pots and fill the air, mixing with the aromas of onions and schmaltz that come from the houses. And again the sounds of humming and singing of Shabbos songs resound—the people sing of the holy Shabbos that gives so much quiet and rest and a delicious meal.

After that Shabbos meal, a coma seems to strike everyone: all sleep. It is a great thing to be able to sleep on Shabbos, and the Jews of the Old City hold fast to that commandment, so that one time during the week they can rest. In the summers, when it is warm outside, people take out old garment, spread it in the shade near a wall, and lie down on it, as their ancestors did in the vineyards; or people stretch out on the little bed of grass that grows in almost every courtyard (if the goats have not eaten it), and a they sleep loudly, snoring through their noses, so that they can be heard in all the streets.

[Page 94]

But the Jews also remember that it was not just for eating and sleeping the God gave them the holy Shabbos. They also had to think of the sacred Torah. People got up and studied. Some learned the chapter of the week, some the Torah portion, and some a page of Gemara, and those who were not adept at the written texts would go to a prayer house or a beis-medresh and listen as the rabbi taught everyone.

Elsewhere in the courtyard, in the shadow of a tree or near a wall, sits a group of women who have worked hard all week, wearing many-colored, flowery Shabbos clothing and different colored headscarves or bonnets. With their hands on their cheeks, they listen to their leader, the "reciter," who sits in the middle with her eyeglasses at the tip of her nose. They are tied to a string from behind. She reads to this Shabbos gathering aloud, with an old bubbishe [literally, grandmotherly] tune. She reads the weekly Torah portion from her beribboned translation of the Chumash.

In another corner of the courtyard, on the short grass, half lying down, is a group of young men and women. One reads aloud Peretz's "Bontscha Shveig." After the reading, they argue, disagreeing about what Peretz meant. And as they calm down, they learn a new song that one of the group had brought from nearby musical Sokolow, where he was recently.

In the evening, everyone goes for a walk. Some dress up and go to the high class city garden. Some go to the city "depth" {promenade] on Warsaw and Kilinska Streets to mix with the more well-to-do and merchant Shabbos strollers. And those who are not so much concerned with showing off, chiefly those men and women who worked hardest during the week, walk in front of their own houses on their own streets. It does not matter, because anywhere one can breathe the fresh air and relax, until—until the first stars appear in the sky, people turn on their lights, the men say Havdalah, the women say "God of Abraham," people put on their weekday clothing, and people return to their everyday lives: the wagoners and droshky drivers harness their rested horses. The porters go out with their handcarts, workmen go to their workshops, merchants to their stores. They are no longer nobility—they go back to being hardworking, troubled, sustenance-seeking Jews.

[Page 95]

* * *

Ancient are the houses and streets of the Old City. Many of them are as old as the city of Siedlce and its Jewish settlement. They show, and advertise, their antiquity, these wooden buildings. Some sit deeply sunken into the ground, up to their little windows, and in order to get inside, one has to use some crooked stairs. One cannot tell whether these houses have sunk into the ground over the decades and centuries or whether the ground itself has gotten higher and trapped the houses in their antiquity. On many of the houses, over the course of time, the doors and windows have come loose and they hang diagonally from the walls like paralyzed, twisted limbs. When one corner of a door lies on the ground by one's feet, the other end reaches your belly. On other houses the walls are hunched over, with pieces protruding, like a pregnant woman in her late months, and it is a mystery how they stand up without falling on the heads of passersby.

To the gray life that is led by the gray people can be added the color of the houses—all are gray and cast gray shadows on the gray streets along with the gray sky that is more visible than in other parts of the city. It creates a harmonious gray entity— the true color of Jewish reality.

* * *

So it was, and so appeared the Jewish Old city in Siedlce before the bloody deluge.

In those dark days of August, 1941, when the shameful judgment to confine the Jews of Siedlce in a ghetto-prison was sealed, fate declared that the poor, deprived, gray streets of the Jewish Old City would constitute the prison.

[Page 96]

The poor, tiny houses of Prospektowa, Yatkawa, Blania, and Browarna, which formerly housed families of five or six people in one dwelling, opened their doors wide and took in their unfortunate sisters and brothers, whom the murderers fist had forced here from all the other streets. Each little dwelling was packed with ten, fifteen, or even twenty people. All the cellars, too, the attics and stables, all the fallen ruins, where there was just a hole that could offer some protection against heat and cold, against rain and wind, and against the wild eyes of the German cannibals became nests for those unfortunate people.

The goals and purposes of the architects of the "new order" became perfectly clear: 1) they had all of the Jews concentrated in one highly controlled area; 2) the packing together of such a great number of Jews in a few tiny streets brought with it epidemics and illnesses, with the result that 3) there was a frightful mortality rate among the oppressed Jews caused by these orders.

* * *

With grieving hearts and tentative steps we wandered through the ruins of the Jewish Old City as one might go through an abandoned cemetery. Each burial mound, each unburned ruin, each wall full of holes, each intact house, each attic, each cellar, and each stable on the grounds that constituted the large ghetto-cemetery—each one spoke of pain and suffering, of blood and death, of ruin and annihilation. Each stone of the road told how many lives were extinguished on. It. From every inch of earth the blood that it had absorbed cried out. Everywhere that a glance fell, everywhere that one wandered, all spoke of destruction, all spoke of how our large community had been destroyed.

A leveled-off mound appears, overgrown with grass—a grave for a row of Jewish houses that were burned and destroyed by those horrible villains. At the top of the mound stands a black, singed chimney. It stands like a black monument—a memory of a slaughtered life. And not far away, buried a little deeper, where there was once a Jewish courtyard with a small workshop, stands a bare, black tree with thin, singed branches stretched high toward the sky like the thin bony hands of an ascetic during prayer. From both, it seems, one hears how they lament over their own disaster and the disaster of their murdered fellows.

[Page 97]

In another spot there lies a mound of refuse around which is a group of chickens that scrape with their feet and pick with their beaks, searching, groping energetically, forcefully. A thought pops into my mind: One should seek there. There one might find something from the ruins of "yesterday." We stand there and scare the poor chickens who perhaps are seeing people for the first time in their lives. In their chicken language they scold the people who interrupt their labors, and they run off. We consider the "treasure" that the chickens have unearthed: a pair of decayed children's shoes, little ones, in which a child may have taken its first steps on the accursed earth. The shoes are not damaged. They are decaying, but whole; a rusty metal Chanukah lamp, the kind that was used by the poor; a few decaying pages of holy books, of holy Jewish books, are scattered around and mixed in with the dirt and the garbage. It is difficult to read any of them. Further on there is some aluminum silverware, shards of plates and and pieces of shattered glassware. Among them, a red piece of glass strikes the eye. I pick it up, wipe off the dust, and I read the dully painted, broken letters: "Cos shel Pesach" [The cup for Passover].

This piece of glass brings up many thoughts: about the beautiful holiday of freedom, Passover, which was celebrated with so much joy and in the poor little houses of the simple folk. It recalls how there was once a whole beautiful, sparkling cup, an inheritance passed from one generation to another like a relic, reserved for use as the cup of Elijah. And it recalls how the sparkling wine with which the poor Jew filled it, fluttered and trembled as people stood up at the seder table, opened the door, and said aloud, "Welcome. Elijah the Prophet is there." And the legendary prophet recalls what the Hagaddah says, "That in every generation they stood to destroy us" and "Pour out your wrath upon he nations that know You not…"

* * *

The remaining houses of the Jewish Old City sit there with their new inhabitants, who came from surrounding villages and from other neighborhoods. They were religious, these new inhabitants, and placed in their windows pictures of holy apostles and crosses. Walls that not long before had been hung with pictures of the Vilna Gaon, of R. Moshe Montefiore and of the Western Wall were now hung with pictures of the "Holy Mother" with her "Child" at her breast.

[Page 98]

And they keep a fire burning before them at all times. It seems as if the religious inhabitants will, with the holy pictures and the holy fire, expel the bitter spirits of the former inhabitants who come perhaps at night in their dreams to disturb their sleep.

Outside, in front of the houses, groups of children play. They cry out when they see us, run quickly into the courtyard and yell, in Polish, "Get away, Jews." Hearing their cry, some mothers come out, calm their children and look at us with womanly curiosity, some with a mocking smile on their pious faces and some with fear: they wonder whether the true heirs of the former homeowners have returned, as has happened lately.

The large number of dogs that the new owners have brought from the villages and from the other neighborhoods are a plague. They are everywhere, these dogs, in the courtyards, in front of the houses, in the streets. They look around, they run, they smell the Jewish passersby and go after them with wild barking, as if to say: "What are you doing, wandering around here, in this Jewish-free city…"

[Pages 98-100]

14. "Children for Children" – in the Ghetto

Translated by Yocheved Klausner

We continue walking through the half-ruined – some entirely ruined – streets of the old city. We stop by the house no. 28 on Oslanovicze Street.

This house was the place where the kitchen for hungry children in the ghetto had been. The kitchen was founded and operated by the children themselves. The story of the kitchen is told by Avraham Halber, his wife Hanke Apel and the sole survivor among the workers in the kitchen, Lusia Gorstein:

The hunger in the ghetto had reached everyone. Masses of people, adults and children alike, swollen and weak, would ramble in the streets from garbage can to garbage can, looking among the waste for something to alleviate their hunger. But soon a group of resourceful children came up with a plan to help their unfortunate sisters and brothers. They decided to open a kitchen and prepare every day some hot food for the children.

The group had a meeting and chose a managing committee: Chanale Eisenberg, (Efraim Tzelnik's granddaughter), Lilia and Salek Yablon (Yissachar Yablon's children), Lusia Gorstein (daughter of David and Ida Gorstein – of the entire group she alone survived), Dina'chke Tchibotzka (Shlomo's daughter), Ida Friedman, Marisha and Koba Levin (Yoel'ke Levin's children) and Feigele Yablon (Yosef's daughter).

A delegation of the children's committee approached the Judenrat, presented their plan and asked for help. The Judenrat gave the children a sum of money, with which the children managed to open the kitchen.

In order to be able to maintain the kitchen, the children sought help from different sources: they asked for regular donations from the Jews in the ghetto who could afford it; pairs of children would go through the streets and alleys of the ghetto and sell various artifacts; they collected food and clothes; in the garden of the house they organized various performances; in the courtyard they held sales; all this produced income that was used to buy food.

Almost all the children in the ghetto were drawn into this important work. Children who still had enough to eat at home would share their meals with those who had not. Many children would not touch their food at home before their parents donated a certain sum of money for the children's kitchen committee.

A group of women decided to join the children in their holy work. They helped obtain products – a very difficult task at that time – and worked in the kitchen as well. Among the women were Ida Gorstein, Bronca Yablon, Andje Levin and others. Some people made important material contributions. Among them were Mr. Parness, a refugee from Germany who lived at the time in the Siedlce ghetto and Mr. Ganzwohl, a Siedlce convert to Christianity who, seeing the terrible tragedy that befell the Jews, repented and returned to Judaism, and devoted himself to helping needy Jews and especially hungry children.

The children's committee worked according to a rigorous plan and followed all the rules of an organized corporation. The management and the secretary properly registered all needy children and distributed food according to plan.

With time, the committee and the kitchen expanded and developed into a central institution in the ghetto, whose aim was to give help to all needy. In those ill-fated days, cold, hunger, poverty and epidemics raged in the ghetto. From alleys, from crowded little houses, from cellars and attics, a stream of hundreds of poorly clad and swollen children would move at midday toward the house on 28 Oslanovicze Street. For many of them the little food they received there was their only meal of the day. Some of them shared the food with their parents, who would wait in a side alley, sit on the ground and silently have their daily meal.

This holy work of the school children, helping their sisters and brothers lasted a very long time in the locked up ghetto. It was savagely interrupted on 9 Elul 5702 [22 August 1942], when the children and their parents were driven by the Germans, the Ukrainians and the other child-murderers to the Umschlag-Platz and from there – to the gas chambers of Treblinka.

[Page 100]

15. At the Ruins of the Butchers' Beis-Medresh

Translated by Theodore Steinberg

And there we are by the ruins of the butchers' beis-medresh on the former Yatke Street.

There has always been an element of dislike between the "fine" Jews—committed Chasidim and scholars—and the common working Jews, simple workers, especially butchers, the greatest number of whom lived on Yatke Street. This antagonism was most greatly felt in the shuls and beis-medreshes, where the "fine" Jews, scholars and well-to-do merchants, considered themselves superior. They took the best seats by the eastern wall, the biggest honors at the Torah reading, and on Simchas Torah they took the most important roles.

The shuls and beis-medreshes were themes sensitive places where the ordinary people were overlooked, when people took up congregational matters.

[Page 101]

They were referred to as the "amei haaretz", a term from ancient times that meant: "Know your place and don't stick your nose where it doesn't belong." Those fine Jews knew what was best in such matters as choosing a rabbi, a shocker, a cantor, and in all other community matters when there were meetings, as was normal, in the shul and beis-medreshes.

To these insults and snubs Siedlce's common Jews answered with a great "revolution." The carpenters, tailors, and shoemakers from Pienkne Street formed their own shuls, such as the "Parkhei Shoshanim" shul. The butchers from Yatke Street also built their own beis-medresh on their street.

With extraordinary love and devotion, these simple folk, the butchers from Yatke Street and the surrounding streets, built their beis-medresh. The building was simple and poor, as simple and poor as its owners and builders. The wall were of simple red bricks and the ceiling was of simple wooden beams. In the middle was a simple wooden reading stand. Because they were the proprietors, they had the whole eastern wall and all the Torah and Simchas Torah honors that they desired. They were happy with their poor spiritual goods because they were their own.

There were no great scholars among those who prayed in the butchers' beis-medresh who could sit and teach. Nor did they have any extra time, because they were always occupied, either going to surrounding towns to find something to slaughter or busy on Yatke Street chopping up the meat for their fancy customers. But before going to the villages at dawn, when it was still dark, or before opening up on Yatke Street, going into the beis-medresh to pray or to recite some chapters of Psalms was considered an obligation for all the butchers, and they were attentive to it. As it says in the verse, "Set up for yourself a teacher (or rabbi)," they paid for a teacher—a poor Jew, learned in the Torah. They paid him a few zlotys a week and he taught them in the evenings between the afternoon and evening prayers—a chapter of Mishnah or a page from Ein Yakov. On Shabbos he learned with them a chapter and explained the Torah portion. And, since the Navaradok yeshiva, which had fled the persecutions of the Bolshevik bullies and had relocated in Siedlce, the butchers arranged for the yeshiva boys to take meals with them on the condition that they would teach in the beis-medresh, and so the sound of learning resounded in the surrounding streets by night and by day.

[Page 102]

* * *

I remember several times when I was in the butchers' beis-medresh, on special occasions: once, as a messenger from the Keren Kayames L'Yisroel, in order to inform the worshippers there about the activities and plans of the KKL in Eretz Yisroel. I cannot forget how much interest the simple Jews showed in the conclusions, how their eyes sparkled with pleasure when they heard that there in Eretz Yisroel, in the fields of the KKL, Jewish peasants worked to grow their own provisions. I felt their spirit that burned with envy that they could not be among those fortunate people.

Another time—this was on Erev Yom Kippur evening put out collection plates to collect funds in the shuls and beis-medreshes. I was charged by the KKL to be responsible for the collection plate in the butchers' beds-medresh. That moment, too, I cannot forget, with what devotion, joy and expansiveness those simple poor folk threw their contributions into the KKL plate. Their beaming faces showed such thankfulness that the KKL had not overlooked them and had given them, these simple Jews, the possibility to add their few groschen and thus take part in the sacred movement of redeeming the earth of Eretz Yisroel from non-Jewish hands.

And another time I saw the Jews of Yatke Street in their beis-medresh in a particularly solemn moment, that, again, I will never forget.

For many years in the beis-medresh, they had added groschen upon groschen, raised from donations for Torah honors, for "Mi shebeirachs", and for other things and they wanted to use those funds to have a Torah written.

When the writing of the Torah was completed, they made a special celebrration such as Siedlce had never seen. Preparations went on for weeks and months. On many evenings, after the businesses on Yatke Street had closed, the wives of the butchers assembled to cook and fry, to bake and roast, They prepared the choicest foods for the celebration; whole days and long nights the daughters of the butchers sat and embroidered with gold and silver threads the holy letters that the scribe had sketched on the dark red velvet mantle for the Torah scroll and on the curtain for the Holy Ark.

[Page 103]

For three days, none of the butchers conducted business, neither going to the villages nor opening their shops. The celebration lasted for three days, with a meal fit for a king, with the choicest dishes and beverages, with music and dancing. Under a chuppah people led the new sefer Torah into the great town synagogue. A group of butchers then rolled up the sleeves of their fancy Shabbos clothing and danced in the streets, as sparks of fire flew from their upturned heels jumped around the circle of dancers and the bystanders.

The sefer Torah, under the chuppah, the dancing crowd, and the musicians playing in the streets were escorted by a squadron of "Red Cossacks" with their red stripes on their pants, with their big black forelocks flowing behind their Cossack helmets, armed with swords and spears. They truly looked like Don Cossacks, not poor Old City imitations.

At that moment it seemed as if the whole world rejoiced with the simple, primitive Jews. Everyone joined in the dancing, especially members of the beis-medresh, where the whole celebration went on. The poor red bricks wall, the wooden beams, the reading stand, the tables, the benches, and everything else seemed to take part in the beautiful dancing circle.

Other beautiful memories of the not-too-distant past that are tied up with various places in the streets of the non-Jewish Old City, with their simple working Jews, with their beloved beis-medresh, all emerge in my memory, scald my heart and mind as I walk these grounds. But they soon dissolve and flee in light of the tragic images of ruin that we encounter with every step.

* * *

The butchers' beis-medresh was not destroyed during the first period of the barbarian rule in the city. Like the great synagogue with its beis-medresh, it served as a home for the poorest and most unfortunate people in the ghetto. There were many hundreds of Jews (possibly even thousands) who, with the loss of their homes and their possessions, also lost the will to to live. They resigned themselves.

[Page 104]

They had not the strength or the courage to fight against all the troubles and difficulties and and they did not know how to find for themselves a corner in some small house, an attic, a cellar, or a stall in the confinements of the ghetto. Those unlucky ones who remained outside without a roof over their heads crowded together in the butchers' beis-medresh, found there their "home" in that small spot, where their broken bodies had room only to sit up.

The unfortunates were packed in like herring in a barrel. Swollen from hunger, filthy from not having a place to lie down or a blanket, without soap, without the most basic human necessities, so that the beis-medresh fostered the greatest number of chronic illnesses and the greatest number of deaths in the ghetto. There was no day when the "wagon" did not have to take away several dead bodies.

The German murderers often visited the unfortunate inhabitants of the beis-medresh. They came to marvel—at first to photograph the packed together shadows of people, and then to take several out behind the beis-medresh wall and shoot them (among them, Abgrahamele the sexton of the great synagogue).

Afterwards, when the unfortunate inhabitants of the butchers' beis-medresh had been transported to Treblinka, during the liquidation of the large ghetto, their "home" suffered the same fate as all the other shuls and beis-medreshes in the city. The German vandals burned it, and the local thieves carried off and stole everything that had been left behind. All that remained were the naked red walls, ashamed, blackened by ash and rain, as an abandoned gravestone that cries out in dumb sorrow over its own destruction and over the destruction of its destroyed worshipers—the simple Jews of the Old City.

When we approach it and look around the ruins through the gaping door and window openings that look out onto the half-destroyed street, like the large eye sockets of a corpse, it strikes the head and the heart with deep gloom—and it strikes the nose with a stinking stale aroma of trash and human waste, left by the neighbors, who thought this was an appropriate spot.

* * *

There is something to tell about the neighboring house at 6 Yatke Street, which was the bakery of Yakov Piekasz:

[Page 105]

In the attic of that house, on the tragic Shabbos of August 22, thirty Jews hid, most of them acquaintances of the Piekasz family and their daughter Chana. Among them were the daughter of Ben Zion Zucker. The attic was well hidden above the bakery and the apartment where people could hide for a time when the barbaric Germans hunted defenseless Jews in the ghetto.

Along with the murder bands who undertook to seek the hidden Jews in the emptied ghetto, there was an SS man from the Sonderdienst, the hangman Bakenstass—a Volksdeutsch, a killer of the first magnitude, who distinguished himself with wild atrocities and sadism in finding Jews, especially young children. He found the hidden thirty Jews in Piekasz's house. With horrible ferocity he forced the unfortunates out into the street, where he sot each of them with his own bloody hands.

Piekasz' wife lived on, even though she had taken several bullets in her chest. She spoke up and begged them to end her life, to shoot her, but none of the murderers was willing to do so. She was thrown alive onto the wagon along with all the dead and led to the cemetery to their grave. From there she was led back into the ghetto, where she at last found an executioner who ended her life.

A similar story befell the painter Federman. He, too, as Binyamin Halberstam recounts, was taken to the cemetery, having been shot but still alive. He also pleaded to be shot. He was taken back from the cemetery to the ghetto, where the chief executioner Fabish was waiting. He called to a gendarme and ordered him to shoot the wounded, half dead Federman. The gendarme refused to carry out the order. I am not certain—the gendarme refused (a wonder!), so that Fabish ended Federman's life himself, shooting him several times.

Another group of Jews who were found in a hiding place were led to the cemetery and there shot. Among them was the young Kuba Levin (son of Yoelke Levin). Somehow the buillets missed him. He lay there in the cemetery, covered by the Jews who had been shot.

[Page 106]

Later he crawled out. For a time he hid in his grandfather's mill, then went back to the small ghetto. Later he fell in Lublin in the underground battle against the Germans.

---

16. In the Former Mikveh

Translated by Theodore Steinberg

And then we were at the home of the former mikveh on Yatke Street at the corner of Browarna. This was the only building that belonged to the community organization in which part of it—actually a single room—was in the possession of the Jewish Committee. We therefore were able to enter freely to rest a bit and to observe.

There was much to observe in this home of the former mikveh that had now been transformed into a central point for all the Jewish "organizations" in Siedlce.

First of all, there was there an "orphans home," not for orphan children—none of these were left in Siedlce—but for the several grown and impoverished orphans, young men with gray hair, pinched faces, and dull eyes who had only recently emerged from underground holes, from bunkers, and from the woods, and for the several poor, broken wanderers who returned from the distant Siberian taigas. They came here seeking someone. None of them had nowhere to go, no corner with a roof for their heads where they could spend the nights. For them the Jewish Committee made this a "home": they divided a room in half and put bundles of straw on the floor. After a day of wandering through the ruins of their destroyed homes and the unrecognizable graves of their near and dear ones in the desecrated, despoiled cemetery, they could come here to rest, the poor cemetery searchers.

It was now noon, and there we met about ten of these shadowy orphan wanderers. They had grown tired and wandered in to rest after traipsing through the ruins. They lay stretched out on the straw in their clothes, quietly, deep in thought with bleary eyes looking somewhere off in the distance…through the windows under which lay their baggage and provisions: a few pieces of bread, a cup of water, and a few pieces of clothing that had received from "PUR" (a Polish repatriation organization) or from the Jewish Committee.

[Page 107]

The other half of the room was itself divided in two. In one half, that is, in a quarter of the original room, stood a table with a chair—this was the office of the Jewish Committee. Each day in the morning hours the committee's secretary, Avraham Friedman, would sit by the table. He registered the newly arrived cemetery searchers.

In the fourth quarter of the room was the office where the technical work of the committee was conducted. The committee's meetings were conducted in private apartments of the committee members, Yisroel Kravetz and Yontel Goldman. They also had an album with hundreds of photographs that the German murderers took of the Jews before killing them. Tragic scenes of tears, spasms, and fainting took place when new arrivals recognized in these photographs their near and dear ones, parents, children, sisters and brothers. They trembled, their blood froze in their veins when they saw our near ones and our acquaintances before their terrible ends: emaciated faces with sharply defined jaws, bent backs, dead-seeming eyes that looked out from a sea of helplessness and resignation, of contempt and horror, like people on the edge of death from whom had been taken the image of God and every belief had been hollowed out.

* * *

The last quarter of the mikveh building, that occupied a corner between the door and the window, had a high purpose: it contained a museum of the destroyed community. At the far corner stood a chest filled with remnants of desecrated holy objects.

With trembling hands I rifle through collection and look at everything. First: a half of a Sefer Torah, naked and ashamed, rolled up on its Etz Chaim, dirtied with mud and unclean hands and—this is hard to say—I think there are flecks of blood. The Committee bought this from a local Christian for a good sum. The other half off the Sefer Torah no longer existed. They used it for some kind of business that the times called for: for light summer sandals, for children's hats, and the rest for hand baskets decorated with Torah strips, which the city and village citizens eagerly bought as a fashion item during the years when the devil reigned.

[Page 108]

Several pieces of such fashioned merchandise, bought by the Committee, lay there in the museum chest and clung to the naked and embarrassed half of the Sefer Torah, exactly as if they wanted to reunite and be as they were before the rape, as they were predestined to be, when they were a sacred thing, clothed in a pure satin mantle and standing in a sacred Holy Ark in some shul or beis-medresh, surrounded by an aura of holiness, serving as as guide for the world with the words that they contained.

People say that when the vandals conducted their wild orgies with drink and whoredom, they often spread out under their feet Sifrei Toros and other holy things as if they wanted thereby to take revenge on "Thou shalt not murder" and the other "Thou shalt nots" that were inscribed there.

Around that half Torah scroll in the chest were a collection of other books and holy writings. Their leather or linen bindings were useful and they lay withdrawn, naked, embarrassed, torn, and muddy, which was a comment on the various metamorphoses and hellish torments they had experienced since the day when they were torn from their bookshelves, along with their owners and protectors until they found themselves at rest in the poor chest in a corner of the mikveh.

My hands trembled, along with my heart as I sorted and examined the desecrated silent "Otzar," that was in the chest. I found a bit of the Talmudic tractate Gittin, folded over, as if it would tell about the destruction of the Second Temple, a ragged Midrash Rabba, a half of the book of Job, a fragment of a Chumash, a Mahzor, a Siddur, a lamentation, a selichah, and several shabby Psalms, coated and stained with tears. It seemed that they were the most common books in the ghetto, along with a few other books.

On some of the books there were inscriptions such as "This book is the property of…." I found there several familiar names of prayer houses and of private people to whom the books had belonged.

As the Committee members explained, there would soon be another organization: a kitchen for the homeless wanderers.

[Page 109]

The kitchen was already functioning. It distributed lunch for the remnant of survivors and for those wandering, returning Siedlce Jews, using aid that came from America and items that the Joint provided through the Central Committee. But the kitchen was located for the time in the attic of a house cat the corner of Stary Rynek and First of May, where they used to hang laundry; they laid boards across trestles to serve as tables; they put other boards on top of boxes to serve as benches. At lunchtime the remnant of homeless people and the wanderers would assemble to eat lunch. Now they were preparing to move the kitchen to the mikveh building.

* * *

From the mikveh building we exited to the half-darkened vestibule that served a number of community purposes: a waiting area for those who came with business for the Committee; a kitchen for guests who were staying there. And the bucket with water, great dishes and cups that stood on the bare ground, as well as the puddles, were evidence that this was a place for washing.

Above, instead of a ceiling, there was a dark black hole that inspired fear and terror.

We went up the ladder that stood in a corner and looked into the dark attic. It inspired a dark gloom with its hot, sticky air. It felt as if the angel of death would have gasped there with his dead black wings. And this is what we learned there:

On that terrible Shabbos of the great massacre, in this dark, stinking attic, under the hot tin roof, seventy unlucky souls took refuge, mostly women and children. They sought safety and a hiding place among the dark attic shadows and the many years worth of spider webs. They were there for three days, tormented by hunger, thirst, and the heat that came from the hot tin roof. These half-dead unfortunates held their breath, stifled their coughs so as not to be noticed and discovered by the murderous trackers who were, with their tracking dogs, running through the emptied ghetto in search of hidden Jews.

On the fourth day, Tuesday, suffering from hunger, thirst and heat, a child, a young girl, left the hiding place and went tremulously to the nearest pump in search of water.

[Page 110]

The poor child was noticed by one of the murderers, the executioner Bakenshtas. Like a sophisticated hunter he went after the child, petted her head, spoke sweetly to her, helped her get some water, gave her chocolate and told her to give some to her mother and sisters. The murderer followed the child and found all of the unfortunate jews who were hiding in the dark attic and he shot all of them all by himself.

God of Vengeance

It pains the heart to see everyone that we find there on the empty, darkened mikveh grounds.

I stand paralyzed on the threshold between the orphanage and the mikveh. I look once again into the dark shadows of death that sweep around and peer down from the vast hole in the mikveh's attic, which was the slaughter house for so many souls. And then I look at the wretched remnant that remains of our community and is now concentrated in three corners of the darkened mikveh building: on these human shadows who lie on straw in their boundless, helpless suffering; I look at the poor broken tables and benches that comprise the central aid organization for the "community" and at the collected holy remnants that lie in the rest in the corner, to which my hand is again instinctively drawn. I pick up a torn page of Psalms. I look at it and I see before my eyes the gilded, tear covered page of Psalm 94, yellowed and soaked with the tears that my simple, annihilated fellow citizens wept before their terrible end. I hide myself in a corner, by the chest of holy relics and I read with devotion:

> O Lord, You God to whom vengeance belongs!
> You God to whom vengeance
> belongs, shine forth.
> Lift Yourself up, You Judge of the earth;
> Give the proud what they deserve.
> How long shall the wicked, O Lord,
> How long shall the wicked exult?
> They overflow, they speak proudly,
> The workers of iniquity elevate themselves.
> They crush Your people, O Lord,
> And they torment your heirs.
> They murder the widow and the stranger,
> And they kill the orphans.

And they say, "God will not see,
And the God of Jacob will not notice…"

[Page 111]

17. The Small Ghetto

Translated by Theodore Steinberg

We cross from one win to another, from one slaughter ground to another, through the Old City, in the days of the destruction, was called "The Small Ghetto." This was the triangle where the corners of three streets converged: Aslanowicz, Targowa, and Sokolower.

Once, before the destruction, the old, small wooden houses were occupied by porters, wagoners, travelers to other villages, and similar poor people. This was the city center of Jewish poverty and need. Later, in the last stage of destruction, this poor quiet corner "merited" being the center of the greatest pain and suffering for the small remnant of our community, who were there tortured during the last three months of their lives.

We consider the few poor buildings and get the idea of how those unfortunate people, who numbered about two thousand, "lived" there, tormented and holding out for a whole three months in such barbaric circumstances as were imposed by the Nazis.

They stand dumb, closed up, the remaining wooden houses of the small ghetto with their twisted doors and windows. They say nothing about the horrible tragedies that took place within their walls.

The open gutters that run down both sides of the street are silent. They do not tell how much Jewish blood flowed through them on each day of slaughter.

The stones oof the sidewalk are silent, the simple stones of the past and also the newer gravestones with their four-cornered holy letters that the vandals brought there from the cemetery to pave the streets.

[Page 112]

They do not tell how much life was torn away upon them during the dark day of the devil's lordship.

Also silent were the few willow and acacia trees that stand there by the crossroads of the deserted, half-dead streets. Blown by the spring wind, they rock back and forth and whisper quietly with their green-leafed heads. Only God knows whether that is a Kaddish for the murdered former inhabitants or they are simply driving away the heat to protect the new neighbors. And perhaps their whispering is a prayer for their health and well-being. But they do not say, the trees, how many of our unhappy fellow citizens lost their souls in these shadows and how many were hanged on their branches.

And quiet, too, is the ground, the slaughtering field of our people. It lies spread out like a silent carcass exudes a stench. It speaks only of the sea of tears and blood that it had absorbed, of the fearful harvest that occurred there and of the innocent lives that were devoured.

The sky over this small ghetto-hell, to which our unhappy compatriots directed their despairing glances and quiet, heartrending prayers and poured out their trembling hearts, with there hands raised to Him in their most painful tragic minutes. The sky, which looked on everyone, saw everything from above—it, too, lies locked up in its deep blue, plays thoughtlessly with the sea of shimmering sunbeams and remains silent.

The new inhabitants of the place are silent. They inherited, aside from the houses of the murdered Jews, also the little grottoes, the legendary Jewish properties—they watch the few wandering Jews with reservations, some with horror, as if they are watching spirits who are returning from the other world. They stand silent and barely answer the questions they are asked.

Silent! Everything is silent! It appears, just as earlier, in the days of destruction, that everything—heaven and earth, the world and nature, people and God, not only did not overturn things, but was not destroyed with our people, but worked hand in hand with the bloody destroyers and quietly went along with their fiendish work. And now, too, after the destruction, everything worked together to confirm that silence, not to reveal anything, so that all will disappear in a sea of forgetfulness, erased from memory, as if it had never happened.

[Page 113]

Is everything deaf, blind, and dumb, or is the custodian of history ashamed to recount it, to record this ugly, bloody chapter?—Perhaps both together.

Perhaps everything would go away in the confusion of forgetfulness if not for the oversight, as in other instances, of a few surviving witnesses who themselves suffered through that hellish period, what the surviving remnant of our destroyed people experienced in the small ghetto—that should tell us, tell the coming generations and tell history, how great human suffering and woe can be and how widely barbaric atrocities and human evil can extend.

And they do tell, those few living survivors:

That tragic Shabbos, the 22nd of August, when the executioners "prepared" the small ghetto for the chosen from the selection, they counted on five hundred seventy people. According to their Nazi calculations, those few small buildings offered sufficient living room for that number of condemned Jews who were to be left alive for only a short time.

That Shabbos night, after the selection, the five hundred seventy chosen, in a convoy, urged on with beatings, were led into the small ghetto. These "fortunate" chosen ones organized themselves in groups of twenty or twenty-five in the ghetto building, in stalls, attics, and cellars.

And although the small ghetto was immediately after its creation surrounded by a squad of Ukrainian Sonderdienst and Polish police, who guarded it thoroughly so that no one could get in, with the help of bribes to the Polish police, individuals at first, then scores, and even later hundreds were successful at entering the small island of life, as people then thought of the small ghetto in the surrounding sea that was ruled by death. It was not long before the number of souls there grew to about two thousand.

Gradually it developed in this way:

[Page 114]

The first who tore themselves from he claws of the angel of death were the few lucky ones whom the orderlies and nurses at the hospital had pulled out as wounded or ill, as well as those who were disguised as orderlies at the Umschlagplatz. Some had meanwhile hidden in the hospital and some managed to mix in with the chosen group from the selection and entered the small ghetto with them.

On Monday the Extermination Squad that had come to carry out the massacre had left Siedlce. The local executioners were left to bring things to an end. With the reduction inn the number of Germans in the city it was easier for some people who had hidden in various hiding places in the large ghetto to convey themselves, in the dark of night, through back ways into the small ghetto by paying off the Polish police.

In the large ghetto bands of Germans and Ukrainians went around with coal Polish assistants and well-trained dogs seeking Jews in hiding places. They dragged them out of their hiding places and killed them on the spot or took them to the cemetery and shot them. This persuaded the unfortunate ones to seek ways to get into the small ghetto, where people had legal "living rights." Many lost their lives in this process, but some managed to escape.

The clearing away of the dead from the streets of the large ghetto and from the Umschlagplatz and loading them on wagons and taking them to the ghetto entrance was done by the "selected ones." It also provided an opportunity to some to leave their hiding places in the dangerous large ghetto, take part in the work with the corpses, and then enter the small ghetto with the "selected."

When knowledge reached the villages of what had been done to the Jews in the city, it awakened the desire in certain portions of the village population to "take action," and they organized raids on the unfortunate Jews who had hidden in the villages or wandered in the woods and fields. The peasants robbed the Jews they found, killed them, or turned them over to the Gestapo. Also, it worked out that many of these unhappy Jews who had hidden in the villages or took refuge in the empty woods and fields, not wanting to be robbed by the peasants, through different means managed in the dark of night to get into that little island of life—the small ghetto.

[Page 115]

No matter how dark and empty life was for the chosen and those who had come to the small ghetto from other places, it was especially tragic and hopeless for old people, women, and children who, on that dark Shabbos, had hidden. They were all condemned. They belonged to the gas chambers in Treblinka. Only men could live legally in the small ghetto, and then only men between fifteen and fifty, no old people, no women, and no children. So where should all these condemned ones go? Should they remain in their wretched hiding place in the liquidated large ghetto, where they would be rooted out by the murderers and suffer certain death? Should they sneak into the small ghetto? What would happen when the Germans encountered them? The whole small ghetto would soon be liquidated, and so would they. The old people, the women, and the children, together with the chosen, would either be sent to Treblinka or stood up against a wall and shot. So had Fabish himself declared.

A tragic situation, with no solution.

Of the two possibilities, the instinct for life led the old, the women, and the children into the ghetto. Some of them sought places to hide—perhaps someone could find them a secure place—and some became depressed and resigned, hoping that by chance they would be among their own, among Jews. Many of the older people and the women fell along the way, but some escaped at that moment.

Among the escaped older men who came to the small ghetto were: Yitzchak Nahum Weintraub, Ben-Zion Zucker, Shlomo Shmuel Abarbanel, Kalman Friedman, Herzl and Nahum Halbershtadt, Henech Goldfarb, Itshe Meir Shochet and his son Yakov, Yitzchak Kagan, and others.

The women dressed in men's clothing (helped by the chosen "legals") and located themselves in the most concealed places in the small ghetto so that they would not be noticed by the Germans, Ukrainians, and Polish police, who seemed to be everywhere. In deathly fear they waited in their hiding places for their fate, which lay in the hands of the bloody murderers.

[Page 116]

The worst was for the little children. They were

hungry and thirsty. It was terrible in the narrow, stuffy cellars, bunkers, and other hiding places, where they cried and cried. Their cries could betray them. The bloody murderers will hear and entrap not only them, the unhappy children, but their mothers and everyone else who was found and lead to the liquidation of the ghetto. How horrible! There were two instances—people say—when little children were strangled by their own parents and others nearby in their hiding spots! To such a level had the murderers led these unfortunate people.

None—no children remain from that bloody epoch.

* * *

There were some who escaped from the Treblinka death transports by ripping off a door or by ripping off the iron bars from the train car windows and jumping from the wagons. Those who were not killed by the Germans and the Ukrainians who escorted the transports or by the larcenous peasants who waited for victims by the train tracks with axes and sticks and killed them managed through various back roads to get to the small ghetto.

There were also some Jews, not from Siedlce, who escaped from Treblinka and came to Siedlce to the small ghetto. They worked at loading the wagons with booty from the victims that the murderers were sending home. Having nothing to lose, they hid themselves among the packages of clothing and shoes. Siedlce was the nearest and first station for the trains headed to Treblinka. The Jews who had escaped from the transport trains sought ways to remain in Siedlce, where there was still a "legal" ghetto with a few Jews.

They also brought with them the horrifying but true news from the "work camp"—Treblinka.

Thus did all the oppressed, all the unfortunate, shut out from the Book of Life, who had somehow escaped to the city and its neighborhood gather in the small ghetto.

[Page 117]

Understandably, with the growth in the number of people, the crowding in the small area became worse, and in the few small building, not only in cellars, attics, and stalls, people were oppressed by the crowding, even trying to find a little open spot on the ground in a courtyard or a garden so they could play down their tired, worn out bodies for rest. This was one of the hardest things to accomplish.

* * *

Mrs. Ida Tenenbaum-YomTov, who alone survived in the small ghetto for the entire three months of its existence, gives the following testimony of that time:

On Wednesday, August 26, Fabish, the commander in the city, issued an order that the small ghetto would continue to exist, on the condition that everyone there would work.

This order was taken to be a kind of amnesty or "pardon" for the "illegals" who had gotten into the small ghetto—women and older people—and for those who were still hiding out in the large ghetto. They could freely, in broad daylight, leave their hiding places and enter the small ghetto.

There was a short burst of excitement after the difficult experiences of the recent tragic days, a spot of hope for the naive: Was it possible? Had they gone far enough?

But like all the German promises of that time, so the assurances of the city commander turned out to be a swindle, a sophisticated killing game, made to lure the hidden ones from their hiding places so they could be killed.

Early in the morning, thirty women and little girls, escorted by the Polish police, went out to work. They were taken to clean the empty houses in the large ghetto and to separate and pack the stolen Jewish goods that the murderers had taken from their victims.

During the day, after this labor, the thirty women were locked up in the ghetto prison—in the former community rooms of the shul. After they were there for several hours, the murderers bound their hands behind them with wire and took them in a truck to the cemetery, stood them up by a wall, and shot all of them on the pretext that they had stolen, that they had donned the clothing of the Jews who had been robbed.

[Page 118]

Only one of these unfortunate women, Esther Spector, managed to escape: with a piece of iron that she had accidentally found in the prison room, she hacked a hole the size of two bricks in the wall, and at the last minute, before they were taken to the cemetery, she managed to get out.

(About the shameful mass murder of these twenty-nine women we will speak in another place, when we come to their abandoned graves.)

Among the women who were shot were Rusze Landau, the wife of the lawyer Yosef Landau, who miraculously, during that week, had escaped twice: on Shabbos from the Umschlagplatz he escaped with the help of the hospital personnel and hid there as a nurse; and three days later—at the time of the slaughter at the hospital. She left behind two young children, also miraculously saved, at the time when their father, Yosef Landau, on the Shabbos of the selection, was sent to the left, that is, to Treblinka.

In the morning, after the frightful slaughter, Fabish gave further assurance that in the future nothing would happen to the women if they would go regularly to their labor and no longer steal. Understandably, since no one any longer trusted Fabish's "assurances," the women went into hiding wherever they could and did not go to work.

Several days later, when people saw that those who went to work returned alive, sometimes with a bit of provisions that they found while cleaning the houses in the liquidated large ghetto, the women emerged from their hiding places and voluntarily went to work.

[Pages 118-119]

A. Labor Camps

Translated by Yocheved Klausner

Various labor camps existed in our town and around it: small ones, where only few people worked, and larger ones, which would employ up to several hundred workers.

The most "popular" camps were:

1.	Reckman – for railroad equipment	about 200 workers
2.	Kissgrube – stone and gravel excavation	" 150 "
3.	Construction works	" 100 "
4.	Army equipment camp	" 100 "
5.	Ralnitche Syndicate	" 30 "
6.	Glass works	" 60 "
7.	Waste collecting station	" 59 "
8.	Wolf & Goebel – concrete works, roads	" 150 "
9.	Railroad inspection & various railroad works	" 150 "
10.	Air force works	" 100 "
11.	General collection center – and several smaller enterprises	

In some of these places, the German supervisors took their workers from the smaller ghetto, arranged for them living quarters in the local barracks and gave them their meals in a common kitchen.

The living conditions in the camps varied, according to the whims of the camp leaders and their wild and sadistic moods.

The general system and the overall goal was, however, the same everywhere: to extract from the Jewish slaves maximum work with minimum food and rest; to exploit their strength as fast as possible, that they would collapse as quickly as possible. This was the wish of the leader, the "Führer," the initiator of the "new order," and all the little "führers" of the camps were dedicated to helping realize the big plan. In some of the camps the "plan" was carried out slowly and gradually, step by step, while in others – swiftly and brutally.

He bloodiest and most cruel of the labor camps in town, where hundreds of Jews from the small ghetto were tortured and killed, was the "Reckman" firm.

The central offices of the firm were in Berlin. The company's main business was building railroads and other transport means for the army, as well as dispatching ammunition transports to the East. Several hundred Jews worked in the Siedlce branch.

[Page 120]

The special tactics of the company leaders concerning the Jews was to torment them through work and hunger until they died. Working without end, without a break, day and night, without food, without rest, along with cruel and continuous beating, the Jews would lay the rails, cut stones, carry heavy loads and unload the wagons. People became swollen and collapsed on the spot when their strength gave way. The dying would be pulled out of the way and finished off one by one, and in their place another person would be assigned right away, and then another and then another. There were enough Jews around – too many, in fact. And, when all the Jews of this region would die, they will bring Jews from countries where there still existed some, for all of them must be used and their lives sacrificed for the new happy order that the Nazis would bestow on the world.

Yudel Ruzhowikwiatt, who had worked at Reckman's for some time, tells that the chief murderer, Reckman himself, would often boast that every morning before breakfast he must kill at least one Jew, otherwise he could not swallow his breakfast.

The healthiest and strongest person was not able to bear for more than several weeks the terrible conditions of hunger, hard work and beating that were commonplace in the Reckman camp. This was not a labor camp – it was a death camp. No wonder that nobody wanted to work there. Thus every morning the messengers from the camp would enter the little ghetto and the terrible hunt began. Every person they put their hands on, even women and old people, knew that their horrible death sentence had been signed.

As a result of these tactics – to wear down people through hunger, hard work and beatings – daily the streets of Siedlce would witness groups of pale and emaciated Jews, in rags, pushing little carts full of other Jews, their faces pale green or yellow like wax, some of them swollen, with very weak signs of life; behind the procession would walk the German watchmen. The Jews in the carts were the workers that the Reckman Company sent back to the ghetto – the tormented and dying Jews that they could not use any longer. They were done, and not needed.

As soon as the cart loaded with the living skeletons would enter the ghetto it was overturned as if it were a load of stones or sand. The wretched bodies would fall out and remain on the ground, unable to move.

[Page 121]

The poor tormented Jews, who had pulled the cart and unloaded the dying people, were led by the watchmen back to Reckman's, to pay with their last drops of blood, until it was their own turn to be carted away by other unfortunate Jews, back to the ghetto. The only creatures that would pay any attention to the still living skeletons were the swarms of flies and worms.

It would happen sometimes, that one of the ghetto residents would furtively give one of the dying persons a piece of bread or a drop of water; seldom would the dying have enough strength left to extend his hand to receive it. It was too late for any help – most of them died the same day.

Leibl Mandelbaum, who worked in this Reckman hell-camp, told his story:

– I worked at digging up and cutting stones. The German supervisor would constantly push the workers, not giving them even a moment's rest. The portion of food we received all day was 80 grams of bread and a bowl of soup – mostly plain water in which we would sometimes find a piece of rotten cabbage or some other vegetable. When I tried to take a few minutes' rest, the supervisor hit me with the shovel over my back so hard, that the shovel broke. I could not move, and Reckman himself, who witnessed the scene, permitted me to rest for one hour, after which I was driven back to work.

Mandelbaum ran away from the camp and went to the little ghetto. He was caught by a policeman and sent back to the Reckman camp and punished by 25 whippings. Several days later he ran off again, was caught and again punished by beating. Feeling that he was so weak that he would soon collapse anyway, he decided to risk everything and escaped for the third time – this time with success. Finally he got rid of the Reckman Company.

B. Life and Death in the Small Ghetto

Translated by Theodore Steinberg

No matter how difficult and bitter life was in these camps, these "special places," it was like Eden in comparison to the life led by those who remained in the small ghetto.

[Page 122]

After a long day of hard work, beset by hunger, blows, and vast suffering, an unfortunate person collapsed in the evening behind the fence, almost done to death, starving and beginning to wonder where he could get something to still his hunger.

No one in the small ghetto thought about regular meals. There was no legal way to obtain necessities. Neither the controlling forces nor the work authorities gave such things a thought. Even if someone smuggled in some provisions, they cost so much that only a few could manage to purchase them. People regarded hunger as a normal thing that would last until they had fallen aside.

After fooling the stomach with a bit of water and some substitute for food—one went to "sleep," so that one could arise in the morning to slavery. One would find a corner somewhere to lie on the ground, with the collar of his disintegrating clothing over his ears, and he wold try to fall into deeper forgetfulness so that he would neither feel nor hear what was going on around him.

Robbed of all of life's necessities—the unfortunate ghetto dweller was also robbed of sleep. Because of the crowding, so that people lay almost on top of each other, on the filth and on the mass of worms that overran the ghetto, as well as because of the constant shooting that the maddened Germans practiced all night to amuse themselves by shooting into the unfortunate clusters of Jews. The victims from this nighttime sport were collected in the morning by the Jewish police and taken for burial in the cemetery.

Beds, mattresses, and bedclothes no one had. They all remained in the large ghetto for the new inhabitants, or else they were stolen. Similarly, almost no one had any extra clothing. Almost no one had any extra supplies.

A particular plague in the small ghetto were the Roma. They had been settled in several two-story buildings that had belonged to Henech Goldfarb that were located in the middle of small wood ghetto houses. They stole from the Jews the last bits of their hidden supplies and then went to Fabish and to the Gestapo with reports and accusations against their Jewish neighbors, which often led to the executions of Jews.

[Page 123]

The city commander, Fabish, and Gestapo head Duba searched the small ghetto every day. After every visit by these two murderers, insane, sadistic proclamations were visited on the heads of the unhappy Jews, or they took with them several victims and a few hours later the Jewish police were summoned to bury the bodies. Generally when the police were summoned to Cuba or to Fabish, they took with them shovels and mattocks. They knew why they were being summoned.

The constant hunger in the small ghetto, the difficult slave labor, and the terrible crowding, the plague of filth, flies, and worms, the complete lack of medications and medical supervision—all of this brought illnesses and epidemics that slashed through the ghetto dwellers like a scythe. No day passed without the deaths of several victims.

In the center of the ghetto, in a muddy courtyard, stood an abandoned wooden pigsty. There in the pigsty, on the muddy ground, they laid out the dead.

Once a week, a large open wagon came to the pigsty. They threw the corpses that accumulated during the week onto the wagon. They were taken to the cemetery and buried in a common grave.

It often happened that s the bodies were being thrown onto the wagon, hands, feet, and other body parts would fall from having lain so long in the pigsty. It also happened that in the dark of night, some of the still-living dead would sneak into the pigsty and take the poor clothing of the dead to cover their own nakedness.

The complete lack of provisions, of the most basic necessities, greatly weakened the ghetto dwellers, so that many died as they went off to the labor.

Then again began the "lapankes." Early every morning, as day was beginning, murderous bands of Germans, Sonderdienst, and police would fall upon the ghetto. They led a wild attack. They pulled out old and young, healthy and sick, as well as women.

[Page 124]

They would beat and torment them mercilessly—with whips, rods, and rifle butts, driving them to labor.

A special wildness and barbarity was demonstrated by the murderers to their victims with the coming of the High Holidays, Rosh Hashanah, Yom Kippur, and Succos. (In general, the Germans, throughout the time of their bloody rule, conducted actions, selections, denunciations, and other torments—as much as possible on Shabbos and on holidays.)

People say that on that Yom Kippur in 1942 a group of exhausted Jews was assembled, including Yitzchak Nahum Weintraub, Itsche Meir Shochet, Ben-Zion Zucker, Shlomo Shmuel Abarbanel, Herzl and Nahum Halbershtadt, Henech Goldfarb, Kalman Friedman, and others, who, like the hidden Jews in Catholic Spain, used hidden cellars in the small ghetto to recite the Yom Kippur prayers with heartrending wails, but in the quietest voices possible (so that the enemy would not hear). Suddenly a fierce band of Germans burst in and began to seize the Jews for labor—to unload munitions wagons for the commander.

When these ferocious man-beasts saw the broken, bent over Jews, with their taleisim around their pale yellow faces, they abandoned the young, healthier Jews, who would voluntarily have gone to the work. Instead they took the older people in their taleisim. That night, at the time of Ne'ilah, the old, worn out Jews were seen. Their pale faces were filthy, black from the gunpowder mixed with blood from the wounds that the murderers had given them during the labor.

C. The New Jewish Council

The condition in the ghetto because of hunger, crowding, epidemics, and savage attacks on the one hand, and on the other the cessation of work outside the ghetto meant that the small number fo rescued Jews, along with the whole ghetto, would be liquidated. This meant that the3 Jewish Council, which had been liquidated together with the large ghetto, had to renew its activities and do something in this approaching fatal situation.

[Page 125]

The three former Jewish Council members who remained in the city were chosen for this work: Hersh Eisenberg (chair), Moshe Ratbeyn, and Anatol Goldberg.

The first job of the revived Jewish Council was to raise several thousand zlotys and pay off the bill that Fabish had imposed: to pay the firemen for their work on Shabbos, August 22, during the selektion.

The actual duties that the revived Jewish Council undertook were to stabilize the supply of bread at normal prices and to get the necessary medications for those confined in the ghetto. In various ways, in a short time these two obligations were carried out.

Fabish had ordered the city committee to distribute ration cards for the ghetto inhabitants. Gestapo head Duba had given the three aforementioned members of the Jewish Council passes to go into the city.

Thanks to these possibilities, they met with bakers about getting bread for the ghetto and with pharmacists about getting the necessary medications. They also had to arrange getting various articles that until then had been considered luxuries that were not available tot he ghetto residents, such as candles (there was no electricity), matches, washing powder, salt, and so on. And then that sophisticated hangman Fabish ordered that the Roma, who were situated in a large two-story house in the small ghetto should leave that building and transfer it to Jews.

In all of these instances, the sophisticated and well-thought out tactics of the Germans were obvious, how to lull the watchfulness of their victims, to blunt their sensitivity, so that the fresh blows that they were preparing would take them by surprise.

* * *

In the small ghetto there were almost no complete families. There were just torn limbs, lonely, solitary survivors of destroyed families. There were sons and daughters whose parents had been killed in front of their eyes or had been torn from them and sent to Treblinka; there were some whose children had been shot before their eyes; husbands of murdered wives; brothers whose sisters had been shot. There were none who did not bewail relatives who had been killed by the bloody murderous beasts.

[Page 126]

All were depressed, broken, dejected and all wanted an accounting of their perilous situation; for the worthlessness of their lives, which anyone, whoever wanted, could destroy and then be rewarded for the act. Before their eyes, there remained the horrible images of the last days, of the mass slaughter at the liquidation of the large ghetto. And then—people clung to their empty lives and seized upon the last German pretenses the way a drinker might seize the blade of a sword. People made peace with their fate and began to accommodate to their horrible situation, to the new circumstances, as if to a "normal" situation. People began to consider how to "make the best of things." Others strove to get reserves of provisions and heating supplies for the winter. Many strove to convince themselves that in any case nothing would happen in the small ghetto over the winter if only because almost everyone would be going to labor—which the Germans desperately needed. They would not kill off the laborers that they needed.

The relentless tension disappeared. A fitful peace fell over the ghetto and lasted until the end of October.

This was a quiet before a terrifying, horrible storm, before the last, final storm in the ghetto.

D. The Last Days of the Small Ghetto

The hard, cold winter began early, with rain, snow, and frost—in that dark year of 1942.

It seemed as if nature itself had joined up with the bloody destroyers, stood by their side as an assistant to torture and plague the last remnant of unhappy Jews.

Just like three months ago, when the condemned community was driven out of the large ghetto to the Umschlagplatz and the bloody murderers had planned the wildest and most sophisticated kind of torture, brutality, and violence—so then the sun came to help them, burning and heating the victims without mercy; so now, too, when the remaining small remnant of the large community was mired in the pain and crowding and filth of the small ghetto, without food, without warm clothing, without bedding, and without fuel for heat—again nature came to the aid of the torturers: in early fall, bizarre cold arrived. Heavy downpours of rain beat down like wet rods upon the ghetto and its inhabitants.

[Page 127]

Thick, heavy snow penetrated the wooden houses in the small ghetto. Through the cracks in the crooked, badly constructed doors and windows of the ghetto buildings and in the half-open stalls, attics, and cellars, where the weary shadows of people huddled, bitter colds winds blew like a great troop of demons into their weary bones and ate away at them, like hungry serpents.

Almost no one had warm clothing, a pair of underwear, a pair of shoes to put on, or a blanket for protection against the winter's cold. Anyone whom the Germans and Ukrainians had not robbed had long ago traded such things with his neighbors for a bit of bread or a few potatoes. Even less frequently did anyone have a bit of coal or wood to make a fire for warmth. The only way to get warmth was to huddle together in a group in their empty ghetto cots, in a pile, and so preserve with their own skin a little warmth that came from the weak, dried up and weary bodies.

People suffered in the horribly long, empty, sleepless nights. Hunger, filth, and cold tortured them; so, too, did the murderous Germans and Ukrainians who went about the ghetto savagely throughout the night and never stopped shooting at random; and they were tortured by their awareness of the unknowable, insecure tomorrow, of the uncertain fate that held them and from which they could see no exit.

After such empty, long, sleepless nights would come a no less empty day with its problems and worries, with its confusion and afflictions that poisoned their lives and turned men into plagued animals.

[Page 128]

Every morning, while it was still completely dark outside, people had to stand there broken, frozen through, hungry, tugging at ripped, filthy rags, barefoot, or nearly so, stamping in the cold, wet mud or snow, waiting for their hard labor and lacking the assuredness that they would return alive to the ghetto.

Thus the empty days and nights seemed like an eternity. Each day was more horrible and tragic than the one before.

The first days of November arrived. Strange rumors spread among the weakened ghetto inhabitants. Something seemed to be forthcoming, but no one knew what or when.

It was not long before people understood that the executioners were not idle. They had only one intention for the small number of Jews who remained yet alive.

As the few surviving witnesses testify, especially Mrs. Ida Tenenbaum-Yom Tov, this is how things happened in those days:

On November 1, the Germans issued an order that five large ghettos were to be created in Poland where all the surviving Jews from the General Government would be gathered. Siedlce belonged to one of the five.

By December 1, all the Jews in the surrounding cities, towns, and villages had to gather in Siedlce, in the small ghetto.

The Jews had a variety of interpretations of the new order. There were some how took them as a good sign. The remaining Jews would remain alive in the ghettos, surely because the Germans needed them for slave labor. Most, however, saw in the new orders a threat, a cunning plot by the sneaky murderers. With the creation of the five large ghettos, the Germans could assemble all the surviving Jews and all of the hidden Jews in concentrated areas, from which it would be easier and less expensive to send them to Treblinka.

Like a horrible eternity, the cold, dismal days and long, dark nights in the small ghetto dragged on. People waited for something, but they knew it was nothing good. The air bore an awful, tragic secret that no one could discern: to be or not to be?

[Page 129]

Life or death? Was the end approaching or would things continue as they were? And could one survive?

---

18. Gensze-Barki

Translated by Theodore Steinberg

On a cold, dark November morning, when the ghetto inhabitants rose, as they did every morning, from their hard, narrow ghetto cots and prepared to go out to their daily slave labor, they heard the latest news that the police brought from the German headquarters: that the small ghetto would be relocated in a smaller and filthier place outside the city—at "Gensze-Barki."

Gensze-Barki lay three kilometers outside the city and consisted of three larger apartment blocs, which the city controllers had one set up between two bare, simple fields and there located people who were of doubtful character and with doubtful professions. The three blocs of houses were a nest for all kinds of thieves, fences, knife wielders, prostitutes, and a variety of underworld heroes from the city and its surroundings. It aroused in all the local working people a feeling of disgust and horror.

All the Jews from the small ghetto had to go there because—according to what the killers said—typhus ruled in the small ghetto and there was fear that the epidemic would move out into the streets surrounding the ghetto.

The transfer to Gensze-Barki was due to happen in several days, on the morning of November 25. People were only allowed to take with them what they could carry by hand.

The unfortunate ghetto inhabitants could only think of the "curse" of three months earlier, of the large ghetto, and they concluded that this meant a similar "curse" according to the way the Germans did things.

These unfortunates were overtaken by a terrible panic and confusion. In the ghetto were a number of children whom people, at great risk, had rescued and hidden. There were also many people who were old and ailing who could not make their way to Gensze-Barki and who would most certainly be shot as part of the "curse." Where could they hide.?

[Page 130]

There were also some who had other concerns. Those rare ones who still had or who had only recently obtained some bedclothes, clothing, or, even more vitally,—a little food, a sack of potatoes—things that were in the ghetto a matter of life or death—how could those things be saved?

There were still several days until the transfer to Gensze-Barki. The crafty murderers made no secret about it and spread the word. Some people tried to get things out of the ghetto. They would smuggle a package to a Christian that they knew, who took it with the understanding that the Jew would be killed and leave the package behind as an inheritance.

Near Gensze-Barki was a glass factory where several score of Jews worked. Some took the risk of bringing their last few possessions. On the last night, people even brought there some of the sick, old people and a few children. The Jewish workers hid them there. On the next morning they were going to move them to the living blocs of Gensze-Barki.

The Gestapo, the gendarmes, and other killers who watched over the ghetto knew what was going on. For a time they closed their eyes, acted as if they knew nothing, and the naive rejoiced in the thought that they were fooling the Germans.

* * *

The last frightful night in the small ghetto arrived. No one slept. Everyone was frightened. All were ruled by the question that tortured everyone, but no one could answer: Did the killers intend to settle this bunch of broken, tortured Jews in Gensze-Barki or was this just a distraction?

After that last painful night, which seemed to last for an eternity, came the terrible day—Wednesday, November 25, 1942.

It was still dark outside when the police read out through the ghetto and sent everyone from their narrow cots into the street, formed them in the usual way into rows of five, hands together, and prepared them for the march.

A cutting wind hit their pale, pinched faces. A terrible cold ate at their bones and nibbled at their emaciated bodies, but the people stood there without marching.

[Page 131]

They waited for the leaders of this bloody act.

At ten o'clock, the chief executioners arrived—Fabish, Cuba, Fricka, and other assistants. They looked over the columns, took reports from their underlings, gave the last orders, and told the Jewish Council what, with great kindness, they were doing for the Jews: they had ordered the magistrate to send a few carts to convey the ill and to carry a bit of baggage.

At around noon came the order to march. A terrible wailing arose: all of the unemptied wells of tears that had remained concealed by the unfortunate ones suddenly opened and out stormed a terrible cry at the beginning of this march of shame. The whole unending mountain of pain and suffering that had gathered during the course of three and quarter years of bloody Nazi rule and made the unhappy Jews into what they now were—all of this broke through at this moment like a volcano, announcing its mighty protest and cry of woe that reached no one's ears. No one heard it, aside from the uncivilized, bloodthirsty killers, for whom the terrible cries of woe and wailing prompted a sadistic pleasure. Also, the neighbors on the Aryan side, who lived in the surrounding streets, through the windows of the warm homes looked on it all—perhaps with pleasure.

Only the bitter, cold, troubling wind that unceasingly hit and thrashed the pale, troubled faces of the beaten, despairing Jewish skeletons carried off the terrible wailing and bore it far away...

* * *

The shameful march of these human shadows took a long time. This train of the living dead took a long time. Some said that they were going to Gensze-Barki. Others said that they were going to Kalushin, where a new work camp for Jews was being formed—this was the way that led there. But instinct said that the murderers intended neither Gensze-Barki nor Kalushin—they intended something else. They meant to drive out the life of the remaining oppressed Jews. They would be beaten and oppressed under the heavy burden of disgrace and woe, of helplessness and resignation.

[Page 132]

People walked in despair and weariness with their last strength. Those who could still think wondered what the murderers were about, what lay under the mask of Gensze-Barki.

And what a wonder! The murderers armed with rifles, revolvers, and whips led the train of shame and surrounded it on all sides—and they also went slowly. They did not rush, and they drove the human shades with no special ferocity. They were satisfied with verbal abuse, curses, and mild blows. From time to time, as if from habit, they would shoot over the heads of the terrified mass of people just to remind them of their status. There were no particular victims on the road.

Before the evening, the procession reached Gensze-Barki.

And again a wonder! The three blocs of houses stood open, without any fencing, without even a police guard.

Many people went to neighboring villages to buy something to eat from the peasants and straw for bedding. No one bothered them. The murderers had withdrawn a little. People breathed more freely. A feeling of hope arose in those who still had the will to live: perhaps they would be left alone. Things seemed good.

* * *

Once again the killers employed their proven tactics, which had truly become a system in their devilish plans—before a mass attack and a mass slaughter of the defenseless Jews, to seem to relax a bit the turning of the hard, bloody screws of murder, thereby confusing the victims, distracting them and reducing their watchfulness and sensitivity.

And as always in such situations, events did not allow for a pause.

Early in the morning of Thursday, November 26, the work office of the district council issued an order that all Jews who lived at their workplaces both inside and outside of the city must by December 1 go to the new "cities of refuge"—that is, Gensze-Barki. Only Jews with a special permit from the Gestapo could after that date be found outside the confines of Gensze-Barki.

[Page 133]

From the whole surrounding area, from all the towns and villages, groups of Jews began to arrive in Gensze-Barki, where the police who had escorted them turned them over to the hands of the Germans and Ukrainians. They were together with the Jews who had been brought from the small ghetto, stuffed together into a single bloc that had been emptied of the Roma who had lived there.

No provisions, especially bread from the city, were provided. There was not even water. The only wells that were in the district, where the Roma had lived, could not provide enough water for all, and the Roma seized the wells as their own and would not allow the Jews to fetch water.

A few Jews who had gone to a nearby village to buy something to eat did not return. They were murdered there by the peasants, who had robbed them and buried them behind a fence.

All of these things were signs of the approaching storm. People heard the steps of the angel of death and the flapping of the wings of death.

* * *

As the surviving witnesses tell us, the storm arrived on the unhappy night of Shabbos, the 28th to the 29th of November (the 20th of Kislev 5703).

That night was horribly cold. There was frost and a blizzard such as seldom occurred in Poland. It seemed as if the whole cold north would take part in the bloody partnership and so had sent its representatives, the heavy frost and the snowy wind to help torture the beaten down Jews in their last days, before they would be killed by the murderers.

The unhappy victims huddled together in the icy, filthy, and stinking rooms in the housing bloc that the Roma had left. The horrible crowding (three thousand beings in a single building), the horrifying cold, and the bizarre darkness brought them all together in a single mass.

They had long ago become accustomed to going without normal sleep, especially in the long nights of the last week when they wavered between life and death and thought that every minute would bring the worst, most frightful things.

[Page 134]

And suddenly, like hosts of devils, those well-known bloodthirsty beings, in the form of the Gestapo, the gendarmes, the Polish police, and specially appointed Ukrainian Sonderdienst bandits all arrived. They formed an iron ring around Gensze-Barki, and especially the building where the unfortunate Jews were huddled together. Like hungry wolves they threw themselves on the unfortunate victims with wild screams, unceasing shooting, and vicious blows, creating a total confusion and tumult, forcing everyone out into the dark, freezing night.

The murderers ordered them to sit on the ground, on the snow and ice. The suffering people sat there for half the night. Over their bowed heads, the killers shot various weapons. And the bitter cold wind never let up from striking the pale yellow, drained faces and cutting like sharp knives into their skin and the drained bones of these human shades.

After many hours of sitting on the frozen ground, the murderers ordered them to stand in rows for a march, in the usual way, five in a column, right next to each other.

Many of the victims at this point could not stand and they remained lying immobile, stiff, frozen to the hard earth. Many, having been shot, lay there in a congealing pool of blood and in the dark were stomped upon by the military boots of the bloody murderers and by the feet of their oppressed fellows.

The unfortunates stood ready to march, on their last way, but they were not allowed to. They heard that at the train station, no wagons were waiting. The killers held a short conference and then ordered everyone back into the rooms of the building, without permission to go from one room to another, to move, to speak, or to look through the windows.

While they were going back into the building, many died from blows and shots from the murderers. The three thousand people were stuffed back into the crowded rooms, massed together, to pass the rest of the dark, empty night, ruled only by the angel of death—the Germans and their helpers.

For the whole of Sunday, November 29, these unfortunates remained without a piece of bread or a drop of water.

[Page 135]

During the day, more groups of Jews were brought to Gensze-Barki, those who worked in more distant labor camps. They were turned over to the bloody fangs of the Germans and Ukrainians. With murderous ferocity they, too, were stuffed into the overcrowded rooms of the single housing bloc.

For the whole day, the Germans never ceased going wild—shooting, hacking, beating, torturing the victims, even for looking through the windows.

Hoda Vaserburg recounts: The murderers took out a group of Jews and shot them. They took out another group of Jews and ordered them to bury those who had been shot, then they shot them. They dragged out other Jews, forced them to bury those who had been shot and so on. This wild bacchanalia lasted the whole time that Gensze-Barki was being besieged.

Hersh Eisenberg—the head of the renewed Jewish Council in the small ghetto—was shot behind the wall of the housing bloc, together with his wife Rachel, the daughter of Ephraim Tzelnik, and their young daughter Chanale. The Germans "suspected" that they would escape…

As was always the case in such situations, when it came to torturing, robbing, and murdering Jews, so this time, too, the Polish police did not lag behind their German and Ukrainian colleagues. The leader of the police, Jankowski, saw that this was the last day for the Jews, just one more day—and done…He squeezed in the packed rooms, called for Avraham Bresler, the vice-commander of the Jewish police, with whom he had had personal dealings. Jankowski led Bresler out behind the wall and shot him.

Another Polish policeman called out an employee of the work office of the Jewish Council, Yosef Sadownik, and shot him.

In this way the murderers "entertained" themselves with the unfortunate victims for the whole of Sunday.

When night arrived, many of the unfortunate victims, who had been massed by the doors and windows, made a last, desperate attempt to escape—they had nothing to lose—by jumping through the doors and windows into the darkness of the night.

[Page 136]

They tried to get through the blockade of fire and death. But only a few merited success. Most fell to the murderers' bullets.

The desperate attempt of the victims to jump through the doors and windows provided the barbaric murderers an opportunity to redouble their devilish efforts, and with the greatest ferocity and bloodthirstiness they took vengeance on the unfortunates. They rampaged throughout the night. The grounds of Gensze-Barki were covered with hundreds of victims.

During the last period, when Gensze-Barki was surrounded by a troop of murderers and everyone knew that the end of the small ghetto had arrived, the end for the last remnant of Jews in Siedlce, many who were weary no longer had the strength nor the inclination nor the will to continue fighting so hard for their poor, bare lives, to bear any longer the awful sorrows and pains, the suffering and shame—they no longer waited for their tragic end, for the tragic epilogue. They ended their own lives in a variety of ways—by taking potassium cyanide or other "means to freedom," as they were called.

We have been told about the couple Yakov Sonschein and his wife Tchipa (the daughter of Aharon Yablon) that in the last hours of Gensze-Barki, they gave their one-year-old daughter Rochele to their Christian friends, Tchipa's school friends Sophia Alaszkowska and Jadwiga Zawaduka. The mother wrote some tragic, heartrending words on post cards for the child, and with potassium cyanide—which their Christian friends had provided—the young couple ended their lives.

Of the many others who in those last tragic hours ended their lives, nothing remains. We do not even know who they were. We know only that their bodies mixed with those who had been killed by the Germans, Ukrainians, Lithuanians, and Polish murderers. They were left in the emptied rooms and outside on the grounds of Gensze-Barki. They were left in wild confusion by the bloody killers, a frightful mass. They were frozen stiffly to the ground. Their poor clothing and shoes were ripped off by the thieving Roma who took over the two remaining blocs.

Mrs. Tchipa Yablon-Sonschein's farewell with her daughter Rochele before taking potassium cyanide

Taking the old and the ill to Gensze-Barki

The Membership of the Credit Society in Siedlce
Sitting, right to left: Mendel Liveront, Shmuel Zucker, Yitzchak Nahum Weintraub, kVelvel Barg, Shmerl Greenberg, Noson David
Glicksberg
Standing, right to left: Asher Eisenberg, Kopracki, Herzl Halbershtam

[Page 137]

The naked bodies lay abandoned for a long time on the grounds of Gensze-Barki and served as food for the wild crows and hungry dogs. Then someone ordered their remains to be collected and taken to the cemetery, where they were laid out and covered with layers of sticks in a pyre and then all burned. Later on, a bitter wind came and spread their ashes in all directions, leaving not a trace behind.

19. The Final Road

Translated by Theodore Steinberg

Early Monday, November 30, the suffering victims were again forced outside. They were arranged in columns and the march began, the horrible tragic march of the last Jews of Siedlce on their final road.

There were no more illusions about the deceitful, hidden "work camps," that at first the murderers had presented to their victims. All now knew their fate, that they were going on their final road. The road that led to the gas chambers of Treblinka. The executioners hid nothing now. Nothing was kept in secret. They spoke openly and cynically about where their victims were headed. Everyone recognized the road they were on. This was the highway that led back to the city, to the train station, to the death wagons.

Three and a quarter years of life under Nazi domination was enough so that the unfortunates were psychologically and consciously half dead, atrophied, apathetic, and indifferent, so that they allowed themselves to be driven like oxen to slaughter. Only a little of their physical strength remained, which allowed them to proceed to their unseen graves—to the never satisfied, bloodthirsty Moloch.

Like a funeral—a large, unending funeral—so went the tragic march of the last remnant of Siedlce's Jews. They marched, these half-dead people, in their own funeral. At the head of this funeral procession went the lion of the fellowship—the old Rabbi Yitzchak Nahum Weintraub, the oldest dignitary, who for half a century had served his community heart and soul, never abandoning the last remnant of his community even now, act the edge of the grave.

[Page 138]

He walked standing fully upright, proudly, with burning eyes. His pale yellow face flamed in spots with holy fire and wrath. The silver-white hair of his head and beard were now even whiter. His blue lips barely moved as he whispered something quietly, so quietly. He was always accustomed, this little old man, R. Yitzchak Nahum, to speak to his community, to say something to his brothers at every opportunity when they were gathered together. It made no difference whether it was a public holiday, a Yom Tov, or a meeting of the community council, or a gathering in the shul to mark the anniversary of Herzl's death. He was always ready to explain to his community a word of Gemara, a midrash, or a chapter of Tanach that related to the matter at hand. So, too, in the last moments of his life and the life of his community, he had something to say. Except that he would arouse the murderers, he would have interrupted the march and explained and expounded to his congregation the great meaning of martyrdom, according to the Torah and to the Talmudic sages, according to the early and late commentators. But the murderers forced him to be silent and to whisper to himself quietly what he could not say openly to his people. He led by the hand his beloved great-grandchild—the only one who remained to him—the little son of Yosef Landau.

Around him went the old ones who had escaped all of the slaughters to this point: R. Itsche Meir Shochet, R. Ben-Zion Zucker, R. Shlomo Shmuel Abarbanel, R. Kalman Friedman, R. Hence Goldfarb, the brothers R. Nahum and R. Herzl Halbershtam, R. Yitzchak Kagan, and others. This group of elders were dressed in white kitties and taleisim. It seemed as if the old leader, together with these elders, led the rest of the community to a huge celebration, for a sacred purpose.

Over their heads were dark gray clouds that covered everything, darkening the heavens, throwing dark shadows on the whole scene and enveloping them in a large black hearse, where the unfortunate half-corpses went on their last funeral procession.

Over the bowed heads of these unfortunates, across the whole dark gray sky, flew hosts of black crows, flapping their wings and crying out: Caw! Caw!

[Page 139]

The bare, green-black poplars and willows that lined both sides of the highway on which the funeral procession traveled stretched out their long branches and sticks like whips against the marching victims, whipping and driving them on.

The sharp, cutting wind laughed devilishly, blew horribly, slapped the unfortunates and forced them to move more quickly, more quickly—as if they would be late for something.

At the little windows of the village houses that were thrown up on the highway, the colored curtains were moved aside and the amazed eyes of Poland's sons and daughters looked at the passing wonder.

* * *

Before noon the funeral procession arrived at the edge of the city, to Warsaw Street. B the train factory the train had made a turn to the left. It was taken to the warehouse of the kerosene business "Falmin," but there were still no wagons.

The frost burned and a wild wind cut and whipped without mercy, tearing at everyone. The earth was covered with a thick layer of snow and ice. The bloody sadists used this last chance that blind, ferocious nature had provided them to torture their unfortunate victims by forcing them to sit down on the frozen ground.

As the elders sat on the snow and ice in their white kitties and taleisim and huddled together against the terrible cold, their leader R. Yitzchak Nahum Weintraub—as Leib Mandelbaum tells it—took out from his bosom a flask of brandy with a glass, poured some in honor of his neighbors, the other elders. Each offered the others a L'Chaim for their trip to the next world, where they were being sent by the bloody executions, and they wished them a dark fate.

This awful suffering lasted for several hours. Finally in the evening the transport arrived with the death wagons. The unfortunates were stuffed into them with the greatest ferocity and bloodthirstiness.

[Page 140]

The Jewish police discarded their hats and other police insignia and wanted to board the wagons along with all the other unfortunate victims, but the executions did not allow them to thanks to their loyal service and aid in liquidating the ghettos, for which they deserved a special death. They received their wagon in the death train.

The doors of the wagons were slammed shut. In a frightfully wild way the locomotive panted and pulled away with the transport of the last Jews on their final journey—in the direction of Treblinka.

[Page 140]

20. Survivors Tell their Story

Translated by Theodore Steinberg

Weary after a day of wandering through the ruins and graves of our destroyed home, worn out by the horrors that we absorbed, upset at what we saw and heard, we went together, the greatest part of the remnant that remains of the Jewish community of Siedlce: a number of wanderers returned from traipsing through the vastness of the Siberian taigas and the steppes of Kazakhstan, dressed in foreign, party Russian and partly donated clothing; some having emerged from underground bunkers and caves in the woods; and some who had suffered through all seven levels of Gehenna pretending to be Aryans on the other side.—Most of them were young men with gray heads, old beyond their years, with creased foreheads and with bulging eyes that glanced around nervously, darting in all directions and focusing on nothing. Each one avoided looking another in the eye, as if people would be embarrassed by them, that they should be called "people," like those creatures, the murderers of our people and our community; and embarrassed that that we did not take that same journey as the rest of our community.

The sun, which followed our wanderings through the ruins and the graves, was as tired as we were, and it set in a tired, embarrassed way behind the distant tree tops and the nearby ruins. Evening shadows grew over the half-ruined city, swallowing up and filling with fear the emptied streets, so that everything gave the impression of homeless, frightening specters.

We did not sit on the earth, everyone wore shoes, on our heads we had no ashes, but our voices were all like the voices of observant Jews from a hundred years ago as they observed Tisha b'Av, sitting on the ground, bemoaning the destruction of their people and their land.

[Page 141]

Their broken hearts were overflowing with such sorrow, sadness, and mournful feelings that we remained suspended in stillness, and it was difficult to speak a word.

We will pass over that dead silence and allow the survivors to explain how they managed to escape from the angel of death.

Melech Halber's Story

On November 30, at the final liquidation of the last Jews of Siedlce, Halaber was loaded together with all the others in a transport headed for Treblinka.

On his way there, Halber took with him a pair of pliers, a small saw, a drill, and other tools that might be useful for whatever might happen.

It was so crowded in the wagon that it was difficult to move. Then, when the train began to move, Halber got to work on the door with his tools. It was not long before the door opened. Without hesitation he jumped from the moving train in the dark night—bruised and bloody from his hasty jump and half-conscious. He saw other people jumping from the wagons and being seized by peasants, who waited for their victims by the train tracks, armed with axes, scythes, spades, and pitchforks, to rob the victims, take their clothing, and kill them.

Coming to himself, Halber got away from the train tracks. Crawling on all fours, he came to a field where there was a stable (a storehouse for grain). He got inside and there encountered Kalman Orszel and Shmerl Feinhaltz who had also jumped from the train. From them Halber learned that he was in the village of Khadaw, six kilometers from Siedlce. His only goal was to get to his brothers, who were hiding in the city at the corner of Stari Rynek and Dluga. On Feinholtz's recommendation and with his help, he hired a peasant who undertook to lead him there for 400 zlotys (80 dollars).

On the horse-drawn cart, the peasant sat in front, Halber in the middle, and in the back the peasant's son.

[Page 142]

In the darkness of the night, Halber recognized that the peasant was not taking him toward Siedlce but in a different direction.

When Halber called this to the peasant's attention, he responded that he was going further, by back roads, in order to avoid the Germans.

The rocking of the peasant's wagon on the soft sand of the road, as well as the cold night wind, cooled and calmed his heated nerves, after his hard experiences of the past several days. Halber fell into a light half-sleep, forgetting reality and conscious of nothing.

Suddenly—Halber continued his story—I felt blows of dull irons on my head. I remained lying unconscious in the wagon, in a stupor. It appears that the murderers thought that I was already dead, so they quickly left the wagon with their spades in their hands and went into the woods to dig a grave for me. As I lay alone in the wagon, I gathered my last strength, jumped from the wagon, and ran across the snow-covered fields. In the blackness of that dark night, I saw that the Liwiec River blocked my way. Feeling the angel of death behind me in the form of the two bloodthirsty peasants who with such alacrity sought my poor life, my shabby clothing, and my few zlotys that they had seen when I had paid them for taking me to the city, I jumped right into the river. Thin thin covering of ice easily broke under me and I found myself half submerged in the water. With my last strength, breaking through the ice, I struggled to the other bank of the river, where I lay inn a faint. I do not know—he continued—if the peasants did not see me and believed that I had drowned or whether they were unwilling to enter the freezing cold river to follow me. I only know that they went away, abandoning their victim, who had escaped from their grasp. Lying there on the snow—Halber continued—I felt terrible pains in my head, my neck, and my face. I felt my head and felt a thick mass of blood that flowed from every side.

My clothing, which had been soaked in the cold water, clung to my skin.

[Page 143]

The terrible cold overcame me. I felt the frost in my bones. This prompted me rise from the frozen ground and start to run as quickly as I could. In a field, I came across a peasant's hut that stood sunken in the sleepy night. I knocked. An old peasant opened the door. He crossed himself and called on all the saints when he saw me standing there bruised, covered with blood, and soaking wet. I answered his questions by saying that I had bruised myself in jumping from a wagon, to which he replied, "That you jumped from a wagon, that I can believe, but from your wounds I can tell that my neighbors did this to you."

This peasant showed Halber a a moving compassion. He sat him by the warm oven, hung his clothing up to dry, helped wash the blood, and in the morning led him by back roads into the city.

Halber continued—I went about searching for the place where my brothers were hidden. I knocked lightly and quietly uttered our chosen password. As soon as the door opened a little, I saw my brothers standing with iron bars in their hands, ready for action, wanting to be armed for what might come.

It seems that my appearance, with rags binding my head and face so that little more than my frightened eyes could be seen, prevented them from recognizing me. They thought I was an enemy and they were ready to attack me. I quickly reassured them through signs and gestures, whispering in the silence, and I barely managed to convince my brothers who I was and to avoid a fratricide.

Melech Halber, together with his brothers Avraham and Yitzchak, hid for twenty months in that spot on Start Rynek and Dluge, until they were liberated by the Red army.

The Story of the Brothers Moyshe and Raphael Kishilinski

At the end of November, 1942, at the liquidations of the small ghetto, the two brothers, together with Mrs. Freida and sister Neche Kishilinski and two children—altogether six people——escaped from Gensze-Barki to the woods and fields outside of Siedlce.

[Page 144]

For a month they roamed around there, hungry and cold, constantly fearing death, not only from the Germans but also from the Poles. They wandered around with other homeless Jews from Siedlce: Yankel and Chaim Ella Dudkewicz, Meir Salzman and his daughter Lola, the Tziglshtein family, Vishnu, and others—altogether twenty-five people. Together they bought a hiding place from the peasant Antony Philipowicz, the village Katun, near Braszkow. This was a covered and hidden mine in the woods for which they paid 6,000 zlotys a month (about 1200 dollars). In time they were joined by another group of Jews from Siedlce who were hidden by the teacher Ashinski in Apala. They had to leave there because they had been detected. These included Dr. Glazowski's Ramek, Dr. Loebel's son Witek, Bracha Ravinsa, Shassenfoygel, and others. They were a group of forty-two and led an underground commune.

For three months they lived "quietly" in the mine. At night, some of them would leave the mine, go to the neighboring villages, buy food and bring water. By chance they had been detected by the Police policeman Marciszewski.

For three months that villain Marciszewski had blackmailed the Jews, extracting money, provisions, and clothing from them by various means and then he sent five Polish policemen after them. Like wild animals they fell upon the mine where the group of Jews were hidden. Aiming their weapons, they ordered everyone out of the mine, then separated the men and the women. The murderers searched each person and took whatever they found: money, provisions, and anything of value. Then they shot all the men, seventeen of them. Among those shot were the Flam brothers, whose father, David, was holding on to them. The murderers left the women and children alive, on the condition that they would go away.

Raphael Kishilinski convinced the murderers that not far away there was gold hidden. They ordered him to get it. He distanced himself from them, leading his twelve-year-old son by the hand. From a distance, he called to his brother: "Moyshe, come help me look for the gold!"—They went into the woods and hid among the thick bushes. There they heard the murderers shooting their neighbors from the mine.

Soon the peasants from the village came to the site of the slaughter tore the clothing and shoes from the dead bodies and buried everyone in the mine.

[Page 145]

Not long after, the peasant Antony Filipowicz was murdered by a band of peasants. This was an act of vengeance by the "A.K." (Armija Krajowa [domestic army])—for having hidden Jews.

Moyshe Kishilinski and Raphael, along with his son, met up in the woods with his wife Freida and her child and sister. These six went to the village of Ostrowiec. There they rented from the peasants Wenedik and Bazur a storage pit for potatoes in a field for 4,000 zlotys (800 dollars) a month. They lived there for eighteen months.

In the winter of 1944, when the Red army cautiously neared the Polish border, word spread among the Gentiles that the Jews would be taking vengeance on them when the Bolsheviks arrived—and therefore all the Jews in hiding should be killed. The owners of the hiding place told the police about the Jews who were hiding there.

On a cold February night the owners, the peasants, opened the pit, created an uproar, and ordered the Jews out.

Outside, around the pit, a troop of bloodthirsty peasants awaited the victims. With murderous ferocity they threw themselves on these unfortunates. Moyshe and Raphael, with his son, in some miraculous way managed to get away from the bloody troop and disappeared in the thick darkness of the woods (Moyshe separately from Raphael and his son. In contrast, the women Niche and Freida with her child were seized by the barbaric peasants and turned over to the Polish police, who were waiting for them. The police seized everything that they had and then shot them.

After losing his wife and child, who were killed before his eyes, and having lost his brother, Moshe Kishilinski remained alone and desperate, apathetic and indifferent. He even went in broad daylight into the city, into Siedlce. He was seeking a Christian whom he knew, a poor shoemaker, Philip Smalenski. Smalenski received him well, gave him food and a hiding place for several weeks without charge.

Having rested for several weeks, Moshe went out to search for his missing brother Raphael and his son. On the road he encountered a band of Ukrainians.

[Page 146]

Out of fear, he hid in a deep bog. He lay there for an entire da. Then he came to the village of Apala and sought some Goyim whom he knew, but no one allowed him in. Lacking any alternative, he went to the village of Katun the peasant Wenedik, whom he knew, the owner of the men where they had hidden earlier. The peasant turned him down, because he had no place to put him. Desperate and resigned, he snuck through the fields until he found a solitary closed up barn with hay. In the darkness of night he climbed onto the roof and lay down for a bit. Through the cracks in the wall he looked out at the darkness. He saw how the peasant Wenedik, from whom he had sought protection and a hiding place for the second time, lay in wait for whom with an iron bar, like hunter trailing an animal. The murderous peasant could not find his victim and left. In the morning he returned with the police. They looked around but could not find him. For three days Moyshe lay hidden under the straw. He heard how the peasant and the police were looking for him. The whole time he had nothing to eat or drink. Miraculously, he also escaped from there alive. Then he met with his brother and his son. They were found another stable in an empty field. They hid there for fourteen weeks. No one, not even the owner of the stable, knew they were there.

On dark nights they would leave their hiding place and go to buy food and water from the peasants. The peasants made certain signs on their wells in order to ascertain whether Jews had come to fetch water. They would lay paper or straw on the surface of the water in the well and then in the morning determine if it had been disturbed. Those in hiding had by this method often been noticed and followed by the bloodthirsty and robbery-minded peasants, who, with weapons and iron bars in their hands, lusted after their miserable lives and poor clothing. Every day these poor people saw death before their eyes.

One evening they went to a peasant whom they knew to buy bread. The peasant told them to come in the morning at a certain time, when the bread would be ready. Arriving in the morning, at the specified time, they were fallen upon by a band from the A.K. who were waiting for them in the peasant's home. They were greeted with shots, In the darkness they were able to retreat and escape.

[Page 147]

But in the process Raphael and his son were wounded in their feet. A bullet went through the hat that Moyshe was wearing.

The Kishilinski brothers had given a fur coat to the peasant Ferkowski, for which Ferkowski was supposed to pay them in installments with a certain amount of bread. At the time of the transaction, the peasant gave them their first installment of bread. When the Kishilinskis came for the second time, they were met by a group of men who began shooting at them. By hiding behind Ferkowski's, they were able to retreat and escape.

Because some of the peasants in the village knew of their hiding place in the barn, they abandoned that place and went to the neighboring woods.

One Sunday morning when Moyshe, Raphael, and his son were lying with bated breath in the woods, they heard one young punk say to another, "Hey, Janek, let's go to church." The other responded, "I'm not going to church today. Today our buddies (meaning the A.K.) are going hunting for the Yids who are hiding around here. I want to be in on that game."

Having heard this conversation and understood what was meant by the "hunt," the Kishilinskis left their dangerous spot, creeping on their knees through the high, thick forest grass and the trees. They came to a thicker part of the forest. They figured that there were Germans there and the A.K. would not follow them.

Raphael Kishilinski had made contact with the good landowner Lipinska, and she gave them food. Late at night, Lipinska would bring the food to the orchard and put it in a designated spot in a beehive. So it went for several nights, until some treacherous goyim took notice and shot at this idealistic Christian as she put the food into the beehive. They warned her that she could be shot for helping Jews.

They were hemmed in all sides. They had nowhere to go. They could not get out. Hunger tortured them. Filth ate away at them. Groups and individuals threatened them. The Germans were nearby. Having been led to the deepest despair, knowing that they had nothing to lose, all three of them, Moshe, Raphael, and the twelve-year-old son, wet to the city of Siedlce..

[Page 148]

But where could they go? Moyshe thought of his friend, the shoemaker Smolinski. He received them well, gave them a hiding place and food. But Smolinski had a worker named Kaminski. He saw the Jews, blackmailed them, and took whatever he could. He threatened them with terrible things. Remaining there would be a danger for Smolinski, and also for the Jews, so after several weeks they had to leave.

They had to go "out into the world," into the hands of blind, savage fate. They headed east, toward the Red army, which was on the march. They approached the front. During the day they stayed in hiding places, in the fields and woods. At night, in the dark, they took small back roads—towards their liberators, who were so near in their desire but so far in actual distance.

They heard that near the Lukower Woods were partisans, and they tried to reach them so they could join them and help them agains their common bloody enemy. A peasant in the village of Szebiszow warned them about the partisans. He told them that they also killed Jews whom they encountered. They had already killed many Jews from Staczek. They encountered Polish partisans, who chased after them in a mob. They barely escaped. They also met Russian partisans, who tried to lure them to a spot where they could be killed. Goyim whom they met on the road went after them, fell upon them, robbed and blackmailed them. When they stopped in a little woods near the village of Semi, they were attacked by a group of A.K., who began shooting at them. Inn this assault, Raphael's twelve-year-old son Leibel was shot when he was several score meters away from his father. The murderers then went after Moyshe and Raphael, wanting to kill them as well, so that there would be no witnesses to their bloody deeds. But they could not find their victims and they left.

There was nothing left for us to live for—concluded the brothers Moyshe and Raphael Kilinski—we have lost everything: our wives, our children, our whole family, all have been killed before our eyes, and we remain alive.

The whole time that we lived in hiding it was a struggle with the angel of death—superhuman sorrow and pain, constant fear of death, trying not to fall into the clutches of the murderous Germans and, even more, of the bloody Poles. Many times were were shot at by bandits and by police, chased by individual killers and organized parties of bandits.

[Page 149]

They would go in groups of 10 to 15, armed with axes, scythes, pitchforks, clubs, and also with guns. Always they were prepared and found our hiding places. We would run from one group that threatened us and we would encounter another. Always we saw death before our eyes. Life for us was horribly ugly, but we always avoided death.

In the village of Ostrawiec, the Poles killed 72 Jews. There was nowhere to hide, so we lay in a swamp, in a deep muddy field. No one approached us there. A little six-year-old shepherd child had pity on us. He brought us potatoes and once a piece of bread. For him we made little cars out of wood and other toys. He kept us a secret, because he wanted the cars. For six weeks we lived in the swamp with the help of the little shepherd. When the Red army arrived, we were swollen and could not move. Pieces of our skin were falling off—so the Kirishilinskis finished their tragic recital—and: nothing. The murderers go free, as if nothing had happened. No one will judge them—"There is no justice, and there is no judge…". [These are the words of the Talmudic rabbi and heretic Elisha ben Abuya.]

The Story of Moyshe Mendel Gora (from Makabid, near Siedlce)

In those days, M. M. Gora found himself in the Wengerow ghetto and was a witness to the killing of the five thousand Jews of Wenegrow.

The liquidation of the Jews of Wengerow was conducted by Germans and Ukrainians, with the full cooperation of the Polish police, as well as the city fire department.

At the time when the Germans and Ukrainians managed and conducted the chief labor, their Polish underlings managed the lesser labor of seeking out hidden Jews and taking them to the slaughter. Not only the police but also the fire department went in an organized manner, under the direction of their chief officer Eichler, to the homes of Jews to find hidden Jews and drag them out. In the bunkers, cellars, and pits, they used their4 fire department tools to blast the hidden Jews with water.

[Page 150]

Then they dragged them out and handed them over to the Germans and Ukrainians, or else they themselves took them to the cemetery and killed them.

Gora was dragged out of a hiding place together with other Jews by the firemen and was taken to the grain storehouse of Yudel Dszewica. When he number of Jews being held reached forty, they were forced to carry a chest of ammunition and machine guns, and thus were these unfortunate victims led to the cemetery.

At the cemetery, a long, deep, broad pit had been prepared. The Jews were lined up alongside the pit and the machine guns were set up. By some miracle, Gore was not struck by a bullet, but when those who had been shot fell into the pit, he, covered with blood, fell with them.

For a certain time, Moshe Mendel Gora lay in the pit among those who had been shot. Then he heard that a group of Polish workers had arrived to cover over the corpse-filled pit. He opened his eyes a little and saw how they searched through the corpses and ripped off their clothing and shoes. He heard the groans of those who were still alive and who were covered with earth, but the groaning became quieter and quieter…

Soon they were near him. He lay immobile, with his eyes closed. He held his breath and waited, knowing that in a few minutes they would be throwing shovelsful of earth on him with the same haste and solemnity that they had used on the others who lay not far from him in the pit. He still lay as quietly as possible in the dark pit—like the others. He heard the cynical counting of those shot by the workers, their obscene talk and joking around; he heard the sound of the shovels that were throwing earth, and he shuddered. He felt it as the men came to him, searched him, pulled the shoes from his feet. He felt strange hands in his pockets. They took out little things, his few zlotys. They took off his jacket, his sweater. They felt his shirt—they were considering whether it had any value. A rough hand moved over his skin. Someone sensed the warmth of his body. Someone cried out: "Are you alive? Run away!" Gora opened his eyes, looked around, and saw everything, everything…

[Page 151]

He pulled himself loose from his dead neighbors. He quickly jumped up and began to run…He thought that they would follow him, seize him, take him back to that pit in the cemetery and bury him alive…He ran across lawns, through fields and woods; he jumped over brooks and swamps. He did not hold still for a minute. He did not look back. He ran for a whole day and a night until his strength gave out. He fell down in a faint, completely worn out, in the darkness of a thick woods. He lay there for he knew not how long until he came to himself. He realized that he was barefoot and naked. Everything had been left behind….ripped off of him. He felt pain in his bare feet, which were filthy and bruised. He saw that he was covered in blood—inn the blood of his neighbors in the massive grave from which he had escaped. He got up and went on. He found a stream in the woods. He washed himself and went on. He went through hidden paths, through fields, swamps, bogs, remote fields, where there were no human beings. Naked, barefoot, and dying of hunger after several days of wandering, he came to his destination—in the village of Chaiczna [?]. There he hoped to find his wife and their three children and his two sisters, who had fled there, as well as a girl from Lodz, sixteen-year-old Natzia Krel, the daughter of Avraham Yakov, who had escaped from Lodz and stayed with him for a year.

But in the village of Chaiczna, Gora did not find his family. He learned that several days earlier, his wife and children had gone to Wengorov looking for him. They had stumbled onto the slaughter of the local Jews and were killed.

At the same time, M. M. Gora met in the village other Jews who had escaped from a variety of liquidated villages. Among them were—his dearest acquaintances, the three brothers Mordechai, Yudel, and Nissen Piekosz, Ben-Zion Vassershtein with his wife and child, three young women from Kolushin—the children of Melech Rimorsz, Yakov Handliosz from Sokolov with his two sisters, Aaronovicz from Kalish with his wife and child, Hershel Jabkowski with his family, and others—altogether about 100 people who were in hiding, some with peasants and some "living" in the fields and woods.

[Page 152]

During the period of the High Holidays, people came together at a secret spot in the woods, and in quiet, heartrending prayers, punctuated with weeping, prayed God to show pity on his persecuted, unhappy Jews…

Thus did people suffer in fear of death and teetered, for several weeks, between life and death.

On a dark, cold November morning, people learned that the Germans, in pursuit of Jews, had ordered a general search for Jews in a radius of fifty kilometers. The village of Chaiczna lay within that area.

Gora found a place to hide, but one of the murderers' bullets found him. Wounded, he ran from one hiding place to another. It was as if jumping out of a fire, he found himself in another fire. The murderous Germans and their Ukrainian and Polish helpers seemed to be everywhere. They would find the unfortunate hidden Jews and shoot them.

Gora could find no place among the living, so he hid among the dead in the village cemetery. He lay down among the graves and, in order not to be noticed, covered himself with the snow that had fallen. He lay there for three days. He survived by swallowing snow. He intended simply to stay there until the end…but cold and hunger tortured him horribly and he left the cemetery. He went to find something to eat, something with which to warm himself. He met his two sisters and their children Yisroel Eizik and Malkah. From them he learned that from the approximately one hundred Jews who had been in the area of the village, after the raid there remained only a scattered few. Almost all had been brutally killed. There was nowhere to go. The peasants, even those who had been good acquaintances, were afraid to take them in. "For a whole day," M. M. Gora continued, "we remained in a field and bemoaned the great misfortune that had befallen us."

In the field was a stack of lupines. We hid there over night and together considered what we should do. My sisters remained there, while in the middle of the night I and the two children went to a peasant we knew, Antoni Karczewski and begged him to rescue us and give us a place to hide. The peasant was very sympathetic, but he had no place to hide five people. He took the two children and hid them.

[Page 153]

He gave me some bread and told me to leave and not return, lest someone suspect that he was hiding Jews.

I returned to the field, to the stack of lupines, where my sisters were hidden. I gave them the peasant's gift—the bread—which we made last several days.

When hunger and the bitter cold again assailed us, I again left our hiding place. I thought of another peasant I knew in Makabid, Waclaw Lisheczki, and although Germans and police were all around, I risked my life and went to him for help.

When Lisheczki saw me in my condition, scratched up, pale, tortured by hunger and by cold, he cried out. First he undertook to prepare for us a hiding place in a pit in his stall, covered with filth. Later on he found for us a better hiding place with a friend, where we hid for six weeks.

On a beautiful morning (but for us it was dark), the police came to Lisheczki, conducted a search and asked where he had hidden his Jews.

When we received this bitter news, we immediately left the hiding places and again for several week we wandered through the fields and woods. That was bitter winter, with heavy frost and snow, which, together with hunger, tortured us terribly. No longer able to bear our troubles, I again went to the village of Makabid, this time to another peasant whom I knew: Jon Gabarek. He greeted me warmly and told me to get my sisters, who had remained in the field. He hid us in a narrow, dark cellar, where we stayed for five weeks. Once, Gabarek came and told us that we had to leave immediately, because Germans and Ukrainians had arrived in the village to conduct searches.

Deathly afraid, we left our hiding place in the middle of the day. Then we realized that from staying so long in the dark cellar, we were half blind. Unable to see the world around us, we ran over the fields and into the woods. We came to the village of Zaliwie. We came to peasant I knew, Jon Dszewalski.

[Page 154]

There we encountered our acquaintances, the brothers Berl and Yudel Vunderbaum. They were wearing decaying rags and were barefoot, with pale yellow faces. Their terrible appearance froze our hearts. Looking at them caused us to burst into tears. They were observant and ate no unkosher foods. They survived on bits of dry bread and water. They consoled us and encouraged us, just as when one sees death before one's eyes, one must not lose the trust that God can help…Even though I had very little, I shared my poor possessions with them. I gave them some garments and a few zlotys. For many hours we sat and talked, speaking of practical matters. We examined deeply the basis of our misfortunes: Did the Holy One, Blessed Be He, intend to annihilate his people Israel? Then who would carry out His commandments, his Torah?—There was no way to understand the ways of God…

The peasant Dszewalski took pity on us and took in my sisters and myself, made a hiding place for us in the attic of his stable, where we remained hidden from February 15 until the end of March.

On an especially cold day, when outside there was a flood of snow, I saw through the window two children approaching. The children were wrapped in torn rags and were barefoot. Their feet were red and swollen as they walked through the snow toward Dszewalski's home. Dszewalski told us to hide. The children must not see that there were Jews with him. The children received something to eat, and they warmed themselves. In our hiding place, we wept over our bitter fate: we saw before us such unfortunate, forlorn Jewish children and we could not show ourselves to them, not offer them a word of consolation. After the children left, Dszerwalski came to us in our hiding place and he, too, wept bitterly. He told us that the children were from

Kalushin. They had been in hiding for more than four months in a stack of straw outside the village of Zaliwie. Fromm time to time they came to him for some food.

Several days later, Dszewalski came to us and said that the two children were no more. The chief of police in Makabid, Mashkowicz, found the children and shot them. One child fell dead immediately. The other ran off.

[Page 155]

The police chief trailed him for three kilometers, until the child, worn out, fell in the snow. The murderous policeman fired several bullets into the child and left him lying there dead.

Another time, also on a cold, wet, winter day, we saw coming to Dszewalski's two young women in the same horrifying condition as the unfortunate children. Dressed in torn, rotting rags, barefoot, pale, skin and bones, they came quietly begging for something to eat. As Dszewalski recounted, the two young women were also from Kalushin, from the Zlotnicki family. I do not know what happened to them.

At the end of March, Dszewalksi was robbed. Then neighbors came by, as well as police, and we had to get away.

After stumbling around for a week in the fields and the woods, tormented by hunger and cold, we came to the peasant I knew, Gabarek in Makabid. He hid us in his attic.

Once, when I was in a deep sleep, I dreamed that my mother stood above me and my sister. She cried and fussed over guys and she said that she was going to the old rabbi of Kalebiel to beg that he would pray for us and beg the Holy One, Blessed Be He, to rescue us from danger. I felt my mother's warm breath, her hot tears on my face, and…a thunderous, wild banging on the door of the peasant's house suddenly interrupted the sweet-sad dream of my old mother. A hot stream of blood rushed to my head. My heart beat wildly and nearly stopped. Before we could come to ourselves and figure out where we were and what was happening, we heard a terrible shout in Polish: "Hands up!" A group of police were standing with drawn weapons just where we were lying.

They took us from the attic and guarded us like the worst criminals, putting us under arrest.

This was on a Sunday morning at the beginning of May. Many of the goyim from the village ran beside us, as if at something amazing, and accompanied us with mockery as we we're led to the village lockup.

We looked through the iron bars and saw how everywhere green grass was springing up, flowers were blooming, birds were chirping and singing. Everything was bursting with life, but we, children of a chosen people, had to right to live on the earth. Our mournful hearts grieved, and we broke out in a confused cry. We wept for a long, long time…

[Page 156]

The door of the jail opened and in cameo a goy whose job it was to prepare pits and to bury the Jews who were shot by the police. He informed us that he had already prepared a pit for me and my sisters. At midnight we would be shot.

We wept over our young lives that would be torn away in a couple of hours. I consoled my sisters—and they consoled me.

And suddenly a thought struck me: one had to try to escape all the time. It was never too late. I lay down on the floor of the jail and began to dig. I pulled off a board and then another. I dug underneath with my hands, and soon my hand was outside. With a little more digging, I was lying totally outside. I pulled out one sister, then the other. We stood up and disappeared like silent shadows in the stillness of the dark night…

Driven on by terror and surprise, we ran through the woods for the entire night. We lay down a bit to rest. Suddenly we heard shooting. We were confused with terror and anxiety—out of the fire and into the flood. We could not decide what to do, whether to run or to lie still. We saw shadowy figures drawing near—human shadows. We looked closely—they were Jews, distraught, suffering Jews bumbling around just like us in the dark, silent night. Surprised, I called our, "Jews! Who are you?" They told us that they were from Lukow. For a third time they were taken from Lukow to Treblinka, and for a third time they had jumped from the death train in which they had been confined for three days without anything to eat or drink. From them we learned that we were not far from the death factory of Treblinka. Completely tired out, they fell to the ground. They begged us for bread, water. We shared our poor provisions with them.

A little rested, we pressed on—in the direction of Lukow—we————we had nowhere to go. Death lurked everywhere. We just distanced ourselves from that spot, from the area of Treblinka.

[Page 157]

We hid in the deep woods. Later, when we reached the fields of corn, we made our "dwelling place in the fields, among the corn. During the day we lay trapped in the field, so that no one could see us. At night I would go 5 or 6 kilometers looking for something to eat. We survived for another month in this way.

Suddenly the sky clouded over. There was a downpour that lasted for three days.

Although it was the month of June, that rain brought with it a bitter cold that tortured us. We were nearly swimming in the water. The tiny bit of bread that we had "in reserve" was soaked and swimming. I was forced to seek help at night. In the distance we saw a fire flickering. I went toward that fire, which led to a peasant's home. We [he changes pronouns] looked through the window and recognized a peasant that we knew. He received me kindly and told me to bring my sisters. He made a fire to dry our soaking clothes, warmed us with hot food, and took us to a stable that stood in the field. There we spent the night.

Early the next morning, the peasant came to us in the stable and, wrapping me in his fur, called me to go outside with him. He took me to his stable, and to my great surprise, I found four Jews there. Three were from Siedlce: Moyshe Bliacheer, Mottel Orlionski, and Chatz from the glass business (at 45 Warsaw Street). The fourth was a young man from Lodz. We were all so happy, and as we spoke, the man from Lodz told how he recently had killed in Siedlce a gendarme with his dog.

He was standing—he said—on Sololow Street with a fellow and explained how to acquire weapons. Then the gendarme arrived. They went up to him and asked him too lend them fifty marks. When the gendarme put his hand in his pocket to take out the money, the Jew grabbed his revolver and shot him. The dog that the gendarme had been leading jumped on him and would not let go, so he received several bullets and lay dead near his owner. As evidence, the Jew showed us the trophies he had taken from the dead German: his revolver, his belt, and perfumed, leather gloves.

[Page 158]

Three days later, a Christian told us that he had been in Siedlce and had heard that a Jew had killed a German.

We could not remain for long in the stable in the field. The place was not secure, so we again went away to a Christian we knew—Stanislaw Kashkewicz—and he hid us for six weeks.

Having gone once to in the middle of the night to a peasant I knew who lived in a village eight kilometers from there in order to sell my sister's coat, a pack of dogs attacked me. I barely managed to beat them off with my thick stick, but I could not stop thinking: Where did dogs come from in the middle of the night? In deathly terror I went on, and by the light of the full moon that was shining then I stumbled over three dead bodies whose throats had been cut lying there in the woods. I drove off the dogs, who had taken chunks out of them. One of them had its entire throat consumed. Trembling with fear, I looked closely at the three slaughtered men and I recognized my friends and neighbors from Makabid: Yisroel Tandeczorsz and the brothers Gedaliah and Leib Goldfarb.

Darkness shrouded my eyes, and my heart pounded. My body felt spasms. The Goldfarb brothers were rugged men—All of the goyim in the village trembled before them—and there they lay slaughters like calves, being eaten by dogs. Such disasters had fallen on us. Today them and tomorrow—me. Such was the end of us Jews!

Trembling the whole way, I returned to my sisters. I told them about the horrible scene. After that, they would not let me leave my hiding place for several weeks.

As we later learned, the killers of my my friends and neighbors were a band of A.K., who had undertaken to seek hidden Jews in the area and kill them.

We could not long stay cut off from the outside world. Hunger and lack of funds forced me from my hiding place. I went to a peasant I knew either to sell something or to trade for food.

[Page 159]

On the way, I had another encounter: I met a young man with a strange appearance: naked and barefoot, with his entire body smeared with lard. His neck and his head were black as coal. From his face, two burning, terrified eyes looked out. By his side hung a bruised hand that he could not move. His appearance made a crazily terrifying impression and made my heart pound.

To my questions, he responded that he came from Amshinov. He was called Menachem, was 24 years old. When he was young he studied in the Wengerow yeshiva. Later on he was a business agent in his shtetl. During the war, he had experienced all seven levels of Gehenna. Recently he had worked in Warsaw with sixty other unfortunate Jews, cleaning locomotives. Several days ago, they had all been stuffed into a train car and sent to Treblinka.

On the way, he jumped from the death train and broke his hand. With great pain and difficulty, he rose and managed to get to a nearby village, where he begged the peasants for help: a bandage for his hand and a place to spend the night. But no one would allow him in. He spent the night in an abandoned barn. In the middle of the night, a group of peasants fell on him, took his few zlotys, tore off his clothing and shoes, and left him barefoot and naked.

On that day I forgot my own sorrows and became occupied with those of the young man. From Christians that I knew, I managed to get him something to wear and some food. I bandaged his broken hand. At night we departed. He went on the road to Warsaw and I to my hiding place, to my sisters.

Early one morning our guardian came to us and, terrified, told us that partisans from the A.K. had raided the milk cooperative and were planning an attack on the village. Therefore we had to leave.

Again it was bad. There was nowhere to hide. The nearest goyim that we knew would not accept us, some from fear and some from hatred, which had flared up against the last Jews more than it had in previous times.

The fear of death hovered over the neighborhood of the peasant Czeslaw Kishelinski from the village of Timianki—a well-known murderer.

[Page 160]

He had received from the Germans a rifle and bullets and he went around looking in all the hiding places. When he found a Jew, he killed him.

Terrible news reached us from the nearest village, Zaliewa. Three Jewish children were hidden by the peasant Dmowski Lirka: 1) Avraham Kasten from Warsaw. The child had escaped from Treblinka; 2) Tzina Goldfarb from Wengrow, 14 years old; and 3) Mendele from Makabid, 14 years old. The Germans had killed his father before his eyes, but allowed him to live. The three children met as they wandered in the woods around Makabid. They found a hiding place by the aforementioned peasant and they did work for him.

In the middle of the night of May 29, 1944, a group of local bandits (most certainly they belonged to the A.K.) attacked the peasant's house. The three unfortunate children were put into a sack and thrown into the Liwiec, the nearest river. In order to ensure that the children would drown, the murderers weighted down the sack with stones.

And then more terrible news reached us.

We heard that the liberating Red army was making great progress. We could live to see the day of liberation, see vengeance taken on our murderers. Desperate, we had no alternative. It was summer. Everything was green and blossoming. Everything called upon life. We again went away to the fields. Again we made hiding places among the cornstalks. If we were too crowded in one spot, we went to another or to another. And in this way, hungry, thirsty, dirty, and always in fear of death, we survived and awaited our liberators, the Red army.

But even after the liberation we had no rest. The few surviving Jews were like thorns in the eyes of our neighbors, who desired simply to be free of them. In the neighboring village of Mord, eight Jews who had emerged from the woods and from underground bunkers were murdered. They were preparing to leave their destroyed, ruined home towns. They fell victim to a murderous band of A.K and were all killed.

Those killed were: the brothers Avraham and Shimon Garbasz, Mrs. Farman, two girls from the village of Czelemen, a woman from Valsha, and two men from Mord.

[Page 161]

Aside from me—continued Moyshe Mendel Gora—there were in the shtetl of Makabid seven other afflicted, worn out Jews who had suffered through the whole Hitler-hell and had escaped from the German axe. They were together in a single room of a Christian whom they knew and were preparing to go to Lodz, where large groups of surviving Jews were gathering. Since the war had come to a halt, communications had improved, so they kept their plan a secret from the village. On the tenth of March in 1945, in the middle of the night, they were attacked by a group of local goyim, who killed them. They were: 1) my sister Leah Gora, who was 26; 2) Yakove Shpodel, 17; 3) Chaim Mordechai Fiatkowski, 25; 4) Eli Piekosz, 18; 5) Chanah Dambak 24; 6) Chashe Szepa, 28; and 7) a man from Wengrow.

During our two years of living in hiding, we had experienced much. We often saw death before our eyes. Many of the goyim betrayed us to the police, many tracked us down, seeking our lives. Bur also many helped us with food and hiding places. Perhaps it is thanks to my profession as a butcher and a dealer in animals that I was often in the villages, where I became acquainted with many of the peasants. The great tragedy of our misfortune its that so many of the Polish murderers, German aides, peasants, firemen, and police who destroyed so many Jewish lives now walk around freely and openly, and there is no one who will bring them to justice.

* * *

Eliyahu Gaszelinski is a young man of 33, but he is totally gray, like an old man, with a wrinkled face, a creased forehead, and dull eyes, the effects of two years of living in the woods.

Goszelinski says:

Until the first aktion, he worked with many other Jews in the village of Drofia, near Siedlce. They did all kinds of hard labor for the Germans. Among other things, they worked by the waters near the city, where Nazi bigwigs, led by Fabish, would go fishing.

On Shabbos, the 22nd of August, Zulof, the head of the criminal police, was with them. He warned the Jews who were in the village that they must not go to Siedlce on that day.

[Page 162]

Later he was working with many other Jews for a rich man in the woods near Lukover. At the second aktion on November 30, the rich man received an order to send the Jews to Gensze-Barki. He released the Jews and told them that by the next day, no Jews would still exist.

There were forty of us—Gaszelinski said. We divided up into groups and hid, some with peasants in that village and some in the woods.

Among those 40, some were from Siedlce: Yenta Gutowski with her husband and brother, Shlomo Freiman, Sholem Zilbershtein with his wife Golde, the two Miller brothers, Esther Goldberg, Yakov Graiantse with his wife, Heniek Adler with his wife Felle, Levin with a child of four, Natke Levin, Moshe Czistaka, Yisroel Dovidkewicz, Eliyahu Gaszelinski with his family of four, and David Figave. The others were people who had escaped from other cities.

In the same neighborhood of the Dominitz woods, there was also a group of Jews, about a hundred, under the leadership of Itsche Rotberg and Shmulke Tempeldiener. Many of them were from Siedlce.

Once, on a cold, frosty morning, when we were huddled in our hiding places, shivering from the cold, that a child was plodding through the snow. A little girl of five or six whom we recognized as a poor Jewish child was seeking a place to hide. We took the child in. It turned out that she was Yakov Vilk's grandchild Chantshele, who had escaped from the slaughter of the recent aktion in Gensze Barki. She had wandered around all by herself in the woods for several days. She stayed with us.

Moyshe Czistoka once went into the village seeking food for our group. He stumbled on a group of Germans. The murderers stripped off his clothing, beat him unmercifully to make him tell where he had been hiding and where other Jews might be. He behaved heroically and gave away nothing, while the killers tortured him to death.

From our sojourn in the woods, we knew about Polish A.K. groups that sought us unceasingly with their attacks and robberies. In order to stand up to them, we had to get weapons. We came in contact with various Christians who, for a high enough price, would sell us weapons and provisions.

[Page 163]

On May 30, 1943, we were attacked by a large band of the A.K. There was a shootout, in which Avraham Bluestein excelled, shooting the attackers with his rifle. But they managed to steal from us many valuable things. I and several other Jews were wounded. Wounded, I dragged myself to a peasant's home, where I stayed for several days as my wounds healed.

In June of 1943 the Germans, seeking Jews, made a raid in the area where we were. We survived this horror. There were no victims.

Because our hiding places became too well known, we left and went tot he woods in the neighborhood of Kalusz. But after a short time we were set upon by Germans. We had enough weapons then, and our fighting instincts were aroused. We put alp a valiant stand and killed two Germans. Three from our group fell.

The Germans left us alone, but we were often attacked by Polish bandits who robbed us and killed many of us.

Poles tracked young Warshawski from Mord for several kilometers, then grabbed him, tied him in wire and took him to the Gestapo.

Seven Jews paused in the village of Kshimus. People from the A.K. found out about them, then attacked and killed them.

In June of 1944, the Germans again made a raid in the area, and they encountered our group. We made a strong stand. In the battle, several of our comrades fell.

In August of 1944, taking back roads and gong through woods, we came upon a large of Partisans, about 450 people, who were led by Nechamiah Galanski from Mord, by Mottel Huberman, son of Bonim Huberman of Siedlce, and by a young woman from Pruszkow. In that group we found many Jews from Siedlce and from its surroundings.

Our last and most violent confrontation occurred several days before the liberation of Siedlce. We were then back in the Daminicz woods. Leib Bergman and I went to village to get potatoes and we encountered a Russian scout, which greatly surprised us and made us very happy. At the same time, we encountered a vehicle with Germans.

[Page 164]
We abandoned our potatoes, threw ourselves upon the Germans, and killed them. We burned the vehicle.

That same day several thousand Germans encircled the woods where we were. They shot at us for several days with artillery and with airplanes. But their battle showed no results and they had to flee because the Russian army was drawing near. Out of anger, they set fire to and burned down the whole village.

Out of 40 Jews, 16 remained alive: Eliyahu Gaszelinski, Sholem Zilbershtein with a nine-year-old girl, Moshe Kaweczki, Natke Levin and Gittel Kaniek from Kikow. All the others were killed by German killers and murderous Polish bandits.

Ziskind Rosenbaum and his Comrades

Hanke and Avraham Halber tell:

Five young men there were who decided not to allow themselves to be led to the slaughter in the Treblinka gas chambers at the time of the liquidation of the ghetto, so they escaped to the woods and the fields. Three of them were graduates of the Tarbus school: Ziskind Rosenbaum, Yisroelik Zucker, Berl Bagagan, Dovid Blustein, and someone from Mezritch (whose name is unknown).

They conducted bold attacks against the Germans. They killed some, took their weapons, created hiding places for Jews who were wandering in the fields, woods, and villages, led raids of revenge against the goyim who had turned Jews over to the Germans or who had themselves killed Jews.

They made a bold attack on the well-known, in Siedlce, Christian merchant Paciarkowski and on a policeman.

This occurred after Siedlce was totally empty of Jews, in the summer of 1943. The Czibucki family, before they were liquidated, had given their possessions to their acquaintance, the merchant Paciarkowski, with whom they had had many business dealings, with the condition that when they were in need of funds, someone from the family would come to him. From the Czibucki family,

[Page 165]
no one remained alive except for Ziskind Rosenbaum (who was the son of Sarah Czibucki).. One day, Ziskind, using hidden back roads, came to Paciarkowski along with his friend Berl Bagagan and asked him for money. Paciarkowski told the young people to wait and he left. In a few minutes, Paciarkowski returned, but not alone. He was with a policeman. The young men quickly realized what was happening, saw that their lives could end, so they quickly took the guns from their pockets and shot the policeman and Paciarkowski. The first died on the spot and the second on his way to the hospital.

Rosenbaum and Bagagan ran to their hiding places and continued their work as partisans.

Later, during that same summer, driven by heat to refresh themselves with cold water, the group of five friends went to bathe in a stream several kilometers from the city. There they wee noticed by several Poles, who considered it a mitzvah to inform on them in the proper place. (This was one of the well-known Polish righteous women.). The enraged police who came after them opened fire on the young people, who were in the water. The water soon turned red with the blood of these young victims.

Only one of the group remained alive. This was young Blustein from Mord. Shot through the hand, he hid in the thick bushes by the river and later returned to his hiding place and lived to see the day of liberation by the Red army.

The Death of Devorah Tuchnitz-Halberstadt

Ittah Radaszinska-Lev tells:

Devorah Tuchnitz-Halberstadt came shortly before the outbreak of the wa with her husband Leib Halberstadt and their child to visit her parents in Siedlce.

After the liquidation of the ghetto, they hid somewhere. The time came when their child was about to be born—one of the greatest crimes at that time.—In the place where they were a birth was not possible.

[Page 166]
So she went to the fields and hid among the plants. The goyim heard her groaning from the birth pangs, and because of her "good" appearance they perceived her as a homeless Christian and took her to the city's Marianski hospital. Several days after she gave birth, a priest came to her to baptize her child. As the priest began to say his prayers over the child, the mother, Devorah, jumped up:

"Don't do that, holy Father," she said to him. "I am a Jewish woman and my child is a Jewish child. Let us be." The priest left. Soon the police arrived, took the mother and her child, and "liquidated" them.

The Apostate Ganzval

Who in Siedlce did not know the photographer Adolf Ganiewski, or, as he was called, Ganzval, with his good-natured eyes, his ever-present smile on his broad face, and his friendly dealings with people? Thus, many Jews quickly forgot his former treachery to his people and went to his studio to be photographed.

But the old apostate, who had converted in his youth and married a Christian, had forgotten that he had a Jewish origins until—Hitler's messengers reminded him.

In view of the greater Jewish tragedy, Ganzval repented: every day he carried packages of food for poor and ailing Jews in the ghetto. He concentrated especially on helping hungry children and gave much aid to the children's committee. Until it was pointed out by one of our always good friends that Ganzval stemmed from Jews and he was transported to Treblinka.

His wife, from generations of Christians, traveled after him to learn of her husband's fate. She thrown alive into the burning ovens of the crematoria.

[Page 167]

21. Non-Jews Tell their Story

Translated by Theodore Steinberg

Jan Filarczuk recounts:

On leaving the desecrated and defiled cemetery, we met the old Jan Filarczuk—who lived in a house that stood right near the cemetery. Old Filarczuk, through his window, saw much of what happened in the old cemetery, and with primitive peasant volubility, he said:

After the 22nd of August, 1942, after the liquidation of the large ghetto, there was never quiet in the cemetery. Almost every day the Germans led in victims, sometimes a few solitary Jews and sometimes more. There were days when they brought scores. The usual procedure went this way: first, the unlucky ones had to dig their own graves. Then they had to remove their clothing, and then would begin the beatings with rifle butts, pointed sticks, shovels, and whatever else was at hand. At first one heard the bizarre cries of the victims. But those cries quickly grew weaker, softer. Then came a series of shots and the graves became totally silent. Many times it happened that after the shooting, some victims remained alive, and those unfortunates were either buried alive or burned alive.

The murderers thus often used the labor of the victims themselves, for carrying off the weapons, the shovels, the ripped off clothing and loading them or carrying them off to the storehouse of stolen goods; And they had to bury those who had been murdered.

Then the murderers shot the Jews who did this work.

He remembered well, old Filarczuk, what had been engraved in his memory, and he offered many concrete tragic facts with dates and numbers.

Not long after the liquidation of the ghetto, the Germans brought to the cemetery a young woman with her child, whom she led by the hand. The murderers flung the woman and the child into the grave and shot them. The woman lay there dead, but the child, either through an accident or on purpose—who can know—remained alive.

For several days and nights, the unhappy child cried pitifully and called for its mama. He bit his dead mother's hand, her face, her breast, until he gradually became silent and his life departed next to his dead mother.
[Page 168]

Old Filarczuk cried and said that for those days and nights when they could hear through the window the pitiful whining of the unfortunate child, he and those with him in the house could nether eat nor sleep.

A little later—continued Filarczuk—they Broughtto the cemetery, directly from the train station, a young, beautifully dressed woman. As usual, she was ordered to undress. The woman protested vigorously and threw herself at the Germans. They hit her and beat her. The Germans beat her unmercifully. Their voices could be heard from far away. Finally the murderers killed her insect a bestial fashion that her body that her body lay in scattered pieces.

Once—he continued—the Germans brought tot he cemetery a group of fifty Jews. They stood them in rows and bade them run in such a way that one would not separate from another. As the Jews began to run, the killers opened fire on them from behind. All the Jews fell dead.

Several days later, Filarczuk, continued, sixty well-dressed Jews were brought to the cemetery, apparently foreigners, with expensive suitcases and handbags. The killers ordered their victims to assemble the suitcases and handbags in one spot, to undress, to put their clothing in that spot, and to do it all within five minutes. The unfortunate ones, you understand, followed the murderers' orders precisely. Then he killers murderously attacked their naked victims. They beat them mercilessly and shouted that they took longer than five minutes. The cries of the suffering Jews could be heard for a good distance in the surrounding streets. But soon the killers let loose with their automatic weapons and their victims were silenced. The executioners loaded up the suitcases, handbags, and clothing and carried them off.

Once Filarczuk passed near the spot where the victims—who were living at Start Rynek—were working and encountered someone he knew—that was Meir Walnowicz, son-in-law of Baruch Mordechai Rubinstein—and they greeted each other.

[Page 169]

For this "sin," the murderers fell upon the unfortunate Walnowicz, beat him with rods, and threw Filarczuk out of his apartment near the cemetery.

Just before the liberation—several weeks before the arrival of the Russians—Filarczuk said—he was walking on Warsaw Street near Polna, and found on the sidewalk a young, fullly-clothed woman who had just poisoned herself (near her was an empty flask of poison). Several hours later, when he went past the same spot, the woman still lay there, but now she was totally naked. The passing neighbors had taken her clothing and shoes.

* * *

A. Ivanowski tells:

In the summer of 1943, as he was walking down a street, a young Jew approached him. He was decently dressed and asked him to show where the Gestapo could be found.

When Ivanowski asked, "Why do you need the Gestapo? Don't you know that as a Jew what awaits you at the Gestapo?" The Jew responded, "Today there is no place for a Jew in the world. No one will take me in. My life is worse than death. I'm going to make things simple and go to the Gestapo."

* * *

Michael Karalowicz says:

When they took the Jews from the Umschlagplatz to the death train to Treblinka, he noticed how a Jew, while going down Kilinski Shenkkewicz Street had laid aside in the square a dead child that he had held. A German, who saw this, had pounced on the unfortunate Jew, beat him terribly and ordered him to take the dead child with him in the train—the beaten and worn out father picked up the dead child and carried him under his arm, like a package—taking him into the train wagon.

* * *

A Christian from the village of Skurszec tells:

[Page 170]

There was a gendarme in the village who was a big shot in seeking out hidden Jews and shooting them. He did this lightheartedly and was always happy and enjoyed his work.

Suddenly he fell into melancholia, went around in despair, sorrowfully, and he told everyone the reason: he had killed many, very many, Jews, which made him quite happy. But one of his victims—a young woman of 18, with dark black eyes and a fair face of read and white—haunted him, would not let him rest, neither during the day when he was awake nor at night when he slept. As soon as he fell asleep, the young woman came, choked him, stifled him, and cried out: "Murderer, why did you take my young life!" He gave up sleeping and fell into melancholia.

* * *

Jashinski from Mord recounts:

In the village of Kukawka Piaski there was a pleasant who throughout the time of Nazi rule was occupied with seeking out the hiding places of Jews, then killing and robbing them. This was his regular "occupation." From this "profession," the peasant became wealthy, which aroused jealousy among the other peasants in his village, who followed his example in minor ways. Scores of Jews died by his hand.

The witness once saw a number of victims of his wild killing. These were three young women. One he recognized as the daughter of Yechiel Stein from Mord. Their heads were smashed in and severed from their bodies. Their hair was cut off and their clothes torn off.

* * *

With a friend who had survived in an underground bunker, we sat on one of the benches that had been placed on the site where once the city hall stood. We were steeped in a conversation about the great destruction. Near us sat a middle-aged Pole in civilian clothing.

We did not pause in. our discussion, and our neighbor began to take part in it. He introduced himself as a member of a socialist party (and to convince us, he showed us his identification papers). During the occupation, he was active in an underground anti-Fascist movement (for which he also had papers). Now he was a high functionary in the O.B. [which he does not explain].

[Page 171]

He spoke emphatically with the assuredness of a man who knew what he was talking about:

"I am ashamed," he said, touching his heart, "that I am a Pole. My fellow Poles played too large a role in the extermination of the Jews. Most assuredly, without their help the extermination would not have been so thorough, so total."
To our question about why the guilty ones were not held responsible, he answered:
"It would be impossible, because one would have to bring to justice of the Polish population."

---

22. Sadism, Ferocity, and Brutality

Translated by Theodore Steinberg

The First Rosh Hashanah under German Terror

From the first day that the German hordes took control of the city, different military groups conducted constant ambushes against Jewish dwellings.

There was not a single night when one did not hear doors and windows being ripped off—and then the despairing cries for help from Jews who were being attacked.

In the dark days and empty nights of Rosh Hashanah, Yom Kippur, and Succos, German ferocity reached its highest state. Throughout the nights, barbaric bands went from house to house, not missing a single Jewish dwelling, breaking doors and windows, pillaging and raping, destroying and plundering. They terrorized the defenseless, unarmed Jews with weapons and with terrible beatings. Despairing voices of terrorized children, of raped women, of beaten men robbed of all their possessions, everywhere and unceasingly pierced the dark night and resounded like a voice calling in the wilderness.

Gentiles displayed crosses and religious pictures in their windows and on their doors.

On Rosh Hashanah the Jews felt what was called the Nazi paws. Only a few days after they had taken the city, all of Jewish life was disrupted, empty, and dark. A Jew could not not be seen in the streets. People were seized for forced labor.

[Page 172]

To all manner of hard work. Jews were seized and sent to Wengrow to the concentration camp. They tortured those who had been seized with hunger and thirst, with ferocious beatings and with terrible humiliations. People sought to hide whenever they could.

On the first day of Rosh Hashanah, a small number of Jews dared to go to shul to pray as a congregation. Soon the shul was surrounded by a troop of Germans. Some went in and threw themselves upon the horrified Jews, tore off their taleisim and dealt them murderous blows. Others assembled by the door and formed a wall. With the greatest ferocity they attacked those who were running out. The Jews who had jumped through the windows were terribly beaten by the barbaric Germans who were waiting outside. The most badly beaten was Rabbi Shlomo Eichenstein. They stripped him naked, led him out into the street and forced him to sweep the street with a broom and with his hands. The ailing Yosef Rubin, who had jumped through the window, was shot.

Around two thousand Jews were seized on the streets and in their homes during the two days of Rosh Hashanah and were sent to the concentration camp in Wengrow.

Wengrow—The First Act of Collective Barbarism

Unending hardship filled the hot days and long nights in the second half of September, 1939. In the first days of Nazi rule, people went into hiding, but lying in hiding was unbearable on such hot days, so people decided that they should voluntarily go to work, before the Germans could seize them.

A group of about sixty or seventy of us went out to the ruins at 7 Shpitalna where the three-storied house of Jagodziinski had stood. It was hit by a German bomb on the first day of their attack on the city.

We figured out that under the ruins of the house, several score of people were buried. As we dug through the debris, we pulled out several buried bodies and laid them out in a row so that their surviving families could mourn their deaths.

Before noon, as we were deeply involved in this labor, we suddenly heard shooting from all around, accompanied by wild cries of "Out!…with your hands up!…"

[Page 173]

Before we could look around, we were surrounded by a group of fierce Germans with guns and revolvers aimed at us. For a moment the Germans stood and looked at the bodies, but then they shouted with loud voices, making a commotion, and distributed blows, moving us into the street.

On Shpitalna Street we encountered many hundreds of people. They were arrayed in long columns, with hands held high. From all sides Jews, and Christians, were added to the columns. They were forced to run quickly with their hands held high, while frenzied Germans ran after them, hitting them from behind with rifles, revolvers, clubs, belts, and other weapons.

There was the Byala rabbi R. Yechiel Rabinowicz, and there they ran after old Dr. Ostrowski with his "Red Cross" armband; there was a sick old Jew, half naked, who had been dragged out of the sickbed where he had been lying, and there was the priest Kabilinski with several other young priests. All, without exception, were forced to run quickly while being hit from behind. The Jews who had been found in hiding places were beaten most severely.

For several hours we stood in those columns on the street with hands high in the air. Anyone whose hands were lowered because of fatigue received blows on his hands and head. Several times the people were searched by the Germans. Whatever they found in people's pockets, they took.

In the evening, we were ordered to march.

When we—several hundred of us—came to the corner of Warsaw Street, we saw large groups of people coming from other streets, mostly Jews, but also some Christians.

It appeared that the Germans had given the order throughout the city and the neighboring area to close off the streets and comb all the houses, take all men 14 years and older and lead them to the prison.

The prison door stood fully opened, and on both sides, from the outside to deep inside the prison, stood many Germans armed with rifles, clubs, iron bars, and belts. They fell mercilessly upon their marching victims, who were followed from behind by other fierce Germans.

[Page 174]

Many fell under their blows and remained lying on the road, under the stampede, in a pool of blood. Among them I saw the grocery merchant Melech Srebrenik—he lay in a broken heap, smeared with blood, showing little sign of life.

They sent us into the prison cells, 20-25 people in a cell that was intended for 4-6 people. We were held in such crowded conditions for two days. Only once during that time were we allowed into there courtyard, again in columns, and given a piece of bread.

In the middle of the night we heard a commotion in the courtyard and soon thereafter shooting. In the morning we learned that the Germans had shot several Christians who had been found with weapons. The Germans sought out several older Jews with beards and sidekicks and forced them to dig graves and bury the Christians who had been shot.

When day began to dawn, R. Nachman Lev and R. Berish Yom-Tov, who were with us packed into the cell—complained loudly—that they had no taleisim and tefillin with which to pray.

R. Baruch Ridel assured them—if God is kind, it won't matter.

On the third day of our confinement, we were taken to the courtyard, and in the street in front of the prison we were ordered to form rows of 5 and we were informed that each of us was a guarantee for the others. If anyone tried to run from the columns, the rest would be shot. We therefore had to assure that no one would run away.

Some high-ranking military man rode alongside the unending long column of men and ordered: "Hats off." At that instant, people were hit over their heads with the usual weapons: rifles, clubs, belts, iron bars, and so on. Woe to anyone who did. Not immediately remove his hat.

Next to the column ran women, young girls, and children. They were seeking their husbands, fathers, brothers. They wanted to give them food or clothing for the road; but the guards would not allow it and drove them away with blows and shots.

[Page 175]

The people marched with bare heads along the Sokolow road toward Wengrow. How many people? Who can tell? But people tried to estimate: The marching column extended for two kilometers, and each row of five people took up 1 meter, so the marchers must have numbered about 10,000.

Nearby marched several young Christians. They tried to get people to throw things at the several score of Germans who were leading and guarding the marchers prodding them and showing their weapons. From their great desire to carry out their plans, they spat on their palms and rubbed their hands together.

It was almost as if they had to calm down and convince themselves that it was a risky undertaking. We ourselves wanted to be liberated, but the Germans would have taken a terrible vengeance on the whole area.

An old, gray-haired Jew was standing in the road, lacking any further strength to go on. He fell to the ground, trying to proceed on all fours. Soon a German ran up to him, shooting at the Jew. The old man lay day on the road in a pool of blood.

There were many instances in which men who were exhausted from hunger, thirst, and pain fainted on the march. Knowing that such people would be shot, their neighbors, who were just as weak, took them under the arms and dragged them.

We marched by fields in which grew carrots, beets, and other vegetables. Some bold fellows dared to run and pick a carrot or a beet. The Germans shot such "criminals" and many paid with their lives.

In a village that we marched through, we saw no one. Farmers tried to bring us water and bread, but the guards shot at them and drove them off.

When we marched through the village of Makabid, there was a great tumult. Many of the men ran off and went into the woods, where they tried to hide in the homes and barns of farmers. The guards began shooting at the escapees. Some started pursuing. Several of the escapees were shot.

In the evening we arrived at Wengrow. At the corner of the shtetl, an armed military unit awaited us. They were arranged on a number of vehicles and gave us an excellent "welcome": for a long time they shot over our heads with machine guns.

[Page 176]

This was so we would listen and fear. It was to frighten the large mass of people.

We were horribly worn out from the long march (40 kilometers), starving from over two days without food, but mainly tortured by the terrible heat and thirst. I greatest longing was for a taste of water. And when the women of Wengrow tried to bring us pails of water, the guards shot at them and beat them unmercifully. The tinsmith Arlantczik took from a woman a little water and he was beaten so badly that he was left there half dead.

In the camp at Wengrow—a large place surrounded with barbed wire and guarded by armed Germans, we found several thousand prisoners—a mix of civilians and Polish soldiers. All had pale yellow, hungry faces and lay on the ground under the open sky.

Tired and fainting, we fell onto the cool, evening ground. But hunger and thirst gave us no rest. We learned that there was a well in the area of the camp, but the Polish soldiers had seized the well and were selling cups of water—20 groschen per cup—but it was hard to get a cup of water because of the congestion, so there were middle-men, toughs, who had the chutzpah and the toughness—young Poles—to push the Jews away from the well, buy cups of water from the soldiers, and sell it to the Jews for 50 groschen. With one cup of water, several Jews were satisfied.

For a whole night the Germans were horribly frenzied. They went among the Jews dealing out murderous blows, seeking Jews with beards and and used knives and shears to cut the beards along with pieces of flesh from their faces. The Polish soldiers helped the Germans in this job.

In the middle of the night there was a rainstorm that soaked everyone. Many became ill and lay on the ground with fever and aches.

The people had to eat—but the Germans would not give in. Still, the Jews of Wengrow, mostly women, who at that time were allowed some movement, disked their lives to bring food and throw it over the barbed wire for the prisoners. This was the only possible nourishment in the camp.

[Page 177]

The food that was thrown over was seized by the strongest and most chutzpadik, mostly Polish soldiers who took "first place" in the camp grounds. The Jews and the weak went hungry.

Gradually people began to seek and also to find ways to escape from the camp. Some dared to jump over the wire fence at night in the dark, when the watchmen turned away. In this way, some were shot or wounded (among them Yenkel Tabakman), some managed to get out as they fussed with a barrel of water: several times in the day, people went with a barrel to get water from a well that was outside the camp. Ten men went out with a barrel, but only four or five would return. They were not carefully watched. In this way, every day several score of men would get away.

Some would escape by bribing the local German mayor. He would come and take people to work in the city, and they, more often than not, did not return. But the greater majority were sent to East Prussia to work camps, where they went through the seven levels of Gehenna. Over all, the camp in Wengrow gave the impressions that it was created only to torture the twenty thousand people who were imprisoned there. In this, the Germans were totally successful.

Wengrow was the first link in the chain of suffering for the Jews of Siedlce.

The Germans Enjoyed Themselves

Yosef Jablonowicz says:

In the winter of 1940, when the lawyer Rubinstein was walking on Pilsudski Street in Stari Rynek, he was noticed by the Germans. They told him to stand still. They took the hat off his head, filled it with snow, put it back on his head, and Rubinstein was forced to stand in this way for an hour until the snow melted, getting him all wet. And the sadists enjoyed themselves, were delighted, as Rubinstein stood there shivering from the cold.

Gymnastics in the Snow

[Page 178]

Quite often, bands of Germans would come out into the streets to amuse themselves with Jews. On a cold snowy day in the winter of 1940, one such band came out into the streets seeking thrills, but they could not find a release, for there were no Jews on the street. All were in hiding. Suddenly two young women appeared, Sabka Benkowicz and Stesha Burstein. The Germans stopped the women and forced them to do gymnastic exercises and ultimately to crawl on all fours—on their hands and feet. This lasted for several hours.

Digging a grave and Shooting for Terror

David Lustik tells:

At the end of 1940 it was forbidden for Jews to travel on the roads. At that time, , Leibl Lustik and another Jew were traveling from Siedlce to Warsaw on a cart. In Milosna, the Germans stopped their cart, took the Jews and led them into the woods, giving them shovels and ordering them to dig a grave. When the grave was finished, the Germans ordered the terrified Jews to stand facing the grave and from behind they opened fire. The Jews felt the burn from the bullets that flew over them but which did not hit them. Then the sadists ordered the Jews to go back and resume their journey.

They Amuse Themselves with Old Jews

Zvi Liverant recounts:

Seizing Jews for all kinds of hard work, or even to torment and abuse them was nothing new. German raids in the Jewish quarter were "normal" daily things under that devilish regime.

But making a raid and seeking specifically old, gray-haired Jews with beards and sidekicks and old women with wigs and caps on their gray heads, that was indeed something new even in those insane times.

Such a raid was conducted by the Germans in the summer of 1941 before the closing of the ghetto. They assembled only old Jews, men and women, and excluded the younger ones whom they encountered every day. They led the old ones to the courtyard of the Szemianski Bank (on Warsaw Street) where the headquarters of the gendarmerie was located.

Germans with sharp rods and whips and shovels forced these old people to crow like chickens, to bleat like goats, to dance, jump around, pray kiss their tzitizs.

[Page 179]

They forced old men to kiss old women and perform other bizarre stunts.

This "social event" was organized by the gendarmerie and was closed to all of the Nazi bigwigs, including the chief sadist, city commander Fabish. They rolled with laughter for several hours.

The Death of Binyamin Hertz

Moyshe Halberstam says:

The Germans showed their greatest ferocity and barbarity to Jews on Shabbos and holidays. On Shavuos in 1940, bands of Germans went out into the Jewish streets to go after Jews. A particular group went around in a truck. On Pienkne Street, before number 41, the iron merchant Hertz and his wife were walking. The truck stopped, several bestial Germans jumped out, and shot at Hertz, who soon fell down dead. The murderers cold-bloodedly got back into their vehicle and drove off.

Desecrated Torah Scrolls

Leon Gliksberg was a witness to this wild act:

At the beginning of October, 1939, a band of 30 German officers came to the great shul of the city. When they found that the should was locked, they sent for the keys, which were under the control of community secretary Herschel Tenenbaum. They opened the shul, and the vandals tore apart the Holy Ark, threw out the Torah scrolls, and with wild ecstasy ripped apart the Torah covers, systematically tore through the curtains and stomped on them.

The Song of Crooked Jews

One evening in the late summer, after the liquidation of the large ghetto, a group of about forty Jews was struggling back from their work on the highway toward Lukow. They were going in columns led by Tzvi Liverant and Lolek Benkowicz. Worn out from a day of slave labor, they longed to go "home" to rest on their cots in the small ghetto.

On the way, they were stopped by armed Germans, highway police, who ordered them to sing.

[Page 180]

The group sang "Hatikvah" as a choir.

This song did not please the Germans. They flew into a rage at the Jews, cursing and screaming: "This is trashy music, caterwauling," and they ordered them to sing "The Song of Crooked Jews."

The group did not understand what the deranged German meant and they began again to sing "The Song of Crooked Jews" to the melody of "Hatikvah."

The Germans were now furious, burning with anger and fury. One stood there like a director and declaimed "The Song of Crooked Jews":

> The Jews go hither and yon
> The war will last longer.
> The Jews have all the gold.
> They wanted this war.

The Death of Henya Kleinman

Wolf Goldfinger says:

Mrs. Henya Kleiman [sic] was found in her hiding places by gendarmes who were seeking a thief. For eight days she was terribly mistreated by the Gestapo to force her to reveal where other Jews were hidden and where she had hidden her possessions. During the whole eight days they gave her no food or drink. Out of hunger, Mrs. Kleiman [sic] bit her finger and sucked her own blood. Finally they took her to the cemetery, forced her to her knees, and shot her from behind.

Forced to Hang a Child and then—Himself

Young Hershel (Shinyu) Klleiman (son of Baruch Mordechai) was hidden in the city by a Christian. In the summer of 1943, such concealment was risky, and he had to move to another place.

[Page 181]

Going down Flarinski Street, a Christian recognized him. She then notified a Ukrainian policeman, pointing out the courtyard into which Kleiman had gone—after searching for him for two hours, they found him in a garden together with six-year-old Livfferant (Shloyme Liverant's grandson). At Gestapo headquarters he was tortured murderously and then he was forced to hang the unlucky child and then—himself.

A Bullet in a Child's Mouth Instead of Chocolate

Yontel Goldman says:

In the winter of 1942, after the liquidation of the small ghetto, the German murderers with their helpers encountered in the village of Yigan (near Siedlce) 90 Jews who were hiding out in various places in the area. Among these unfortunates was a woman with a small child in her hand who was crying bitterly from hunger and from the cold. One of the Germans who was guarding the victims held a piece of chocolate to the child's mouth. When the starving child opened its mouth, the German shot a bullet into the open mouth and left the child dead in its mother's arms.

At the exhumation of the 90 dead in Yigan in n1946, Goldman recounts, they found in the open communal grave a young woman, a mother with her small child in her arms, held tight. The child still had its mother's breast in its mouth. They also found a couple of young children who held fast to each other. From the documents that people had found, they recognized that these were the sister and brother Wiczkowski from Kalish, Fabriczna Street number 1.

Near a body with a smashed in head, they found a document with the name Kellman from Prague in Warsaw, Torgowa Street. The majority of the martyrs were beaten with dull weapons and had split-open skulls. They had also been shot.

The Bestial Deaths of Thirteen Jews

Tzvi Liverant says:

In July of 1942, some weeks before the liquidation of the large ghetto, the Gestapo accused the Jewish Council of sabotaging its orders to assign Jews to all sorts of forced labor., After a check of the Jewish Council's lists of laborers, the Gestapo ordered them to select thirteen Jews who they claimed had been exempted from going to work.

[Page 182]

After several days of being tortured in captivity, the thirteen Jews were led back to the ghetto one dark night, taken through the opening in the fence on the side of New Siedlce that served as the entrance into the ghetto reserved for Gestapo personnel, whose headquarters were in New Siedlce (at 4 Prussa).

They ordered these unfortunate Jews to go home. lAs they started to go, the executioners shot at them from behind. Twelve Jews fell dead. The thirteenth was struck by a bullet, but he remained alive and dragged himself to the ghetto hospital. The Gestapo ordered the Jewish Council to locate the thirteenth Jew. When they heard that he was in the hospital, wounded, they made thew Jewish Council responsible for putting him on their list and exempting him because of his wounds.

The executioners, however, would not wait for their victim. Several days later they ordered him to be brought to their area in New Siedlce, there he was shot in the sick bed on which he had been carried.

(The names of the thirteen victims are not appropriate nor reveal, but people know that they were among the poorest and weakest and therefore lacked the strength to work.)

[Page 182]

23. Gentiles who Saved and Gentiles who Murdered Jews

Translated by Theodore Steinberg

It would be wrong and a great injustice if we would be silent about the closest faithful assistants and helpers that the mass murderers found among the Poles, Ukrainians, White Russians, Lithuanians, Latvians, and other people who took to heart the "idea" of killing the Jews. They, the Germans, could not have achieved such a result if they had not had such devoted, true assistance.

But it should also be said that there were some cases when Poles rescued Jews, hid them, gave them food and even risked their own lives.

[Page 183]

Many cities and towns had a few such righteous people who were not swallowed up in the sea of hatred and wickedness that flooded the world but instead helped to rescue Jews. So it was over the whole area of the slaughtering ground in the country of Poland, and our city was no exception.

One cannot generalize about the righteous Poles who stretched out their hands to help a tormented Jew and showed that they listened to him—or to some ideological or social voice in the Polish society.

For the most part, these were the exception, who showed their individual humanity and raised themselves from their poisonous surroundings and ideological attitudes. Some were from the rich, prosperous camps whose daily ideology was always a wild hatred of the Jews; some were working people from the socialist camp; some were individuals farmers from a village; some were mid-level city clerks; and some were poor—a washerwoman, a servant, or a butler.

* * *

Thus we know that the well-to-do Alexander Woitaszewicz, a well-known merchant in the Siedlce area, had, in Gut Szianna, near Braszkow, hidden the Jews Yehudit Kwiatek-Greenwald, David Lustik, Yisroel Orlantszik, Levi Orlantszik, with their wives and Henech Banalewicz from Braszkow. He hid them with food and an apartment, comforted them, and gave them strength to persevere and survive. Trusting that the war would not last long, he stated formally that they worked for him. This lasted from 1940 until 1942, when the small ghetto in Siedlce was liquidated and their further stay with him in Gut was no longer possible. He sent Yehudit Kwiatek, Levi Orlantszik, and David Lustik with their wives to Warsaw to his former farmhand. Woitaszewicz often came to them in Warsaw, bringing necessities and supporting them with an open hand. He did all this without thought of reward, only out of humane feelings.

Possibly because of his humane attitude toward Jews in those unhappy years, Woitasewicz paid with his life. At the end of 1943 he was attacked by an armed group, who shot him. Since nothing was stolen from him, people assumed that this was a political murder by the A.K. as revenge for hiding Jews.

[Page 184]

* * *

In Roskow, at the well-known Siedlce magnate Count Stephan Humnicki, a group of 50 Jews worked. They were treated humanely and correctly. On November 29, 1942, when the group was forced to go to Genszi-Barky, some Jews still remained with Humnicki. Among them were Aaron Perlman from Loszic and the two Feinholtz sisters from Siedlce (the daughters of Gulf Feinholtz). They were hidden and cared for my the count and his wife Sophia until the liberation.

* * *

Shomer and his wife Anna, owners of a brewery and a sawmill in Sarnak (in the vicinity of Siedlce), hid and cared for several Jews (among them the brothers Yoel and Berl Liberman) until the liberation. When their hiding place was suspected by neighbors, the Shomers took the Jews to their relative Josef, in another village, and all survived.

* * *

The owner of Chwalatszice near Loszic hid several Jews. The neighbors betrayed him to the Germans, who hanged him for this transgression and shot the Jews.

* * *

In the village of Kszimos (near Siedlce) a group of hidden Jews were discovered by the A.K. The Jew ran, and the A.K. people shot after them. Eliyahu Gaszelinski, after being shot, dragged himself to a second farmer who hid him, cared for him for a long while, and healed his wounds.

* * *

In the village of Glucha-Piaski, the innkeeper Jaszinski hid seven Jews.

* * *

When Moyshe Mendel Gora and his two sisters were wandering around, starving and weary, in the fields and woods, they found a hiding place and a bit of food with farmers they knew, Antony Karczewski, Waclw Liszecki, Jan Dszewalski, and others.

* * *

[Page 185]

Zubrowicz Josef, from the village of Kszimos, near Siedlce, recounts that a farmer from the village had set aside weapons and provisions for Jewish partisans, a group of 450 who for a while had lived and conducted their partisan activities in the woods near Kalusz. The Germans seized the farmer and shot him.

* * *

Yitzchak Bornstein and Zatorski survived in a bunker in the thick of the Mezritch woods thanks to a religious monk who provided them with food.

* * *

The teacher Aszinski from Apola near Siedlce, known as a socialist activist, hid a group of young Jews from Siedlce in a pit: Dr. Loebel's son Witek, Dr. Glaszwski's son Ramek, Lola Salzman, the brothers Yisroel and Leibl Wisznia, the young woman Shassenfoigel, and Bracha Rawinska from Apola. For two months the bewildered Jews found a hiding place and protection with the idealistic Christian. They were recognized by the neighbors, however, and had to leave. They went to the village of Caton near Braszkow. For a long time they hid together with the Kiszelinski brothers. Later on they were killed by the murderous Polish police.

* * *

Theophile Ruszinski, a well-known pauper in Siedlce, hid and cared for the young Berl Rabinowicz (a son of Yishayahu Rabinowicz) until the liberation, with no care for himself. One time, they saw through the window that Gestapo members were going by in the direction of Ruszinski's apartment. The frightened Rabinowicz was sure that he had been detected and that they were coming for him. He wanted to run outside in order to prevent the detection of his protector, but the idealistic Christian did not allow him to, saying, "What happens to you will also happen to me."

* * *

When Moyshe Kiszelinski escaped from the slaughter that the Polish police had carried out when the pit was discovered in the village of Katon, where nineteen Jews were murdered, he found a hiding place with the poor shoemaker in Siedlce, Philip Smolinski, who kept him for several weeks without payment. Later, when Moyshe and Raphael Kishenski and son escaped from the death that threatened them from all sides and had nowhere to turn, they again found protection and a hiding place with that same Smolinski, until they were detected and had to flee.

[Page 186]

* * *

The poor Christian woman in Siedlce Jadwiga Budna hid six Jews in her poor apartment, without payment: the three brothers Avraham, Melech, and Itsche Halber, two Galicki brothers, and David Greenberg. The hidden Jews gave her money solely to buy food. After the liberation, this Christian woman married Mottel Galicki, whom she had saved.

* * *

The Christians Sophia Alszakowska and Jadwiga Zawadzka inn Siedlce took from the parents Yakov and Tchipa Sonnschein their one-year-old daughter Rochele. The parents committed suicide in Gensze Barki. This Christians protected the child, took care of her, and after the liberation went to the Jewish congregation in Poland and to her relatives in Israel to hand over custody of the child and for her education. (This child lives now in Israel, in a children's home in Nahariyya.)

* * *

The Christian Maria Kowalska for two years in her home hid Mrs. Leonia Greenspan-Halberstat, receiving compensation only for her actual expenses.

* * *

Mrs. Gutsze Szinalawa and her daughter Lily, who had managed to get to Chentshin, survived with a poor beggar, Karl Kitszinski, who was 68 years old. He created a hiding place for them in his home. Later, because of security concerns, he hid them in a camouflaged grave in the cemetery. The beggar did not have enough food for himself, so he went around to houses and begged from the farmers. Whatever he collected he shared with the hidden women, who survived thanks to the goodhearted beggar. After the liberation, the beggar begged Mrs. Gutsze and her daughter to leave him so that no one would know that he had saved Jews.

* * *

Even in view of the conquest, stealing, or inheriting Jewish possessions, which was so normal for most Poles at that time of extraordinary "good fortune," there were also some exceptions.

[Page 187]

Such a one was the Christian Bunik Antony in Siedlce, to whom the Do a brothers had entrusted various articles and valuable. After the liberation, he sought relatives of the Do a family and returned everything.

* * *

There was also an occasion when a man from the Polish underworld extended a hand to save a Jew.

Moyshe Rotbein and his daughter decided in the darkness of night to get away from the ramp where together with thousands of Jews they awaited the loading of the trains that were headed for Treblinka. They crawled away on all fours, unnoticed by the killers who surrounded them in a thick cluster and they managed to get to a nearby garden. There they were accosted by an unknown man. They lay there as if they were dead, motionless. The man came near them and said, "I know who you are, unfortunate beleaguered Jews. Come with me. I will take you to safe spot." And he took them by back roads to his friends who were waiting outside the city. He brought them food and helped them escape. Rotbein offered the unknown man money, which he refused to take, saying, "Keep your money. You'll need it. I have more money than you." It later turned out that their rescuer was well-known thief from the Siedlce area.

* * *

There were certain cases in Siedlce and its surroundings when Poles either rescued or helped to rescue a Jew in that sad, hellish time. However, these were exceptions by individual righteous Christians, whose like Avraham our father sought in Sodom and our unfortunate sisters and brothers south and very seldom found.

Instead, if one looks, one finds the evil and bestiality that our neighbors showed to Jews in those dark years, their active assistance to the Germans in their extermination efforts.

And just as one cannot pinpoint the ideological camp or social faction to which the individual righteous Christians who helped Jews belonged, so one cannot pinpoint the ideological camp or social faction to which the great number of wicked Christians who helped the Germans rob and murder Jews belonged.

[Page 188]

They came from different factions of Polish society and were drawn to their deeds in a variety of circumstances. Sometimes it was greed for Jewish possessions, the desire to steal Jewish goods. Killing a Jew provided the opportunity to steal from him his clothing and shoes, to take whatever money he had. It was worth whatever kilograms of sugar he had, or flasks of brandy with which the German killers rewarded the murder or the turning in of a living Jew. Sometimes it was the product of bestial instincts, the thirst for blood that the Germans awoke in certain portions of the Polish population. But mostly it was the result of the confirmed hatred of Jews that certain circles had long instilled in the Polish masses. And they, the masses, had finally found the opportunity to unload this amassed hatred, to set their hands to making real the slogan "Poland without Jews."

Immediately in the early days of the occupation people heard at every turn from the greatest part of their Polish neighbors threats, backed by the specter of the Germans. Betrayals and interventions by outsiders became daily occurrences.

Even small children would gather around Jewish homes and yell, "Jew," indicating to the Germans where Jews lived and helping the Germans seize Jews for work or help those seeking Jews who were in hiding.

* * *

In October of 1939, a German with a Polish wife held a sexual orgy in the courtyard of 25 Pienkne Street. The neighbor of that house, the shoemaker Arszech, in total ignorance, happened to wander past and took in the spectacle. The neighbor, whom the Jew knew well, not wanting anyone to know of her good deeds, told the German, who seized the Jew, led him to the Gestapo, and told them that the Jew had attacked him. The Jew was taken to a court martial, which called as a witness the German and the neighboring woman. You have to understand that the Jew's guilt was "proven."

[Page 189]

A special notice was pasted up on the streets of Siedlce announcing the death sentence that was carried out against the Jew for attacking the German soldier.

* * *

Long-time acquaintance and friendship were no help, even when people had been school friends, studied together, or worked together in business.

Avraham Nadwarna decided not to go to the ghetto, not to be locked in the ghetto-cage that had been established in Siedlce. He got Aryan papers and left for Lukow so as not to be in his home town where he would be recognized. Sitting one lunchtime in a Polish restaurant, he was recognized by a Christian whom he knew, who immediately reported him to the Gestapo. Nadwarna was tortured for four days before he died.

* * *

The same thing happened to Salek Tabakman (the son of Avraham Tabakman). He also provided himself with Aryan papers. He did not go to the ghetto and he avoided the first slaughter in the Treblinka gas chambers. After the liquidation of the ghetto, Tabakman arrived at the train station in order to travel to Warsaw. He had a good "appearance" and good papers, and no one would know he was a Jew. But there he ran into a school friend who had studied in gymnasium with him and attended lectures together. The school friend called a German gendarme and denounced Tabakman as a Jew. Tabakman exclaimed to him, "My colleague, what are you doing?" To this his colleague responded, "Shut up, Jew!" The Germans did not hesitate to arrest Tabakman, remarking that he did not look Jewish. They warned the young Christian that he would have to face a higher power if he freed a Jew. This former school friend was not released until Tabakman was shot.

* * *

The fiendish attitude toward the beleaguered Jews and the unwillingness to help them afflicted all classes, as much among the village farmers as among the educated intelligentsia.

[Page 190]

Sarah Goldfinger (daughter of Baruch Mordechai Kleinman) tells that Dr. Butszinski, who was a house doctor for the Kleinmans and a close acquaintance, turned her out of his home when she came seeking a place to hide. As Mrs. Goldfinger tells it, Dr. Butszinski, desiring to be free of her, have her tea to drink mixed with poison, which she detected at the first swallow.

* * *

A large number of Poles did very well for themselves in the Jewish tragedy, having sought to acquire goods or wealth by dealing in unclaimed Jewish property. All methods of obtaining these were considered "kosher."

The young Siedlce Christian Tofek Artik put together a treasure in sacred objects: Torah scrolls, megillos, mezuzahs, tefillin, taleisim, religious books, and many other sacred things, telling people that American Jews wold pay a lot for them. Nothing interfered with his achieving his goal.

* * *

Professor Buchholz, a Pole of German ancestry, well known in Siedlce as an antisemite, was named by the Germans as guardian of the stolen, movable property of Jews. This position gave him the opportunity to gather valuable Jewish objects, from which he grew rich. With particular industriousness he gathered Torah scrolls that later, after the liberation, he sold them to Jews for a good price.

* * *

The poor teacher Henryk Chrominski also decided that people should take advantage of the seldom-good "circumstances" and simply use his position once and for all to become wealthy. With the help of his wife, who had a flair for business, he opened a secret mediation office. The oppressed ghetto Jews would bring him their clothing, linens, jewelry, and furs, which they would trade for groschen.

At the liquidation of the ghetto, he would get Aryan papers for those who could pay him well. He also dealt in hiding places. He created a hiding place for Mrs. Yehudis Greenberg and her daughter, for the Kleinman family, and for others.

The poor teacher made a fortune. After the liberation, he bought up many houses that had belonged to Jews, including the house of Mendel Cohen.

[Page 191]

The well-known Siedlce merchant of electrical accessories, Leonard Oskerka, always maintained that being an antisemite was a key to business—and he always stood by his slogan of "What's yours is yours" [i.e., one should patronize one's own people]. With the arrival of the Germans—as Moyshe Halberstam tells it—he reached new heights and he created terrible troubles for Jews at every opportunity, cursing and beating them, saying "Now my time has come. This is the end for you Jews."

Even wilder and more brutal was his son. He betrayed Jews to the Gestapo and the Sonderdienst with whom he was friendly, and he was responsible for the deaths of many Jews. He often cam to the ghetto with the Germans to help them. He ceaselessly embittered the lives of the Jews in whatever ways he could.

After the liberation he was seized by a Polish court martial and at his trial he had to give an accounting of his deeds. His mother, however, utilized various protections and interventions until her brat was released—he was afraid to remain in Siedlce and went to Bratislava. There he resumed the wild actions to which he had become accustomed in the years of "good conditions." He committed acts of robbery and murder until the Polish government condemned him to death.

* * *

Sarah Yom-Tov Halberstam, before she entered the ghetto, left her best clothing with a Polish family that she knew, the Mazurs. At the beginning of 1943, when she had to leave Siedlce, she sent a messenger to the Mazurs and asked for her clothing, to which the Mazurs replied that they had no idea what she was talking about. No one had given them clothing. And when, one dark night, Mrs. Halberstam came to the Mazurs for her clothing, no one would even open the door or let her into the house. They warned her that if she did not leave, they would call the Gestapo. Right after the liberation, fearing the consequences of their actions, the Mazurs returned the clothing.

* * *

Most of the Gentiles who helped Jews did so for the high prices that Jews paid them for help or for other self-interested reasons.

[Page 192]

Many Jews who gave away their possession to Gentiles for safekeeping were turned out into the hellish streets (if they were not simply killed) after their goods were taken, because the Gentiles knew that the Jews did not matter and were not protected by the law.

* * *

My brothers Shlomo and David made a deal with Christian whom they knew, who lived int he woods, that he would hide them for a high price. After being with him for several days, he took their possessions and threw them out.

* * *

The brothers Raphael and Moyshe Kishelinski paid a Gentile in the village of Astrawek, near Siedlce, four thousand zlotys a month to allow them to make an underground bunker in his field. That was the equivalent of 800 dollars a month.

* * *

Moyshe Rotbein, Tsirl Kaplan and others had to sign over their houses, aside from the large amounts of money they paid the Gentiles for protection.

* * *

And when the fifteen-year-old Idsze L. found her way to her father's Christian acquaintance Kardowski and asked for help in hiding, he cynically agreed to do so for a price—that she should give herself to him.

* * *

Yisroel Orlanczik, who was hidden by the prosperous Wotaszewicz (near Siedlce) went to a neighboring village, Chlewisk, to see his wife, who was hiding there. He was noticed by Gentiles whom he knew. They informed the police, who surrounded the house where he was hiding. Orlanczik was dragged out and shot.

Before that, Orlanczik had left his five-year-old child with Christians whom he knew. The Christian himself killed the child.

* * *

Yosef Kesselbrenner, who went around disguised as a Christian in various villages, as a shepherd, as a tinsmith, as a carpenter, as a miller, as a janitor, came to the village of Faganow (in the Lukow area). He arrived a half hour after two gentiles from the village, Mircah Krasicki and his partner in killing Jews, Witkowski, had murdered his 20-year-old grandson Alter Zakalik.

[Page 193]

Witkowski bragged to Kesselbrenner the "Christian," who had to control his feelings over the death of his grandson, that this was the eighth Jew that he had killed with his own hands (as he showed him his bloody hands).

* * *

Yosef Zubrowicz tells: In the village of Kszimos, two families from Siedlce were hiding with a farmer: the Finkelsteins and the Konopnes, altogether eleven people. The farmer Wachowicz found out about this and went to get the Germans and showed them the hiding place. The Germans shot the Jews.

* * *

Young Asher Warszawski from Mord fought from under the German oppression and ran away, but Gentiles pursued him for several kilometers until they caught him and brought him to the Germans.

* * *

Kuba Ellberg says: The Pole Radzikowski Kaszimiesz, who lived outside of Siedlce had lured to himself Jews who had fled from the slaughters and from the death trains. He made empty promises of providing hiding places. When Radzikowski had enticed 40 Jews, he turned them over to the gendarmes, who killed the unfortunate Jews.

* * *

Natke Levin-Kutin tells us:

Her sister, Felle Levin-Adler (daughter of Yehoshua Levin) and her four-year0old child Chanale were hiding in a stable in the village of Mircha. Once, her husband Henpeck came to her. Gentiles saw their hiding place and informed the village magistrate. This resulted in a wild pursuit by many peasants with scythes and axes. They dragged their unfortunate victims frothier hiding place, put guards over them, and sent a messenger to the police in Skurszec with the news that they had captured three Jews. The police took the three victims to Siedlce, to the Gestapo, where they were shot.

* * *

[Page 194]

In October of 1942, Felek Goldberg and Frimet Rotbard were working in Rolnik, They did not go to the small ghetto to sleep but to a Christian whom they new in Siedlce, Sztszor at 10 Loti Street. The owner of the house, Glusztszak, found out about this and and he informed the Gestapo, who came at midnight, dragged the victims to the Sports Plaza and shot them.

Sztszor and his wife were arrested for hiding Jews. He was shot and his wife was sent to a concentration camp.

* * *

Chantshe Dvash-Miedziinski from the village of Plifk near Siedlce recounts:

Her father Mottel Dvash was for a time hidden by a farmer he knew in the village of Plifk. After a certain time the farmer threw him out. He roamed through the fields with nowhere to go. Eventually he went to another farmer whom he knew where his daughter and her child were hiding and he begged to be hidden—or at least to be allowed to stay for a bit with his daughter and her child. The farmer, the murderous Tadeusz Orszelowski, killed Dvash with an axe, took his body into the woods and buried it.

* * *

Four young children—Shmilke, Yossele, Shyele, and the little girl Peshke Dvash—were hidden in a stable at the farmer Tadeusz Rumkominski in the same village. One day the farmer went to the police and told them that four Jews were there and asked them to come and kill them. When the police, who knew them, refused to do so, the farmer went off to the Germans and told them. The Germans then ordered the police to go and shoot the four children. When the police arrived, they told the children to flee and then shot them from behind. The farmer buried the children nearby.

* * *

The two brothers Shmuel and Simon Dvash from Siedlce, who found themselves in a village, were seized by the murderous farmer Franzishek Korpus, who forced them into his stable where he struck them in the head with an axe.

Two women—a mother and a daughter, both from the Dvash family—sought a hiding place in a haystack in a field. They were noticed by two farmers, Czibulski and Kszimosik, who killed the unfortunate women.

* * *

Twelve Jews lived in the village of Plifk. They were all killed by local murderous farmers whom they knew.

[Page 195]

* * *

In the same village there were several other Jews hiding in different spots, among them a woman, Manya, with her child Sevik from Warsaw, a young woman Chnshe from Nashelsk, a young man from Siedlce who had just eaten in the village restaurant. The local farmers went after them—then brought them into a barn and killed them with axes..

* * *

Shimon Shanshein, who survived in the woods around Sarnak, near the Bug, tells: The farmer Jan Grigorczik in the village of Floskow near Sarnak hid nine Jews, for a high fee. The hiding place was in the farmer's house in a cave under the floor. On January 20, 1943, after the Jews had been hidden there for three months, the farmer opened the cave and in a horrible manner killed the unfortunate Jews. The Farmer poured boiling water that he had prepared over the Jews in the cave. Those who had remained alive after the horrifying executions he ended with blows of an iron bar to the head. One of the victims—Eliyahu from Loszic—who was scalded, fought back against the murderous farmer. He went to the village magistrate and begged to be taken to the gendarmes. You must understand that the magistrate obliged him. At the gendarmerie, Eliyahu told them about the horrifying slaughter by the farmer in the cave. The gendarmes made an inspection at the farmer's and and found weapons. For that infraction (and not for killing eight Jews), they arrested and executed him.

* * *

At the same time a second farmer in the same village, Teodor, observed what his murderous neighbor Grigorczik had done and he killed several Jews who were hiding out with him. People found a chopped off woman's head and recognized her as a young woman from Sarnak—Dvorah Zilberstein. There was also the body of Aaron Shvartzbard from Blashki.

* * *

Sarah Yom-Tov Halberstam recalls that to the Krinskis in a village between Siedlce and Mord, at the time of the liquidation of the ghetto there came a Jewish woman, a seamstress from Mord.

[Page 196]

They hid and supported her while she made all kinds of clothing for the whole family. When the woman completed her work, they tied her up, took her into the city and handed her over tot he gendarmes, who immediately shot her.

* * *

After the liberation, there occurred in the Siedlce courts a trial for the Wengrow firemen with their leader Eichler—for their bloody actions. There were no Christian witnesses—the Gentiles feared retribution if they testified against their neighbors. Of Jewish witnesses there were almost none. They had all been killed. Only one Jewish witness, M.M. Gora, was at the trial. He related the deeds of the firemen. The court acknowledged their guilt and the leader of the firemen was sentenced to eight years in jail and his helpers to two years.

* * *

In the numerous trials of Polish murderers that occurred after the liberation, people learned the dreadful details about the murderers. Thus did people learn that in a village between Siedlce and Lukow, several Jews were in hiding with a 70-year-old farmer. During a winter night, the old farmer and his son used scythes and axes and to kill the group of Jews. While they were burying the bodies, they realized that according to their count, one Jew who had been in hiding was missing. The murderers searched around in the snow and found footsteps and drops of blood. It was clear to them that the footsteps and the drops of blood were evidence that the Jew was still alive and was fleeing. The old farmer followed the footsteps and the drops of blood in the middle of the night. They led to a farmer in another village. He went there and demanded that they return "his" Jew, and when the farmer refused to hand over the Jew, the old killer threatened to go to the Germans. This was effective and the Jew found himself again in the murderous hands of the old killer, who took the Jew into a field and killed him.

People learned of this bloody killing later on, when the second farmer, from whom the unfortunate Jew had sought sanctuary, told the story. The old murderer and his son were put on trial in the Siedlce court.

[Page 197]

At the trial, the farmer-witness—fearing vengeance—withdrew his testimony and the killers were acquitted due to a lack of evidence.

* * *

Yontl Goldman tells:

Farmers in the villages were stubbornly silent and would not reveal where in their fields or courtyards Jews who were killed by Poles were buried. They feared that they would have to be witnesses against their neighbors. But they willingly revealed the places where Jews killed by the German murderers lay buried.

* * *

A horribly bloody chapter concerned the participation of the "grenadiers" and their prominent contribution to the extermination of the Jews. Armed with their ancient, deeply instilled hatred for Jews and having the extraordinary opportunity openly to kill and to steal, they left nothing to chance either in their destructive activities either in the whole of Poland or in our destroyed home. They did all this voluntarily and on their own initiative. They showed great industriousness in the days of liquidation by surrounding the ghetto and ensuring that no Jew could escape. They actively cooperated at the Umschlagplatz, at transporting victims to Treblinka, and, like bloodhounds, going into the city after the liquidation, as well as into the villages, the fields, and the woods, seeking Jews in hiding and killing them.

All of the surviving Jews know and can relate how the bloody hands of the "grenadiers" killed more hidden Jews than even the German murderers did.

* * *

David Listik, who at first was hidden in the area of Braszkow, says: When the transport of Jews from Kalusz on the way to Treblinka went through the station in Braszkow, a young man jumped from the train. In jumping, he injured himself severely and remained lying by the train tracks in pain. He could not get away. His groans, like an evil wonder, attracted a group of Gentiles. He begged for someone to help him get away from the train line, to which they responded with wild laughter. Instead, they found someone to go to the police.

[Page 198]

The remaining Gentiles meanwhile tore off his clothes. When the police arrived, they found him naked. They shot him.

* * *

The same police in Braszkow shot Yisroel Orlanczik, who was betrayed by Gentiles whom he knew when he went near the village of Chlewisk to see his wife—the police surrounded the house where Orlanczik was hiding, pulled him outside and shot him.

* * *

People tell: In the village of Stak-Lanci, during the winter at the end of 1942, there was a pretty young woman, Leah. A Russian partisan, Shura, took pity on her and hid her in nearby woods. He took her to himself and hid her in his own hiding place in the woods. A Polish policeman learned about this. He searched for the young woman and shot her.

* * *

Forty-two Jews who were hiding in Kotun were discovered by the police agent Marciszewski. He blackmailed them for three months, took everything they had, and in the end he sent in five policemen who killed nineteen of them.

Six of the survivors, the Kiselinski family, while they were hiding in a pit in the village of Ostowek, were fallen upon by Polish police, who killed two women and a child.

* * *

When Moyshe Mendel Gora and his two sisters were sleeping in a hiding place in an attic in a barn, they were set upon by Polish police. The police arrested them and prepared a grave for their victims, who were due to be shot. Through an astounding chance they escaped by digging under the village's prison cell and ran away.

* * *

One cold, wet winter day, when hunger and cold drove out from their hiding place two unfortunate young people, half-naked children on whom the village farmers had taken pity, given them a bit of food, they were seen by the local murderous police commander Moshkowicz, who followed them for three kilometers through snow and water, shot at them many times, the killer did not stop until the unfortunate children fell dead.

[Page 199]

* * *

Getzl Vaysberg from Sarnak in his testimony before the tribunal in Munich said:

Jumping out from the death train that took the last transport of Jews from Siedlce to Treblinka, he met up with his cousin Noson Goldbert and his friend Gedalyahu Moncorsz by the train plant. They had also jumped from the train. They stayed together and went to their home town of Sarnak seeking a hiding place from farmers whom they knew. When Noson Goldberg went to one farmer asking for a bit of bread, other farmers saw him. They informed on him to there Polish police. When they found him, he began to run. They pursued him and shot him.

Gedalyahu Moncorsz went to a second farmer, who told him to come alone, without other Jews, and he would find a hiding place for him. After the liberation, people learned that for about two months he lay in a potato pit. Other farmers saw him and informed on him to the Polish police. The police found him half dead, with frozen hands and feet, and they shot him.

Because n o farmer that I knew was willing to take me in—continued Vaysberg—I went to the fields. I arrived at a barn, where I heard a quiet voice. I stood still and was shocked at what I heard. It was Yiddish. I knocked and begged to be let in. They opened up for me. I was with them for several days. But the farmers learned about us and told the Gestapo. At noon the police attacked us. They ordered us out of the barn. We were hiding in the straw. They began to tear off the doors and to shoot at us. In great despair I opened a door and began to run. They shot after me with different kinds of guns—but they did not hit me. When the other six fellows saw that I was escaping, they left the barn. Running through fields, three of them were shot. One fell wounded and a Polish policeman beat him with a club. Two of the six continued to run. Two days later, one of the six was shot.

[Page 200]

The other was with me in the woods. On November 15, 1942, he was also shot in an attack.

For four months I hid in a pit that I made in the stable of a farmer I knew. On March 21, 1943 I went into the woods. There I encountered 25 Jews and we were together. On May 25, 1943, Polish police attacked us in the woods. Six Jews from Sarnak were shot: Gavriel Zucker, 33; Shmuel Chibowski, 27; Markl Rosenberg, 18; Moyshe Rudzki, 35; Yitzchak Wladower, 18; and Velvel Wladower, 22.

At the time of an attack by the Gestapo and the Polish police on November 15, 1943, three more men were killed: Yidel Chibowski, 29; Hershel Chibowski, 20; and Ezriel Moncarsz, 22.

When the day of liberation arrived for Siedlce and its surroundings—July 30, 1944—the liberation affected only a small number of JewsThey had been murdered by German and home-grown murderers, mostly by Polish police.

* * *

Lilka Lautenberg recounts:

In the village off Zakszwuek, where she was living with her husband and father as "Aryans," a rich innkeeper saw how his neighbor, a poor innkeeper, had begun to dress better and was leading a better life. He began to observe him with curiosity and he noticed that in the middle of the night he messed with the ground outside of his house, dug in it and then covered it up.

The rich farmer informed the police about this. The police came, conducted a search and brought the farmer in for an interrogation. The farmer, without much thought, explained the matter:

One time a man came to him and asked to spend the night and get some food, so he complied. At night, he saw how the stranger went away to a corner to say prayers, just as Jews do. Then he understood that the stranger was a Jew. Later, when the stranger was sleeping, the farmer took an axe and cut off his head. He found that the stranger had some pieces of gold, continued to run.

Two days later, one a little money, and other valuables that he took and used to better his material condition.

[Page 201]

He buried the Jew near his house. The police shook his hand in appreciation of his being a good and brave patriot and asked him to prepare a meal. They went to the village magistrate and then had the meal with brandy and other dishes.

As they became more inebriated, one of the police asked the magistrate to sell him the beautiful rug that was hanging on the wall. He would pay whatever was asked, but when the magistrate refused the offer, the drunken policeman tore the rug off the wall and thereby revealed a secret door that the rug had covered. The police went through the door and, to everyone's surprise, brought out six Jews, who were hiding behind a double wall.

Everyone suddenly sobered up. The police forgot about the rug. The unfortunate Jews were led out to courtyard and under the observation of many peasants who had been drawn to this spectacle, the police shot the six Jews.

* * *

In a nearby village, where the Lautenbergs were hiding, a farmer was hiding several Jews. The farmer had thereby gotten a lot of money. After the farmer had used the money to buy a horse, a cow, a farm machine, and so on, he went to the police and confessed to them that his material condition had been bad and he wanted to better it. Just then the Zhids came to him and paid him well, so he took them in. Now he was delivering them into the hands of justice.

This farmer also received congratulations from the police, who shot the unfortunate Jews.

* * *

Out of the large number fo Polish police who were "active" in the city at that time, almost all were active participants in the extermination of the Jews. They sought to distinguish themselves by killing more Jews.

On August 22, the day of the mass slaughter, at the Umschlagplatz.

[Page 202]

Two days later, one Soszniak, a policeman, spent the whole day shooting at the crowded mass of Jews. When his hours were up, he boasted to a second policeman who had come to replace him: Today I killed a hundred Zhids. Now show what you can do."

* * *

And when the policeman Jankowski saw that in Gensze-Barky that the end of the Jews was near, he called out Avraham Bressler, the assistant commander of the Jewish police, and shot him.

But they, the bloody police murderers, no one judged. They took care that no witnesses to their bloody deeds remained. No one could call them to justice and they remained the guardians of law and order.

The sacred "idea" of killing and robbing Jews also possessed the partisans—Poles and Russians who went to the woods and the underground so that they could from their hiding places assault their common enemy. Many of them forgot their primary purpose and made deals with the A.K. and with other murderous groups or they took it upon themselves to take the light and at that time popular way of killing Jews. Russian partisans who lived in the Polish woods and in the villages forgot, in that poisonous atmosphere of the Nazi epoch, the Soviet teaching about the brotherhood of all that had been drummed into their heads for three decades, and they renewed the old motto of czarist Russia, "Get the Jews."

Yontl Goldman tells us: The village of Gola-Piaski, a group of Jews hid. Polish and Russian partisans in the area found out about it. The partisans set fire to the house where the Jews were. As they ran from the fire, five Jews were shot by the partisans. Some were burned, and two Jews were forced to run. The local farmers buried the Jews who had been who had been shot and burned. Several days later, Polish police came from Mord. Together with the local farmers, they dug up the corpses, ripped out their golden teeth, took their clothing and shoes, and reburied them.

In the forest of Mord there was a Russian partisan named "Franek," whose murderous deeds caused terror in the whole area. He would seek out hidden Jews, then kill and rob them.

[Page 203]

Sarah Yom-Tov Halberstam knew a young man from Warsaw who had jumped from the death train on the way to Treblinka. He hid in the woods around Mord. All of a sudden, his dead body was found, naked and barefoot. His clothes and boots were being worn by the murderous partisan "Franek."

* * *

The Gentiles from the villages around the train lines leading to Treblinka distinguished themselves with special ferocity, bloodthirstiness, and greed.

From the transports that rushed with such speed, taking the victims to the death factory, many showed courage and tore off the doors, broke the iron bars on the small windows, or made other kinds of openings in the death wagons and then jumped from their blind fate. But there, by the train lines from Siedlce to Treblinka, waited, lurking like hunting dogs, were camps of bloodthirsty and robbery minded peasants who, with extraordinary wildness and ferocity, through themselves upon their unfortunate victims, whom they murdered and robbed.

We hear much about them from the small number of people who jumped and by some miracle were saved from the murderous onslaught and survived, such as: Melech Halber, Leib Mandelbaum and his wife Itta, Sheyna Sarah Goldfinger, Getzel Vaisberg, and others.

As they tell it, the area around the train lines resembled a slaughter house for people, littered with corpses swimming in blood, twisted in the agony of death. Around them, working feverishly, were groups of human beasts, pawing, seeking, cutting, ripping off clothing and shoes, pulling gold teeth out of dead and half-dead mouths, and throwing themselves on a still living victim who had been hiding amid the dead. One threw himself quickly on the victim with an axe, clearing the way for another killer who wanted to get his hands on the clothing. Having finished, they moved on to another victim, then to another, and on and on.

Others stationed themselves in fields, under bushes or trees, and awaited their prey who had escaped from the first batch of kiilers, from those who lurked by the rail lines, and who managed to run further and further away from that road to hell, only to find death.

[Page 204]

There were others who did their work more quietly. They led their victims away from the slaughterhouse, from the rail lines: they led them home to their villages, where they promised them a place to hide, seeking to gain the trust of their victims. Then they led them into a part of the forest or just a field and there ended their lives.

Then there were others who used horses and wagons for their murderous and thieving purposes, as was the case with Melech Halber. His farmer, for a good price, took him almost to Siedlce, where Halber wanted to join his brother in hiding. The farmer took roads that he did not know. In the woods near the Liwiec River, the farmer and his son, whom he had brought along for assistance, attacked him with an iron bar. Only through extraordinary luck was Halber able to escape from the killers.

Many, very many, darted to jump from the rushing transports, from the death wagons, and escaped from the clutches of the Germans and Ukrainians, escaping from the road to the gas chambers. But they fell into the clutches of the homegrown murderers and thieves on the roads around Treblinka, who waited and threw themselves upon their victims and treated with equal ferocity as had their German and Ukrainian exemplars.

Few survived to tell of the bloody deeds of these homegrown thieves and murderers who terrorized the roads that led to Treblinka.

* * *

In this "sacred" work of helping to exterminate Jews, women, young people, and children also played a role, if not directly with their own hands, then by betraying Jews to the Germans or to the police.

* * *

And as the young Kleiman (Baruch Mordechai's son was forced to move from one hiding place to another, he was recognized by a woman on Florianski Street. She informed the police and showed them his hiding place. They seized him along with the six-year-old Liverant child and hanged both of them.

* * *

In February of 1943, when Sarah Yom-Tov Halberstadt was hiding at Mrs. Wohlgemit's, she told her that in a store where she was recently, a young man came in to buy something.

[Page 205]

A young Gentile who was in the store recognized the young man as a Jew. He quickly called a policeman, who took the young man out, stood him against a wall, and shot him.

It appears that that young man was from a group of slave laborers who were allowed to live. They worked for the trains and were not allowed to leave their workplace or the barracks where they were stationed.

* * *

Mrs. Sarah Karcz-Charnobroda with her son managed to escape from the Umschlagplatz and went to the former servant in Raskasza (outside the city). They spent the night there, and early in the morning the servant's mother arrived. She threw them out. She would not allow them to stay until the evening, as they requested.

In the street they were besieged by Polish children who ran after them yelling, "Zhid, Zhid." The children left them and went to find Germans to inform them about the two victims. They were saved by chance when the Polish policeman Jurek happened to come by and arrest them, Mrs. Karcz and her son.

She begged him to let her go, and she offered him money, to which the policeman responded, "Come with me to the police station. Nothing will happen to you." Truly they had no confidence in the police, but they had no choice and had to go with him. He locked them in a cell, but that night he let them go free.

* * *

On a hot summer day, when Yontel Goldman emerged from his underground bunker to get a bit of air and stretch with a short walk, he encountered a group of young toughs. They followed him like shadows, going after him with shouts of "Zhid, Zhid." These young people who had been poisoned with antisemitism were ready to find a German and turn their victim over to him. Goldman, who was ready to die, saw from a distance, on Pienkne Street, a German. He went up to him and started talking. The children saw this and left him—a Jew, they thought, would not go up and speak to a German. Goldman was thus spared from certain death.

[Page 206]

Even priests—the preachers of goodness and love for neighbors—were also (not all of them, of course) caught up in the wild pursuit of Jewish lives.

Dvorah Tuchnitz and her child to whom she gave birth in the Mariansk hospital after the liquidation of the ghetto in Siedlce was killed thanks to a priest who had come to the hospital and saw that she was a Jewish woman. The holy father informed on her to the police.

* * *

Fourteen-year-old Dvorahle from Mezritch, who through some miracle escaped from the mass killing in her city, went from village to village and finally found a resting place in a village restaurant, where she worked as a server. The local priest subjected her to an interrogation to see whether she was a Christian girl, as she had claimed. When he determined that she was Jewish, the holy father became angry at her deception and ordered the owners to turn the poor girl out of their house.

* * *

The Jewish tragedy also served as an entertainment:

In December, 1942, when Sarah Yom-Tov Halbrstadt was in a village near Mord with the Naszilowskis, who thought she was a Christian, a bedraggled Jew who had jumped from the last transport to Treblinka showed up and asked for a drink of water. The Naszilowskis drove him away and chided: "Get away, Zhid. You want the Bolsheviks to come. Go to hell, to the Bolsheviks." The Jew searched in his pockets and pulled out his last possession—a little box of shoe polish—and asked for a little water in exchange. The transaction was made. When the Jew left, after drinking his water, the Naszilowskis immediately released from their chains their fierce dogs and set them upon the unfortunate Jew. While the dogs tore his clothing and bit him and bloodied him while he wrestled with them, the Naszilowskis stood by the window and fully enjoyed the fine spectacle.

* * *

[Page 207]

There often came "comedians" who supported themselves , mainly by mocking the way the Jews grimaced and shrieked when they were being tortured by the Germans. In such a way, one Christian depicted how after the war, all the Jews from the entire world would go on foot to Treblinka, take a bit of dirt inter hands, kiss it and say, "Oy vey, this is my father this is my grandfather, my grandmother." He demonstrated how the Jews would do this, and everyone got a kick out of it.

Among the peasantry who stood around talking, there was one who was regarded in the village as a wise, "cultured" person—he read newspapers and loved to talk about two things: politics and Jews. As he maintained that there should be a Bolshevik Poland, he considered himself a communist—only without Jews—he solemnly maintained. "We have enough of them."

Another time, the conversation was directed by a young Christian student who was there on a visit. Believing that Sarah was a Christian, he spoke freely and openly, maintaining that the Poles should long ago have made an end to the Jews. Enough with them! "But we Poles, as Christians, with Christian feelings in our hearts, would not allow ourselves to do so. But," he concluded, "we should be happy that the Germans have done the job for us. We Poles should always be grateful to Hitler."

Everyone nodded in agreement.

* * *

Both before and after the liberation, large camps of robbery-inclined peasants from the area around Treblinka and on the roads leading there abandoned their home duties and their work in the fields and devoted their time to the most profitable labor at that time—digging cup dead Jews on whom could be found gold or other valuables. For a long time this was the chief occupation of whole villages of peasant vandals.

Yontl Goldman, who, after the liberation, took on the obligation of exhuming widely scattered corpses from the fields, roads, and woods and bringing them to Jewish cemeteries, tells us that in many cases there were indications that the dead in their graves had already been sought after, with their teeth ripped out, fingers hacked off for rings, clothes and shoes taken, and women's hair cut off.

Even in 1946, when we came to the desecrated cemeteries, we encountered open and dug up graves of the Germans' victims, all the work of local vandals who sought the money and the valuables of dead Jews.

[Page 208]

* * *

With the approach of the Red army, rumors flew around that the Jews would take vengeance on the Poles, who helped in the killing and who themselves did the killing of Jews. Thus the bloody rampage against the hidden Jews grew stronger—in order to eliminate any hint of living witnesses.

* * *

Yontl Goldman and other survivors relate: In a village between Siedlce and Loszic, a farmer hid two Jews. A few days before the arrival of the Russian army, the farmer fooled the Jews into going to the woods, saying that he had prepared for them a better hiding place. He took one of the Jews first, then the other, and one by one he killed them.

After the liberation, when the farmer quarreled with a relative, the relative went to the police and informed them about the terrible murders. The police arrested the murderous farmer, but inexplicably the farmer was allowed to escape and disappear.

* * *

On May 29, 1944, local bandits drowned in the Liwiec River three children wo had been in hiding with the farmer Lirka Dmowski.

* * *

Moyshe Ratbein tells: In the last weeks before the liberation, he, along with the other inhabitants of his bunker, noticed that the farmer who was hiding them was "making preparations." They saw this in all of his actions, felt it in all of his words, in the fire of his eyes. They expected every minute that he would arrive with an axe or a scythe and all would be over—therefore they, the partners in the bunker, who had no more money, gave the farmer written assurances that they would give him their homes. That worked, and the farmer calmed down.

* * *

Slowly the days passed for the small number of surviving Jews. They awaited the dreamed for day of liberation.

[Page 209]

No more of the wild German beasts!

They emerged, the skeleton-Jews, from the dark underground bunkers, from the damp, stinking cellars, pits, and holes. They emerged lamenting the destruction, the tragically cut-off lives of those near to them and their own loneliness and orphanhood.

They wander around in the cities and villages, the few living shadows, dried-up skeletons with yellowed faces that betray years of hunger and pain, young men with gray hair, old before their time, with dull, half-blind eyes that for years saw no gleam of light. They seek the hidden graves of their dearest ones. They wander around like in a world of confusion between dream and reality. They have no homes to go to. Their homes are ruined, burned, and if there is anything left—it is now occupied by thieving Gentiles. There is nowhere for them to go. The air is suffocating, poisoned from the stench that the Nazi angel of death left behind. It is hard to breathe. It constrains the soul, desolate on the ground, where they where they encounter cold, hostile looks of mockery and contempt, of hate and ridicule, and in the best case of pity and sympathy in ways that disgust and disturb as much as the hatred and ridicule.

They search, these lonely shadows, these solitary survivors of whole families. A communal fate of loneliness and sadness, all equally tormented and crushed, brings them together in a single place that some Christian has provided so that in collective sorrow they can bemoan the destruction and their own fates.

But these survivors see something, something distinct, in the eyes of those who still desire a "Poland without Jews" and who can in no way make peace with the thought that after all that has happened there still remain "so many Jews," from whom they need to be free. And since they would be free of Jews, they know well the homegrown killers. They saw not long ago and learned from their ideological friends—the Germans and Ukrainians—and too they attack these surviving Jews and they kill them with no less frenzy and terror than did their German and Ukrainian teachers.

There is variety in the murderers of the surviving homeless Jews. Sometimes they are solitary practitioners of theft and murder, which has been their profession for many years. Sometimes they form nameless bands dedicated to the "sacred task" of robbing and killing Jews, which brings them together and unites them.

[Page 210]

But most are groups with nationalistic and "ideological" coloring, remnants of the half-defeated fascist militia who now call themselves by such resounding names as the A.K. (Domestic Army) and N.S.Z. (National Armed Force).

Formerly they had been corroded, these demoralized bands of helplessness against the powerful German enemy. Now they were corroded by the that Poland was freed thanks to the victorious Red army, by the hated Bolsheviks. They took out their sacred regrets on the last remaining Jews. They attacked at night and in the light of day. They attacked in the homes and in the hiding places, in the cities and in the villages, on the roads and on the trains. Anywhere that they could find a wandering, surviving Jew, they lusted after his life and killed him. There was a saying: "To kill the few Jews that Hitler did not kill will free Poland of Jews once and for all…" So ordered the Polish pro-fascist government in London, and so ordered their own rotten consciences.

David Lustik, Shimon Shanschein, and many others who came in contact with Poles at that time read the order from the government in London that was published in the underground press and spread among the Poles and the few surviving Jews. A large portions f the Polish population took this order to heart and followed it eagerly.

* * *

Eli Gaszelinski, who survived for nearly two years in the woods with a group of partisans, tells much about the problems that his group and other Jews had in withstanding the bloody deeds of the A.K. who rampaged through the villages, fields, and woods around Siedlce. He gives the impression hat their sole activity was to search for hidden Jews, to rob them and to kill them. They did so through the whole period, but they did so most fervently in the last days before the arrival of the Red army and after the liberation.

* * *

After the liberation—March 10, 1945—seven Jews who were preparing to go to Lodz were killed.

[Page 211]

* * *

At that time in Mord, eight Jews, worn out after their liberation from their hiding place in bunkers, paused for a rest. As they prepared to move on, they were attacked by the A.K. and all were killed.

Those killed were the brothers Avraham and Shimon Garbarsz, Mrs. Furman, two young women from the village of Czelemin, a woman from Warsaw, and two Jews from Mord.

* * *

Shiimon Shanschein tells:

Yehoshua Kalan from Sarnak survived in the woods, having gone through all seven levels of Gehenna as a hidden Jew in the bloody era of Hitler. Nine months after the liberation, while he was at home asleep in his bed, in the middle of the day, he was attacked by people from the A.K., who shot him.

On the same day, Polish killers dragged out from his home the 23-year-old Shepsel Kleidermacher, who also had survived in the woods. They took him to fields outside the shtetl and, after torturing him, buried him alive.

* * *

Nineteen-year-old Yisroel Shulmeister, who worked for the police, was sent to a village near Sarnak. He was killed by A.K. men on the way.

A Russian military unit went to the village after the killers. A battle broke out between them and the A.K. and seventeen soldiers were killed.

* * *

Eli Gaszelinski and Yosef Zubowicz relate that in the village of Kszimus near Siedlce there were seven Jews after the liberation. They had survived in the local woods. The A.K. attacked and killed them.

* * *

Two women from Kolibiel, Rude Granatower and her daughter Feiga, survived in a hiding place with a farmer in the village of Glupianka. When they emerged after the liberation and went to their own home-on the first night they were attacked and murdered by locals.

[Page 212]
Henech Chanalewicz, who survived by hiding with the landowner Witaszewicz on his estate Shiano, came outside freely after the defeat of the Germans. He was murdered by farmers he knew in the village.

* * *

Kalman Oszel, who escaped by jumping from the Treblinka death train that had left from Gensza Barki, dragged himself with his last strength to the village of Pruszin to his teacher from the gymnasium. The Christian professor remembered him well as as his best student. He sent him to another Christian whom he knew, where he hid for a long time and—survived. After the liberation, he moved back to his own apartment at 38 Aslonowicz. He married Rusza Szubrowicz and he worked as a secretary in the police department. Once—on February 2, 1945—as he was returning from work at around 5 in the evening along with his friend, the prosecutor Fimek, he was near his home, near his bedroom window, there were three rapid shots. His wife, who had heard her husband's cry of "Oy," quickly came out to the street and, seeing him lying on the ground, she took him immediately to the hospital, where he breathed his last. His last words were for his wife, whom he left in difficult circumstances.

* * *

Mottel Orlanski had escaped through some miracle from Treblinka, where he stood with the rest of his community before the open doors of the gas chamber, ready to be forced inside. He went through all the tortures of Gehenna until the liberation. He came out of his wet underground bunker an ill and broken man. A year after the liberation, while he was traveling on a train, he was kidnapped by a band of Polish killers, who tortured him, and no one even knows where his bones are.

* * *

Yosef Vunderbaum from Radzin, a Jew of thirty-some years, was traveling three years after the liberation from Radzin to Siedlce. Near Lukow, several armed Poles came along looking for Jews. They took Vunderbaum off the train and shot him.

* * *

[Page 213]
At the same time, Mendel Steinberg from the village of Kreszlin, a police employee, was traveling outside the city with the Christian Sokolowski. They were attacked by an armed band who mistook Sokolwski for a Jew as well and shot both of them.

* * *

We have conveyed here only a selection of horrifying facts that speak to the bloody deeds of our neighbors in that time regarding the area of our destroyed home town, to their active participation in the extermination of Jews. We are more or less certain about the truth of these tragic stories, and they show how it is incumbent upon us to collect all such stories. The greatest portion of such horrifying stories have remained hidden, taken by the murdered victims into their unmarked graves.

We must never forget and always remember the few righteous Poles who rescued Jews—but we must not forget the greater majority of Polish murderers who killed Jews and helped in their extermination.

When people recall the bloody deeds of the Germans that destroyed our nearest ones, our community, and our people in Europe, they should not forget who their helpers were. Without their aid, the extermination would not have been so nearly total.

---

24. At the Graves of our Fathers

Translated by Theodore Steinberg

Like a thriving, spreading forest, there stand before our eyes the many institutions and organizations, societies, and fellowships, philanthropic and cultural, financial and social-economic, medical and educational, political and religious that over the generations our tragically cut off community created in our once so beloved and now cold, strange, and ruined home town of Siedlce.

Those institutions and organizations formed a protective belt, a kind of armor, that the instinct for self-preservation called to life in order to defend the national, cultural and religious uniqueness, the social-economic positions that were constantly assaulted by the hostile voices of their surroundings.

[Page 214]

Each one of these many organizations that we had in our destroyed home town, some to a greater extent and some to a lesser, had an important function. Each was loved, dear, and important. But there were some among them that had particularly deep roots and grew especially broad and tall, like some mother trees that tower over their smaller neighbors and grow deeper, wider, and higher with their won atmosphere, shade, and aroma.

Now not one of those beloved institutions remains. They were cut off along with those who created them and with those for whom they were created. Hardly any of them have left behind a embarrassed silent monument in the ring, or a surviving building where they were once located that now has brand new owners and new institutions. But most of them have left no trace. They were erased, wiped out in the chaos of destruction and will never exist again.

We should recall the most outstanding of the institutions on the day of remembering and give them the honor they deserve and visit the graves of the fathers of these now-gone offspring.

A. The Talmud Torah

As we leave the home of the former mikveh, later on the slaughterhouse, where so many of our unfortunate fellow citizens were killed, and which now serves as the poor lodging for the remnant of wandering souls and community organizations—our desolate thoughts are interrupted by joyful, ringing children's voices—a mixture of song, laughter, and dance, that comes out into the street through the open windows of the great Talmud Torah building that stands there in its wholeness, just as it did in earlier times.

For a moment our hearts tremble. We are captured by the childish happiness that comes from the Talmud Torah. It seems to be the singing of hundreds of young boys who once studied there.

[Page 215]

The Moyshes and the Shloymes, little Jews with pale faces, black eyes that remind us of days past, of little birds. They sing while they learn for Shavuos the strange, difficult vocabulary but well understood poem "Adams," the sweetly beloved hymn in honor of the Torah that they study for the whole year, which states that "if all the heavens were parchment, all the woods pens, and all the seas ink, still we could not inscribe all of Your greatness."

And then the voices change suddenly, take on a form full of rhythm and cadence, singing out in chorus the song that the congregation of Israel sings for its beloved, for the Holy Torah, in the springtime Peach Song of Songs, "in the poem that is the greatest of all poems, the poem that is the Holy of Holies, because it was sung by the sage son of a sage, by the prophet son of a prophet, by the king son of a king."

And again there is a change in the chorus of hundreds of voices. They turn to a sweet, melancholy elegy, to a gnawing longing that runs through the blood, through the heart, and through the soul. A tune that comes from times past, from thousands of years ago, ancient but still inflaming the young hearts, lighting up their young eyes with sparkling fires as they all sway over their Chumashim and sing out together harmoniously: "And I, and I, although I am concerned with my burial, I did not do so to your mother Rachel when she died on the way to Padan Aram and I buried her along the way, as was the will of the Lord of the world, so that when Nebuzaradan sent the Jews into exile, she could leave her grave and weep before God over the fate of her children."

But be silent! Who suddenly breaks into the sweet melody of the pale little children and throws into the midst of the fantastic choir such alien, strange tones? Whence comes such strange music in the sanctuary of the Torah? Instead of those dreamed-of boys, with pale, drawn faces, dark eyes and black hair, looking through the open windows of the Talmud Torah are playful girls, laughing, with round, rosy cheeks, blue eyes, blond hair, wearing white blouses, whispering mischievously. How did they get here? This is a place for studying Torah for young boys, and "All who study Torah, it is as if they study prayers. So what are these girls doing here?

[Page 216]

Their playful laughter woke us from our sweet, beautiful dreams interrupting our thoughts of the long ago when from there emanated the Torah-inspired voices of hundreds of young boys, children of Jewish poverty, with their ringing voices filling the surrounding, darkening streets with their always penetrating, nostalgic melody that began at Mount Sinai.

The large sign in Polish in front of the entrance: "Trade School for Girls" tells us without doubt who the current owners are and who are now the students in the Talmud Torah, which for fifty years was a place dedicated to teaching the Torah to schoolchildren, created by the former Torah luminaries and donors in Siedlce: R. Yakov Dovid Korona, z"l, R. Shimon Greenberg, z"l, R. Berish Ekheizer, z"l, and other scholars, God-fearing and righteous, who believed that they were founding a building that would last forever.

I do not know if they wanted then and there such a visitor, but it was difficult to hold back. I went in. It was still "our" Talmud Torah.

In the hallway and on the steps, carefree girls were whizzing around. They came to the entrance, regarding me with amazement, as if I presented them with a puzzle. They themselves had seen all the Jews there on the Umschlagplaltz and also how they were later herded to the death trains to Treblinka. So did Jews get here? Perhaps they rose from the grave—the resurrection of the dead? I can read the questions in their puzzled eyes.

I enter a few classrooms. Yes, all is the same as it once was: the same walls, the same school benches, but no more Palle, black-eyed and black-haired eager little Jews. There are only blue-eyed and blond-haired mischievous, carefree girls.

Where are you, pale Jewish children with your dreamy, sparkling eyes? What bloodthirsty god or what terrible devil needs such young, innocent victims? For what sin? Whom did your sweet nostalgic melody harm, the melody you hummed as you immersed yourself in the passage about "two people who find a tallis" [a passage in the Talmudic tractate of Baba Mezia], about "an egg that was laid on a yom tov" [from the Tractate Beizah], or about "a woman becomes betrothed in three ways [from the tractate Kiddushin]? No one ever interrupted that melody, not Nebuzaradan and not Antiochus, not Titus and not Haman, but it was now interrupted by the last bloody oppressor—the Germans?

[Page 217]

For hundreds of years were you the object of heartfelt prayers from our religious fathers and grandfathers. They stretched out their hands to the heavens and pleaded, "Do it for the sake of our children," "Do it for the sake of the innocent infants and children"—were all those prayers in vain? Dispersed like smoke, it is as if they had never existed.

A bell rings noisily. Girls run, jump, dance, sing with mischievous glee. A secretary comes. She looks like one of the older students. She asks how she can help me. I want to say to her: "I have come to see my little brothers who studied here," but my tongue does not work.

Many blue-eyed looks are directed my way by the mischievous girls, but I see before me black-eyed boys with deeply thoughtful, pale faces—a song rings out, girls singing together "Rata," but I hear the fervent, sad sound of hundreds of voices that sing together, "And mother Rachel will leave her grave and weep before God over the fate of her children…"

B. Ezras-Y'somim [The Orphan Home]

At 17 Dluga Street, in a poor apartment of two small rooms, lived the then famous teacher in the city Avraham Hersh Osina. Avraham Hersh was a great Jewish scholar and a greater Maskil. He knew Hebrew, Russian, Polish, German, knew the literature of these languages, and was so devoted to them that he spent on them his meagre earnings as a teacher. Although Avraham Hersh was an observant, careful Jew, sporting a beard and sidekicks, praying with two sets of tefillin, and guarding all 613 mitzvos, religious Jews would not support him, implying that he was a secret heretic, and they would not send their children to study with him.

Rather, the children who studied with him had more enlightened parents, partial and total maskilim who wanted their children to have a taste of secular education aside from Torah from the hidden mask Avraham Hersh Osina. Studying with him were: Paltiel, the son of R. Moyshe Abbe Eizenstat; Misha, the son of Shmerl Greenberg; Aaron, the son of Yakov Lerner; Dovid and Berl, the sons of Leibl Kanapna; Yakov, the son of Shimon Ridel; and others.

[Page 218]

At the teacher Avraham Hersh's lessons there was, in addition to several of his own children, a lonely, impoverished child, an orphan who was related to him. Because of the poverty of his guardian, he went around in torn clothing, nearly naked, barefoot, and hungry.

Avraham Hersh Osina's were very concerned about the fate of the poor lonely orphan who was in their rabbi's room. They shared with him the snacks that they brought to school, and the small pocket change that they received from their parents they collected in a little box and used it to buy clothing for the poor orphan.

This activity of the of Avraham Hersh Osina's students grew so much that they were able to help several other orphan children whom they knew suffered from hunger and need, and they provided meals for them and sometimes bought them clothing.

* * *

At that time, on a winter evening in 1903, when it was bitterly cold, there were visitors in the house of R. Zalman Greenfarb, guests of his sons Moses and David and his pretty daughters. The guests were their friends from the different schools they attended, such as: Shia Zilbergleyt, Vulf Tuchklaper, Minia Weintraub, Madzia Kahana, Liebe Zeidenzweig, Berl Mintz, Yechiel Greenberg, the Nietzwiedsz brother and sister, and others. They had gathered to play cards and other games, and to take turns reading from the latest literary works and to sing.

With their sentimental and poetic voices, David and Moses Greenfarb and their sisters sang this currently popular song:

> It was snowing and raining
> And running quickly down the street
> I met a young girl
> Who was half-dressed, half-barefoot in the street…
> With her unshod feet
> She pounded on the cobblestones
> And though she was annoyed,
> Her childish glance shimmered…

Having sung this, someone called out, "Today, in our terrible cold, I met such a child on the street. That child tramped through the snow with swollen, red, bare feet, and extended to passersby frozen, red hands, begins for a couple of groschen, for something to eat."

[Page 219]

"I, too," someone else said," several days ago encountered such a poor child, wrapped in rags, begging in the street. When I asked the child who he was and where were his father and mother, he became embarrassed, lowered his head, and whispered, 'I am an orphan. I have no father. I have no mother. I have no home.'"

Another said, "I think this is the time to do something for such unfortunate children who have been shamed and ignored by fate."

The money that this group of young people had brought to play cards and other games was quickly collected and put into a chest as a fund to aid poor orphans.

* * *

At 22 Dluga Street, under a thatched roof in an attic of two rooms, there lived a poor workman—Reuven Blacharsz. He had agreed to give one of his rooms as a home for orphans whom people had brought together.

A delegation of the young people had gone to the Jewish community organization where they presented to the directors (Moyshe Temkin, Y. N. Weintraub, Hershel Shlipka) their plan to create a home for orphans, and there they received their first help. They bought several beds. Generous, more prosperous men and women from the city donated household items, some clothing, underwear, and food. They brought together twelve poor, deserted orphans who huddled in the study houses or slept in the streets. People washed and dressed them and thus was formed the "Ezras Y'somim," the Home for Orphans.

From the very time it was established, the "Ezras Y'somim" was received sympathetically in the city. From the aforementioned people, with the aid of the young students from R. Avraham Hersh's school, leaders emerged who participated in this sacred philanthropic work.

[Page 220]

The circle of people who took an interest in the fate of these unfortunate children grew, and the Ezras Y'somim became one of the most important institutions in the city.

For several years the Ezras Y'somim was located in the poor apartment of Reuven Blacharsz.

The poor attic at 22 Dluga Street became too small. The number of children whom fate shamed by taking their parents increased. There was no place to take them. People therefore went to the community organization, which gave them two rooms under the rabbi's apartment that had previously served as the Beis-Din. The Ezras Y'somim moved there.

The Ezras Y'somim grew even larger in its new premises in the center of the city. The directors were joined by Alter Kaminski and Monish Ridel; residents of the city helped by establishing a monthly contribution. The Jewish community organization and the city administration gave stable subsidies, and the number of orphans continued to grow, so that the locale was too small. The directors had a big problem trying to find premises large enough to house all of the city's orphans.

To the rescue came the generous donor R. Fishl Frankel, z"l. He purchased a house on Shenkawicz Street (Ogradowa) as a home for orphans and the aged.

This house consisted of two smaller houses: one was designated as a home for the aged and the other for the orphans.

In these rooms of the house on Shenkawicz Street, the Ezras Y'somim again saw further development. There was surely more room for taking in lost orphans, whose number reached fifty. The personnel increased and teachers were engaged. The number of executives increased. Social events were organized, and again people saw that the premises were too small. The house was simply too small for such an institution.

In 1925, the directorate, along with an ad hoc building committee, proceeded to build on the site of the smaller house that had been donated by R. Fishl Frankel, z"l, a large, modern building that would be designed for the needs of the institution.

[Page 221]

These city dignitaries belonged to the building committee: Yitzchak-Nachum Weintraub, Asher Orszel, Yisroel Gutgold, Velvel Barg, Dovid Rubinstein, Ephraim Zelnick, Alter Kaminski, Bunim Rottenberg, Hershel Rosengarten, and—for many years—Monish Ridel.

The work of building began with great excitement. Hundreds of observers came to the ceremony of laying the first stones. With open hands, the Jews of Siedlce brought their contributions for this magnificent building that they believed would last forever, an eternal home for unfortunate orphans.

They built a beautiful modern two-story building with all the modern conveniences, large bright rooms with a beautiful hall where musical evenings, theatrical performances, literary evenings, party gatherings, lectures, and other events could be held. Thanks to the "Poland for Poles" atmosphere, such events could not be held elsewhere in the city. Many hundreds of Jews came to the dedication of the building. They rejoiced in this great accomplishment of the institution and generally donated beds, bedclothes, underwear, and other necessities for the orphans.

With the establishment of this large building, the number of orphans increased to 70. Cooks, cleaners, and teachers were engaged. In addition to the normal education of the Folk School, the children learned various trades. They prepared for the time when they would leave the orphange so that they could maintain themselves throughout their lives.

The most important men and women of the city took an interest in the fates of the orphans. At the yearly meetings in the last years, the directorate included such dignitaries as: Yitzchak Nachum Weintraub, Asher Orszel, Yisroel Gudgold, Ephraim Zelnick, Velvel Barg, Alter Kaminski, Avraham Asher Kwiatek, Nachum Halberstadt, Bunim Rottenbrg, the Bialer rebbitzin Chavale Rabinowicz, Chaya Tenenbaum, Faya, Rabinowicz, Esther Levenstein-Czarnobrode, Gutshe Ferster, Yakov Yom-Tov, Leibish Weinstein, Hershel Rosengarten, Avraham Bressler, Berl Konopna, Yehoshua Zucker, and Monish Ridel.

These directors of the Ezras Y'somim, the members of the steering committee, thee teachers and educators, intended to be for the orphans the parents that fate had taken away from them.

[Page 222]

The directors would dine and celebrate with the orphans. On Pesach the most important citizens would come and celebrate the seders with the poor orphans. The venerable R. Yitzchak Nachhut Weintraub often delivered talks and lectures to them.

People showed affection and warmth to the children. They strove to create an atmosphere that help them to forget their somber fate.

Still, because the biggest job and the highest goal of the institution were to remove these children who were victims of fate from their deplorable situation and make them into useful citizens, the Ezras Y'somim was one of the most beloved institutions in the city.

* * *

After the first four weeks of Nazi rule in the country, parts of the Red army spent several week in Siedlce. The staff of the Ezras Y'somim took advantage of that time and evacuated the facility to Russia with almost all of the children and personnel. At first they were in Minsk, where the government took care of its upkeep. With the German attack on Russia, the Ezras Y'somim collapsed. Some of the children were evacuated deeper into Russia and survived. But some remained in Minsk, where the bloody paw of the Nazis reached them and they were killed.

Some of the personnel, along with the educators who went with the children and could not be evacuated, were also killed. Among them was the director of the Tarbus School, Bronstein, who at that time had taken over the direction of the Ezras Y'somim.

Some of the surviving children remained in Russia. Some of them returned from distant places to their destroyed home town and went to the building that was built specially for them, where they had found a warm home, but now they found the doors shut. There was no place there for abandoned Jewish orphans. Now it was the "Polish Artisans School"—so said the new sign by the doors in place of the former inscription: "Ezras Y'somim—Foundation Donated by R. Fishl Frankel, z"l."

[Page 223]

These returning orphans pass by and look with distress at the building that not long ago was their home. They have no where else to go in their orphanhood, which has now become greater and more painful.

They pass by, these gray, homeless orphan wanderers, having emerged from bunkers, from woods and taigas, and they look with pounding hearts at the building that not so long ago was the pride of Jewish Siedlce and should now be their home.

They go, these homeless orphan wanderers, to the current orphan home that is located in the building of the former mikveh, and from there they wander further away in search of a new orphans home.

C. Ha-Zamir

As we wander through the ruins, we remain standing by the building at 61 Warsaw Street. The building is intact, and we ask the neighbors who live there-both Jewish and non-Jewish: does anyone know what happened to "Ha-Zamir," which was the largest and oldest cultural institution in the city? Where is the library with its accoutrements that cultural Siedlce had assembled over the course of decades? We asked many passersby on the half-ruined street. We asked the few surviving friends, former members of "Ha-Zamir," but no one knows whether that treasury of books from the library was stolen by the Germans for Rosenberg's and Goebbels' purpose of "Researches in Judaism" or whether homegrown thieving neighbors stole it for scrap paper. Or perhaps local and German punks made a joint auto-da-fe and burned the Jewish secular and sacred books that they hated for generations.

[Page 224]

What became of the treasured musical instruments that the music section of "Ha-Zamir" created with such devotion? Did the vandals steal it and send to their homeland, prepared to use it for playing their victory march, when the "New Order" would rule over besieged Europe? Or were the instruments in the surrounding villages, in the storage chests of thieving peasants, who take them out for their Sunday amusements to play for the dancing young men and women their polkas and mazurkas on the "Jewish instruments." Or perhaps the last members of the music section of "Ha-Zamir," the students of Aaron Shpilfidel, took the beloved instruments with them into the death trains along with some linens and food, in the naive belief that they were being sent to labor camps, so that in their new, unknown exile they could play a new version of "By the rivers of Babylon."

These and other questions were ask of those among the living whom we encounter. We seek answers, too, from the silent walls that lodged Ha-Zamir. But no one can answer our painful questions.

We have some foggy notions: At the beginning of the destruction, when the German hordes entered the city and began their murderous and thieving attacks on Jewish homes, they also ripped off the closed doors of Ha-Zamir and rampaged through it: they ripped from the walls the pictures of Grandfather Mendele, of Peretz, of Sholem Aleichem, Bialik, and the picture of the founder of Ha-Zamir, Mordechai-Meir Landau, z"l. Because they did not find any living Jews there to torture, they took out their murderous Nazi rage against the pictures: they tore them up and stomped on them with their brutal nailed boots. They took many books from the library shelves, ripped and shredded them.

A group of young men who often accompanied the Germans as they robbed and pillaged Jewish homes helped to steal whatever was left.

In those first hellish weeks, one often found shameful ripped up pages from and Jewish and Hebrew sacred and secular texts blowing around in the gutters.

At the end of December, 1939, after the Germans burned the shul and the beis-medresh, along with the community office, the Jewish Council was moved to the premises of Ha-Zamir. Some supporters of Jewish culture came and packed up the remaining books and instruments in chests, sealed them, and took them to the attic—they might yet be useful…

But that did not last long, for the Germans commandeered the premises.

[Page 225]

They ordered the Jewish Council out. Together with the Jewish Council, the chests left their ruined home and ended up in a variety of places.

At the closing of the ghetto, the dispersed Jews took with them the remnant of the spiritual possessions of Ha-Zamir into the enclosed ghetto and distributed them in cellars and attics wherever there was a little room for the disgraced chests of books.

With he liquidation of the ghetto, also liquidated was any trace of the great, rich cultural institution. It disappeared into the chaos of the destruction to an unmarked grave, just as its creators, members, readers, and friends disappeared.

Ha-Zamir and its library had existed for thirty-three years, After great effort and many intercessions, in 1906 the cultural activist Mordechai Meir Landau, z"l, was able to obtain permission from the czarist government to open a library in Siedlce.

Earlier, people would be able to obtain a book from a beis-medresh bookseller who would have secretly in his home some books like Shomer and Bluestein's "moral" novels that he would lend out for a few groschen a week. From a modern teacher with maskilik leanings one could also obtain Mendele's "The Nag," Smolenski's "Burial of the Ass," and Linetzki's "The Polish Boy," but until Ha-Zamir, there was no normal library in Siedlce.

So it is no wonder that the opening of such a library, where people could get hold of the best books in Yiddish and world literature in a variety of languages, was regarded as a great event and the culture-hungry young people formed the bulk of its readers and members.

Beginning modestly with a few hundred volumes, with limitations imposed by the rules of the czarist government that oversaw such institutions as if they were dangerous, half-revolutionary undertakings by a seditionist movement, even so the library developed and grew until it became the most important cultural institution in the city.

[Page 226]

At that time, the road to education was closed to Jews: there were quotas for the mid-level schools, quotas for the high schools, so the library was everything—the beginner's school, the middle school, and the high school. It provided a little taste of the forbidden to a yeshiva student; a forbidden socialist book for a worker; an exciting novel for a young bride; Enlightenment literature for live-in son-in-law; a book of metaphysical speculation for an old heretic. But everywhere the books of the library brought knowledge and enlightenment.

After 1915, as the reactionary czarist government began to withdraw, so did some of its restrictions on Jews, and Ha-Zamir took another step in its development.

As the number of readers and the number of books increased, a drama division was formed under the direction of the writer Yakov Tenenbaum, where such artists developed as Nina Goldfarb, Moshe Grabia, and Rusze Tenenbaum, who presented the best works from the Yiddish repertoire. A music section also developed with a choir under the direction gifted violinist Aaron Shpielfiddle. There was a chess club that produced such masters a Zukerman. New young people contributed: Asher Livrant, Berl Czarnobroda, Levi Gutgold, and others, who devoted much if their time, knowledge, and energy to the development of the library; literary evenings were organized with the participation of the greatest writers and authors; musical and artistic undertakings where noted musicians and artists took part.

Ha-Zamir attracted the best young people in the city and conducted an enlightened cultural life for its members and readers, whose number eventually reached a thousand (four hundred members and six hundred readers).

The library contained twenty thousand volumes in six languages: Yiddish, Hebrew, Polish, Russian, German, and French.

All of this was destroyed by the Nazi axe and sank into chaos and destruction.

Founders of Ezras Y'somim in 1903

Sitting, from right to left: Simcha Rubinstein, Moses Greenfarb, Yitzchak Eli Zucker, Dr. Moyshe Temkin
Second row: Shia Zilbergleyt, Vulf Tuchklapper, Minia Weintraub, Madszia Cahana, Libba Zeidentzeig,
Berl Mintz

Tarbus Administrators and Teachers
At bottom: Sitting, from right to left: Yakov Yom-Tov, Chanuch Ribak, Gitl Veyman, Asher Orszel, Tzvi Bakser,
Ch. Levenstein, A. Wlodowski
Middle row: Rubin, Yehoshua Eckerman, Finkelstein, Fishl Popowski, Yitzchak Freilich, Leib Mendiszecki, Flaashin,
Moshe Yudengloibn, Levi Gutgold
Third row: Elimelech Feinzilber [author of this book], Moyshe Rotbein, Moyshe Yom-Tov, Rachel Heller, Velvel Lev,
Avraham Alternberg, Yosef Gutgold, Hillel Schwartz

[Page 227]

D. Tarbus

On April 1, 1925, the nationalistically aware Jewish world throughout the Diaspora celebrated special day: on that day, the Hebrew University in Jerusalem opened.

Zionist Siedlce was not left out. With a great parade and solemnity people in the city marked this historic moment. With a torchlight parade through the streets of Siedlce by all the Zionist and pioneer organizations led by the oldest Zionists—Yitzchak Nachum Weintraub, Moyshe Abba Eizenstadt, and Asher Orszel; with lights illuminating all the Jewish windows; with a solemn academic meeting in the city club with the participation of delegates from the Zionist Central Committee in Warsaw, Yosef Grawicki. The solemnities concluded with a banquet in the home of Moyshe Orszel that lasted until dawn.

In the celebratory speeches at the banquet, for the first time people spoke openly about a subject that from time to time had long been spoken of quietly at meetings of the Zionist Committee and in private conversations among friends: that it was now high time that the eighteen thousand Jews of Siedlce should have a normal Hebrew Folk School where Jewish children could receive a truly Jewish education and which could serve as a source of students for the newly formed university.

The foundation for such a school had long been prepared. The Hebrew teachers Akiva Goldfarb and Vulf Tuchlaper had for a time conducted Hebrew evening courses for teenagers. And Dovid Morgenstern had a small school. Later, in 1915, supported by the Zionist executives Weintraub, Orszel, Nehemiah Malin, and led by the young and energetic Asher Livront, Levi Gutgold, Yehoshua Eckerman, Chanah Spektor, and, for many years, Paltiel Eisenstadt, Baruch and Mordechai Yaffe, Yudel Tenenbaum, the Hebrew evening courses grew to be an important site of learning, where hundreds of young people acquired significant knowledge of the Hebrew language.

Helping to prepare the ground for a normal Hebrew Tarbus school, there were also many developments in and around Eretz Yisroel: the Balfour Declaration; the later decision in San Remo Conference to create for Jews a national home in Eretz Yisroel; the increase in emigration after the First World War [trans. note: He says "Second" World War, but that must be an error.]; and also the development of Zionist thought in Siedlce and the growth of pioneer youth organizations.

[Page 228]

Another factor in the creation of a school was the growing antisemitism in the country that was also manifesting itself in the public schools and creating a fiendish, uncomfortable atmosphere for Jewish students.

The last impulse toward opening a Tarbus School was given by the celebration—They opened a Hebrew University, and what about us?...

Preparations went on for over a year. In meetings between the Zionist executives and representatives from the pioneer organizations, they considered this question: Where would they get children? There was a fear that parents would not trust such a school where children would learn not the traditional holy tongue but modern Hebrew. There were pessimists who feared that such a school was not viable because of financial considerations—parents would not want to pay at a time when there were Polish public schools.

The always enthusiastic Yehoshua Ekerman and Yosef Gutgold visited parents who had school-aged children, so that at the beginning of the school year in the month of Elul 5686 (1926), 20 children gathered together from different families at the premises of the Zionist organization at 20 Kilinski—there was no other location for the school then—and the newly engaged director, the well-known teacher and scholar Yosef Akun (now in Israel), opened the Tarbus School.

In about another month there were 100 children enrolled in three classes in furnished rooms in a building at 15 Florianski Street. Three teachers worked with the director, and when they were not sufficient—Levi Gutgold worked as a special teacher.

At the beginning of the second school year, in 1927, the Tarbus School had 180 children enrolled in 6 classes with five teachers, among whom were such educational stars as Salita, Kushlan, and Joselewicz (all now in Israel), and to the previous locale was added the building of Avraham Sukenik at the corner of Pienkne and Florianski.

At the beginning of the third school year there were 250 students in the school. There were also new teachers, Rachel Heller and Flashin (the latter of whom was killed in a tragic motorcycle accident in Israel). The director Yosef Akun left Siedlce.

[Page 229]

He was replaced by the talented young teacher Tzvi Bokser (who later became an inspector for the Tarbus Schools in Poland).

At the end of the 1930 school year, there was a celebration with a large parade for the first graduates. Nineteen students, boys and girls, were there, some of whom today fill important positions in Israel among the builders and fighters.

In a short time, the Tarbus School had earned great popularity among all levels of the Jewish population as the best school in the city. Former opponents became supporters. All kinds of people sent their children: Orthodox parents from the Agudah, Bundist working people, even secret communists. From year to year the number of children increased, new classes were opened, and the teaching staff grew. The school gained a large new building with a huge hall for assemblies in the center of the city at 60 Warsaw Street.

In the last year before the flood of blood, the Tarbus School had 360 students in 10 classes, and nine first-class teachers, led by the director Braunstein.

From its beginning, a stable committee of Zionist executives was active in the school: Asher Orszel, Levi and Yosef Gutgold, Yehoshua Eckerman, Sholem Zaltzman, Moshe Yom-Tov, Avraham Altenberg, Chanuch Ribak, Moyshe Yudengloiben, and, for a long time, Fishl Popowski and the author of this book.

When they were needed, the Zionist activists Yitzchak Nachum Weintraub, Nehemiah Malin, Vulf Tuchklapper, and Dr. Schleicher and Dr. Bergman were also involved.

The constant concern of how to improve the school, its continuous growth, the great duties regarding financial matters allowed them no rest. They forced the committee to be on guard, to be creative, really to invent new ways of dealing with things. They organized social events, literary, musical, and artistic evenings, concerts and garden entertainments that were marveled at in the city—all of this made the Tarbus committee the most creative organization in the city.

A committee of parents also assisted at the school. It's members organized the yearly meeting of parents and took part in all undertakings.

[Page 230]

There was also a young people's group at the school that consisted of representatives from all the pioneer youth organizations in the city and assisted the committee in its efforts.

The Zionist leaders conducted a constant battle with the Orthodox community majority to gain a respectable subsidy for the school.

Tarbus was not only occupied with efforts for the school. It developed a broad range of cultural activities in the city. It created Hebrew evening courses for young people who were not able to attend the school, it created a good library, and it organized artistic evenings; literary reviews of a very high level that appealed to the most intelligent people in the city; there were regular Friday evening gatherings with a program that impressed the young people and drew them in great numbers. There were often entertainments on literary or scholarly subjects; there were special educational lectures and talks for parents.

The school children also from time to time conducted artistic and cultural evenings in the great halls of the city. The school had a Hebrew drama club where pieces such as "Jephtha's Daughter," "Samson and Dalilah," "Saul and David," "Martyrdom," and others were performed. These were admired by theater people and the young actors were referred to as The Small Ha-Bimah.

Also impressive were the Lag b'Omer celebrations that Tarbus would organize. At Tarbus' invitation, children from other schools and youth from the pioneer organizations would come. The celebrations would begin a night early—in clear rows the children marches through the streets with lights and torches in their hands. Early in the morning, all of the invited children and the pioneer youth would gather at the courtyard of the Tarbus school and with the Tarbus pennant at their head, about two thousand of them would march through the streets to the woods of R. Yitzchak Nachum Weintraub, pitch their tents, and celebrate with dance and play the holiday of Lag b'Omer.

On the streets of Siedlce, one often overheard young people speaking Hebrew.

[Page 231]

Thanks to Tarbus, Siedlce was one of the most Hebraicized cities in Poland.

The successful work of the Tarbus endeavors led its directors to further challenges. The last effort of the Tarbus committee before the bloody deluge was to try to prepare a Tarbus gymnasium for the new school year.

* * *

We go past the grave of our beloved Tarbus school that gave so much joy and pleasure to our dear children, instilling in them the fire of belief and hope for the future and bringing light and security into the gray, careworn homes.

We travel along the road where our dear, beloved Moysheles and Shloymeles, Sarah's and Chanahles went every day, dancing and singing with their book bags under their arms, fire in their eyes, and belief in their young hearts that they would encounter a better tomorrow and a better future for them and for their people. We come to the courtyard where there was once a school that burst with song and life, to the ground where their young feet, in the intervals between one lesson and the next, danced the hora, and they sang together:

> Never again will the chain be detached;
> The chain continues
> From fathers to sons,
> From generation to generation;
> The chain goes on and on.

[These are Hebrew verses from a song written by Yitzchak Lamdan.]

Hidden away in a corner the school garden lies crushed and buried where the children used to sing lustily and happily with their ringing voices, "Hurray, hurray for the little garden!"

Empty and deserted lies the schoolyard, like a little abandoned cemetery. In front stands the ruins of the once beautiful school building, burned and falling apart, like a large, black tombstone that cries silently for the young students, the teachers, and the administrators who have disappeared.

[Page 232]

E. Yitzchak Nachum Weintraub

As we wander through the ruins and through the sites of our destroyed, overgrown homes, we come to spots that force guys to pause and to think about the former owners who used to live there…

On the flat, overgrown empty spot on Warsaw Street, where before the destruction stood house number 53, which belonged to R. Yitzchak Nachum Weintraub, z"l, we stop. We cannot go on. It forces us to pause and think about the original Jew who lived there and who became, for the Jews of Siedlce, a legendary figure.

R. Yitzchak Nachum Weintraub came from a small shtetl—Terespol, near Brisk. He was taken as a son-in-law by the well-known philanthropist and distinguished citizen in Siedlce R. Noson Shimon Greenberg, z"l.

Weintraub came from his shtetl with many virtues: zeal for Torah learning; a love for people; a desire to work for the needs of the community; and devotion to the idea of returning to Zion, which was in its early stages.

These traits made him popular in the city and he was quickly absorbed in the circles of those who studied and those who worked for the community.

While still young, he became a Dozor in the Jewish community organization and worked to satisfy the needs of the common city together with the other executives and community activists in the city, like R. Moyshe Temkin, z"l, R. Hershel Shlifka, z"l, and others.

R. Yitzchak Nachum Weintraub became famous for his lifesaving work for the good of the community in 1906, at the time of the pogrom. Under a hail of bullets, when the czarist pogromists went wild in the city, R. Yitzcham Nachum was at the forefront in the city of slaughter together with the rabbi R. Mordechai Dov Analik, z"ll—he knocked at the doors of the czarist power brokers; he went from home to home of the pogrom's victims and brought them aid and security.

Weintraub was a member of the delegation that then traveled to Petersburg to seek justice from the czarist government. He was received by the then prime minister Stolypin and presented to him the story of the pogrom.

[Page 233]

Weintraub was involved in almost all of the existing institutions and brotherhoods in the city. He was active everywhere, and he helped to create several new organizations.

In his early years, he created an aid organization called "Secret Gifts," to help distinguished but needy Jews. Each winter he led a movement to distribute wood and coal to needy Jews—in the form of secret gifts.

He attracted the most distinguished leaders to his efforts, such as : Moyshe Temkin, Dovid Greenberg, Meir Frankel, Mottl Halberstadt, Moshe Eizenstam, Noson Dovid Glicksberg, Getaliah Orszel and others.

From his early youth, Weintraub was active as a Zionist. He went to conferences, worked to raise funds for Zionist causes, and was for many years the chair of the Zionist organization in Siedlce.

Weintraub was everywhere one of our chief speakers. He had something to say at every opportunity: at the meetings of the Jewish community organization, where he served as a door for half a century; at the shul and in the beis-medresh; he often gave talks for the children at Ezras Y'somim; he spoke at a variety of undertakings and celebrations in the city; at all Zionist meetings and celebrations; and on the twentieth of Tamuz, for the anniversary of Herzl's death, he always delivered a eulogy to the Zionist leader in the Great Synagogue at the memorial service.

Thanks to his simple demeanor and his courtesy to people, he was much lo9ved by all levels and circles in the city and people therefore lovingly called him "the Uncle."

Jews used to say, "Go to the Uncle," when someone needed advice or had to consult. His home was open to everyone. Jews always came to him for advice. He wold listen closely, contemplate, and often told people to return the next day so that he could give a concrete response or good advice.

He believed strongly in the mitzvah of doing good deeds, which he did with a free hand to anyone who turned to him. He either gave cash or he signed promissory notes, and in many cases he paid the fees for those notes.

Weintraub was a great philanthropist. He generously supported many organizations in the city and especially funds for Eretz Yisroel and Zionist causes. He owned a small forest outside the city where pioneer youth and children from the schools and Talmud Torahs would celebrate Lag b'Omer.

[Page 234]

That little bit of woods gave him great concerns: he paid taxes on it, and he had to hire a guard because the peasants from the surrounding villages would steal wood from the "Jewish forest." When people asked him why he held onto it, he answered, "So the children would have a place to go for Lag b'Omer."

Although R. Yitzchak Nachum Weintraub was a man of the old-fashioned observant and studious world, he had a strong inclination for the Haskalah and the requirements of the time. He read Hebrew books and newspapers, kept up with sports, and gave his children a modern education. He participated and supported all kinds of cultural activities and organizations in the city and therefore he aroused hostility in religious Chasidic circles.

His daily routines operated on a strict timetable. He awoke early, and, in both summer and winter, he went for a several kilometer walk outside the city. In the summer he went to the Weselka River to swim. In the winter he would do exercises in the snow. After breakfast he would do his regular weekday work for his business. Every day before lunch he would chop wood or do some other physical labor. Then he would study a lesson from the daily Talmud passage in the beis-medresh or in R. Yisroel Hill's little beis-medresh with a group of Jews, studious citizens with maskilik tendencies. In the evenings he would be busy with the needs of the community. He would go to meetings, to conferences, and to other gatherings, and if he had no meetings—he would do more study in the beis-medresh.

Yitzchak Nachum Weintraub kept diaries in which he wrote copiously. He wrote down the talks and lessons that he had delivered on various occasions. He wrote memoirs about events in the city, about the 1906 pogrom, about community activities, and about the activities of other organizations that he either led or participated in. He also wrote about his own life and the life of his family.

These diaries covered fifty years in the story of Jewish Siedlce, and the leading role in them was taken by he himself, R. Yitzchak Nachum Weintraub.

* * *

The first days of the war were for him quite tragic. At the first German air attack on the city on Thursday, September 7, his house was destroyed by a bomb, and buried under the ruins was his beloved daughter Freyda, the widow of Mordechai Meir Landau. She had lived with her father since her husband's death.

[Page 235]

The elderly R. Yitzchak Nachum spent long days, working alone, trying to clear the debris of his collapsed house until he could extract the body of his daughter, who had been killed.

At her funeral he said: "In the misfortune of my daughter, I see a punishment from heaven for my not having kept the vow that I made at the open grave of her husband, Mordechai Meir Landau, that I would take my family to Eretz Yisroel."

True to his habit of always serving as an advocate for his community in times of trouble, in October of 1939, during the first weeks of Nazi rule, he headed a delegation to the German in charge of the city asking him to order that Jews should not be removed from the lines that were forming at bakeries to obtain bread, since segments of the Polish population were doing so, with the assistance of the Germans. The delegation consisted of Shmerl Greenberg, Dr. Henrik Loebel, Eliezer Levin, Hershel Tenenbaum, and Leib Glicksberg. It was headed by Weintraub.

This elderly advocate later went several times to the German rulers of the city to intervene in various difficult matters concerning Jews, but it was not long before he realized that it was beyond his capability to fight against the Nazi sadists, so he withdrew and left this job to other, younger people.

This older man survived many tragic events in the prison-like ghetto. He often saw deaths. On that dark Shabbos of August 22, he was hidden in a cellar. Later he hid in the small ghetto together with his only surviving grandson, the young son of his beloved, the lawyer Yosef Landau.

People say that in the small ghetto he had no clothing or linen except what he was wearing. This fastidious old man often removed his clothing and underwear and washed them, then hung them out in the sun to dry.

On Yom Kippur he was seized while he was praying in secret with other older men. He was taken to the train station to load coal. There the German murderers beat him badly and covered him with coal dust. People also say that throughout the time of the Nazi regime, and even more in the last months when he was hiding in the small ghetto, he wrote a great deal and greatly troubled because he could not be sure that his writings would not remain in the hands of Jews, so that people would know how a community of Jews were killed as martyrs.

[Page 236]

At 80 years of age, this leader and advocate met the fate of going on the last journey of the last remnant of the Jewish community, of drinking from the cup of pain and sorrow to its dregs. He went through the hell of the small ghetto, of Gensze Barki, and of the wagons to the Treblinka gas chambers.

[Page 236]

F. Lawyer Landau

As a member of the Jewish Council, the lawyer Yosef Landau led the division for social aid. This was perhaps the only labor of the Jewish Council that appealed to the conscious and the idealistic character that he inherited from his father Mordechai Meir and from his grandfather, Yitzchak Nachum Weintraub—to help the poor, the suffering, the unfortunate. He devoted himself totally to this work, as people tell, doing as much as was possible in those conditions.

As a young lawyer, Landau was very popular with his Christian colleagues, both judges and lawyers. The judge Gala told L. Glicksberg that on the tragic Shabbos of August 22, several of his colleagues came to the gate of the ghetto and told him that they had prepared a hiding place for him. If he could get out, they would rescue him. Landau thanked them heartily and said, "Sadly, I cannot accept your offer of help. I must be there with my community." And he went with his community to Treblinka.

[Page 237]

G. Dr. Henryk Loebel

Born in Cracow in 1897 to intellectual, half-assimilated parents, who gave him a secular education: studied medicine at Cracow University, graduated as a gynecologist in Vienna, served as assistant to the famous Professor Rossner, published a great medical work on gynecology and often published scholarly medical works in a variety of Polish and German periodicals.

He married the daughter of the Zionist leader in Pszemiszl Meir Honikvaks and then drew close to the nationalistic Jewish world. Was active in different groups in Pszemiszl, especially in B'nai B'rith while practicing as a gynecologist.

In 1933, when the Jewish community in Siedlce sponsored a competition for director of the hospital, Dr. Loebel took the spot, presenting himself as a well-organized, generous doctor who acted as a friend to his patients.

He devoted his entire time and energy to the development of the hospital and did not take part in community activities or political life in the city, except as a military man (with many commendations) who created the association of soldiers.

* * *

In October, 1939, when the Germans ordered the formation of the Jewish Council, Dr. Loebel was fated, as a man of great energy and cultural qualifications regarding the greater European environment, to be the chair of the organization.

As people relate, in the course of his activities in this difficult and responsible position—between the hammer and the anvil—he showed great tact and consistency. His bearing was so full of Jewish and human dignity that it aroused sympathy for him among the persecuted Jewish masses.

While he was chair of the Jewish Council, he remained in his position as director of the hospital, to which he had devoted so much. He gave it his time, strength, and energy, so that he not only healed his suffering patients, but he also brought them security and hope.

[Page 238]

On that black Shabbos of August 22, when the hangmen ordered all Jews to the Umschlagplatz for the selection, Dr. Loebel came along with everyone else, although as director of the hospital he had the right to remain in the hospital building with the ailing, where the hangman Fabish had assured him he would remain unharmed.

When on that tragic Shabbos in the Umschlagplatz there were so many Jews who had been beaten and shot, the determined Dr. Loebel intervened with the German killers and received permission that people from the hospital could come to the aid of the unfortunates and of the many wounded. At that time many who were uninjured also found rescue in the hospital building.

That same Shabbos evening, when those chosen for the work detail were led into the small ghetto, Fabish ordered Dr. Loebel to leave his living quarters in the hospital and go to the small ghetto, to which Dr. Loebel proudly replied to the hangman: "I will never leave the hospital. I will share in the fate of my ailing sisters and brothers."

And he did share their fate.

Two day after the liquidation of the ghetto, the hospital, too, was liquidated.

After all the patients were shot in their beds, including the little children, while he was forced to stand by, Dr. Loebel and his wife were forced to stand against the wall in the hospital courtyard and they, along with their fellow workers, doctors, aides, and nurses, were shot.

In the last moment of his life, Dr. Loebel called out: "Death to the killers. The Jewish people will outlast you." He fell like a true soldier at his post.

[Page 239]

H. Hershel Tanenbaum

His reputation as secretary of the Jewish community organization, where so many people came day after to day to look after their interests, each with his own each with his own claims and complaints—some about tax payments, claiming their taxes were too high, some from organizations whose subsidies had not been increased, or because they had not been paid on time. This has to be taken care by the pompous donors with their particular party ambitions and personal caprices, according to which each one desires that only his orders should be followed, while the desires of the other doors are not worth a shred of tobacco…And so the duties of his position made him nervous, often destroyed his equanimity, so that he responded bitterly, in an upset way, so that people often realized that they were dealing with a furious Jew.

In his private life, Hershel Tanenbaum was a totally different person—friendly, intimate, a good companion, very sentimental. Over all, he was a warm-hearted mensch.

Often it seemed that people saw two men in him: one was an official who sat in the office and gave official answers, bitterly and angrily, and the other was at home, friendly to his guests, and in community or party groups he was friendly, good-natured, smiling.

He was a man with the split personality of a clerk in a Jewish organization who had no great pretensions in his life, no great aspirations, not for wealth, not for honor, and not for fame.

He outgrew that division when the great misfortune of the Nazi plague befell the community for which he had worked so long.

A bitter, tragic duty was his fate—he was called on to serve as the liaison between the Jewish Council and the Gestapo; to spend days and nights waiting outside their doors, getting from the wild sadists their crazy fantasies and orders that the Jewish Council had to carry out.

This contact with the Gestapo—in the very nest of the greatest impurity and bloodthirstiness, of robbery and murder required that every day he stick his head deep in the wolfish maw and withstand the greatest indignities and offenses, terrible physical and spiritual suffering and indignity.

[Page 240]

Tenenbaum had to furnish it all: the most fantastic food and drink, the most expensive clothing, shoes, linens, furs, jewelry, furniture, cookware, assessments, workers, dwellings, and anything else that their wild fantasies demanded.

Normally these orders for robbery ended with a warning—if they were not carried out, this or that number of Jews would be shot. Tenenbaum, trying to prevent such executions, would go around a beaten, defeated man to the beleaguered Jews in the ghetto and carry out the orders of the Gestapo thieves.

With the rebuke that the robbery was not conducted on time or that the things were of poor quality, the contemptible villains often beat Tenenbaum and abused him. They often forced him to eat the animal food that their dogs left behind.

Tzvi Livront recounts: In December of 1939, the Gestapo officer Karl gathered together in the square of Stari Rynek a hundred Jews and announced that they would be shot because the sum of 20,000 zlotys that the Gestapo had imposed on the Jewish Council had not been paid. Some people had alerted Hershel Tenenbaum, who told the murderer Karl: The Jews were not guilty. Only I am guilty for not getting the money together on time. Shoot me."—In this way he bared his heart. The German was so confused that he released the Jews, gave Tenenbaum a good beating, and extended the deadline for another eight days.

People tell of many instances when Tenenbaum risked his life to save Jews, often resulting in his being beaten and debased and putting his own life in jeopardy.

On the last day of the ghetto, early on August 22nd, Hershel Tenenbaum received his last order from the Gestapo. He brought chicken, wine, beer, and pastries for the executioners' lunch at the selection table. He received no more orders. He, his wife, and their two sons were sent with the rest of the community to Treblinka.

[Page 241]

25. Once There Were in Siedlce Three Jewish Cemeteries

Translated by Theodore Steinberg

It is an ancient custom among Jews on days of introspection and spirituality to go to the cemetery and have a discussion with those who have left us forever. On the anniversary of a death, on Tisha b'Av, on the High Holidays, and at times of spiritual feeling such a need would be aroused, so all the more, after wandering for several days through the ruins of our ruined home, we felt a call to visit the graves of our fathers. If it was not actually possible to go to those whose burial place is unknown—still, we will visit those who merited to die before the Hitler deluge, to be buried in a Jewish cemetery and to have an address.

After a painful, sleepless night—like all our nights in this ruined home—full of bitter and empty dreams, early in the morning, when the sun was shining (in stark contrast to our moods and feelings), shining shamelessly as if nothing at all had happened, we went off to the cemetery.

We had already been at the oldest cemetery, near the shul courtyard, when we went looking for traces of the great community that had been sent to the gas chambers of Treblinka. We knew that the cemetery with its old surrounding walls was no more. In its place was an open passageway, a no place, where the surrounding neighbors dug the white sand. So we went to the second one.

Like the first cemetery near the shul yard, the location of the second was also once, a hundred years ago, outside the city, and similarly, over time the city grew around it, so that the cemetery was now in the midst of the city. As old people tell us—having heard it from their parents—it must be hundred years since this cemetery was closed and had ceased to receive the dead.

Because the surrounding land had belonged to the community, several community buildings were built in the area, for example: the superb Jewish hospital, which was for many years the pride of the Jewish Siedlce, where hundreds of ill and suffering people found healing and a warm home. There was also a building known as the "Community Shop," which extended from Pienkne Street, through the market place and to the hospital.

[Page 242]

In addition, the city directors had built around the old cemetery shops and cabins and had put a market hall in the large plaza between the cemetery and the prison and designated it as a market place. Thus, amid the ongoing tumult and confusion of shops and market business, amid the stalls of merchants and the wagons of peasants with sacks of potatoes, carrots, and fowl, the older generations of Siedlce's Jews continued in their eternal sleep.

Like the first cemetery by the shul yard, the second cemetery cultivated those plants specific to cemeteries. The graves were sinking, the monuments were half sunk in the soft earth of the cemetery, A person had to make a real effort in order to read the old inscriptions—the names, the praises, and titles that had been ascribed to the dead on their tombstones.

The enemy's fires, that had devoured almost all of Pienkne Street—along with its Jewish inhabitants—did not affect the community buildings or the hospital. It left them alone. They stand there with their shops and workshops just as before. But instead of their former Jewish residents, they are owned by new strangers, who are full of gratitude to the events that provided them with such an unexpected inheritance. And on the hospital building, where there was once an inscription reading "Hospital," there is now a sign reading in Polish "Hospital for Infectious Diseases."

Today is a market day, as shadows float past me—I and two other grave-seekers—among the stands with merchandise and farmers' wagons, we are the only three Jews in the great Siedlce market and we feel the mocking looks of the fresh-baked merchants and the half-witted smirking eyes of the village farmers and their wives.

At the corner of Szenkewicz and Szwientojanski we encounter a newly erected gate (before the destruction it was not there). We slink around unnoticed, like thieves, looking all around, seeking signs of the former cemetery and finding none. But built near the gate is a barracks, suitable for an office with an area for a guard. By the fence there are large, long shops where people work with cement and concrete roofing, bricks and pipes.

[Page 243]

Over the whole expanse of the former cemetery are huge stacks of lumber, bricks, chalk, tar, and other building materials. People stand around these stacks, carrying, laying down, measuring, counting, weighing. A carnival! The earth is paved with the tombstones that used to stand at the head of the now desecrated graves. They are spread throughout the roadways over the whole area of the cemetery, and cars and trucks loaded with merchandise and building materials travel over them. Other monuments are scattered among the stacks of bricks and boards underfoot in the dust.

Amid the banging of thrown boards, bricks, and iron, and in the tumult and chaos on the other side of the fence from the market, it still seems that one could hear the silent murmuring that came from the dishonored, desecrated graves, from the dishonored and desecrated tombstones with their sacred letters, trodden upon by human feet and the hard hooves of horses.

While I was steeped in reading the worn down inscriptions on the tombstones that lay under my feet and those that were incorporated in the cobblestones so that I could learn from them the secret of our destruction, my thoughts were interrupted by a question:

"What is the gentleman looking for?"

"I'm looking for the old Jewish cemetery that was here," I answered brusquely.

"There is no more Jewish cemetery. Now there are only the warehouses of the building materials cooperative," the gentile tells me with a face that reflects his satisfaction.

That answer tells us that no one wants such seekers there. Followed by unfriendly looks, we leave that desecrated holy place.

* * *

We proceed to the last cemetery, to that which was the most "lively" of all the cemeteries in the city.

The many tombstones that we find along the way, incorporated in the cobblestones and in the sidewalk, indicate that there, too, the hands of the murderers reached out, and our hearts tremble with painful anticipation, as we think: Will we be able to find the graves of our near ones?

This did not last long until before our eyes stood the whole terrible picture in its grossness:

[Page 244]

The cement wall around the cemetery for the length of Szkolner Street lies broken apart, smashed, thrown into piles of debris. From there one perceives a sea of smashed and crumpled pieces of white and gray marble sticking out among the high, wild grasses. Far and wide, the whole extent of the cemetery looks like a jungle of broken stone. With bloodshot eyes and pounding hearts we begin to move in that sea of fragments and wild growth. Soon we find ourselves in white sand from dug-up graves. We cannot tell if this is the work of grave robbers who sought the golden teeth of the dead or whether it was done just for its own sake: when there were no more living Jews to torment, did they torment the dead Jews in their graves? Who can tell? There is no one to ask.

We are in the area where Siedlce's rabbis and rabbinical authorities of many generation rested in their "ohalim" [translator's note: this Hebrew word for "tent" is used for the structures that were built over the graves of important people]. As people used to visit this place, so are we filled with a feeling of the greatest respect and honor for the graves where the bones of famous Torah scholars in Siedlce used to lie: Rabbi R. Mordechai'le z"l, the famous lover of Israel, who was famous for his self-sacrifice for Jews at the time of the 1906 pogrom; Rabbi R. Shimon Dov Analik, z"l; the last rabbi in Siedlce, the great scholar and fine man R. Yehuda Leib Ginsburg, z"l. There, in their "ohalim," rested the famous Polish rabbis: the Biale Rabbi, R. Hershele,z"l; the Szelekhower Rabbi, R. Gershon, z"l; the Partszewer Rabbi, R. Noson Dovid, z"l. Thousands of Chasidim would come here to pour out their hearts and cover the graves with a flood of written messages. Of those "ohalim" and tombstones no trace remains. One cannot even recognize their graves, which lie, like all the others, desecrated, covered with rocks and wild plants.

We difficulty we move on and find among the fragments of tombstones a piece of broken marble with the inscription, "leftist Poalei-Tzion in Siedlce." This encouraged to seek further in the area and we found another piece wth the inscription "Yosef." We sought further and found another fragment inscribed "Sluszn." From a large number of such pieces, we reassembled a tombstone that the Leftist Poalei-Tzion organization had set up over the grave of its leader, the leader of the Jewish workers movement in Siedlce, Yosef Sluszny.

[Page 245]

In a similar fashion we reassembled fragments of other broken up tombstones, where we read the name Avraham Greenspan (who was shot in 1920 by the Polish army) and other names that we knew.

In that great sea of fragments we also found several whole tombstones. We have no idea how they escaped destruction by the vandals. They were torn out of their spots and trampled on among the detritus and sand of the desecrated graves. We read there several names that we recognized: R. Avigdor Ridel, z"l; R. David Rubinstein, z"l,\; editor of the "Siedlce Vokhenblat" Asher Livrant, z"l; and other names that we recognized and some we did not.

We approached the cement wall of the cemetery on the eastern side, where we gazed at fresh leaves that marked the magnitude of our tragedy: this section of the cemetery that had been fertilized recently with blood. It grew with thick grasses and was used by the neighbors as pasture for their animals. Who would stop them? A young shepherd lather on the desecrated graves warming himself in the rays of the springtime sun, whistling a carefree tune while his animals grazed.

Not far from there, in the midst of a green field, there was a white area. We went over and stood before a place where recently, driven by wild hatred and evil, people had brought the bodies of our dead. And who knows: perhaps also our living sisters and brothers? The wind had not yet driven away their ashes. So there lay the white ash, piled up as a memorial to our burned up lives, mixed together with burnt pieces of bone, human bones, and pieces of burned shoes and unburned coal.

We stood as if turned to stone, made dumb by this accursed auto-da-fe spot, and we thought…we thought…We were joined together in our current thoughts with the thoughts of our nearest and dearest about God, people, and the world, about the desecrated and destroyed thousand-year ideals, about the eternal ethical values, at the moment of their greatest torment.

[Page 246]

And…not far away there was a huge shaggy dog, and soon there were many, a whole host of dogs in the grass, sniffing, seeking things in their doggish fashion. We went in their direction and came across a large open pit with a pile of bones from different body parts of different sizes: skulls, hands, feet; bones from children, even very small children, all strewn around at random, gnawed on and dragged around by the dogs who were frightened and retreated somewhat at our approach, regarding us with their fierce eyes, outraged that we were disturbing them. But they did not run away. They waited for us to leave so that they could complete their canine meal…

While we gazed at the dried up bones that were strewn about in the small valley of the desecrated cemetery, each pile of bones reminded us of our poor forefathers, who after the destruction of the First Temple filled the valleys of Babylon, and we thought: one needed to be winged with such spiritual bravery and prophetic faith as was the prophet Ezekiel in order to believe that these dry bones that we see before us will be revived at the resurrection of the dead.

We went from one slaughter place to another and found ourselves by that section of the wall that had served as the execution wall for hundreds and perhaps thousands of our unfortunate fellow citizens. The earth there was freshly dug, full of mounds and pits, all of it soft. When one talk a step, the earth quivered, just as those lives that were cut short quivered when they were thrown into the graves that they had had to dig themselves. Through the thin layer of earth that barely covered them we could see the contours of their tortured bodies that had gone through the seven levels of Gehenna. They told us so much, those grave contours, so much…

And even more than the ground, the dumb wall spoke, the wall that stood athwart the tortured martyrs, telling the magnitude of our disaster—innumerable bullets are contained in that unhappy wall, bullets that jumped from the pierced bodies of our tortured sisters and brothers. They are buried deeply, those lead bullets, and sparkle in the sun like living, burning letters on a huge, long tombstone. Other bullets only grazed the wall, making small pits and then falling into the cemetery grass.

[Page 247]

And then we read other inscriptions on the large, dumb wall that is a monument to the executions—these are the inscriptions that were put there by the blood of the holy and pure who were killed near the wall.

They tell the survivors:

Several days after the liquidation of the large ghetto, when the Jews of Siedlce had been transported to Treblinka, in the small ghetto, where the small remnant of the Siedlce community were crowded together—a band of the murderers came and took thirty women and girls who were there to the emptied out ghetto to sort and pack up the Jews' abandoned and stolen goods for the killers. While doing this work, the women would pick up a piece of clothing or a jacket or a bit of linen to share with those in need in the small ghetto. The chief executioner of Siedlce's Jews, Fabish, discovered this. After detaining the "criminals," he ordered the women to be killed. His murderous aides brought the unfortunate women to the shul building that served as a prison in the ghetto. Only one of the women—Esther Spector—through a miracle escaped. The other twenty-nine women, with their hands bound behind their backs, were taken to the cemetery, were forced to dig graves, and there, next to the execution wall, were first beaten and tortured, and then shot.

These are their names:

Rusza Landau, Sarah Jablkowicz, Chana Piekorsz, the two Stolawa sisters, Sarah Wakstein, Ferster-Vayman, Sarah Gelbfish, Yenta Lederhendler, Golda Goldring, Chava Felzenstein, Felzenstein-Miadownik, Chana Kromarsz, Gitl Kromarsz, Bronstein, Sarah Grinvald, Suchadolski (wife of Nachman), Bracha Radushinska-Neiman, Rochel Zuckerman, Rivkah Felzenstein, Rochel Kahn, Sarah Kleinlerer, Rochel Einemer, Toiva Epelblat, Esther Kishelinska, Niunia Felzenstein, Perl Ribak, Karnicka.

Their names are not inscribed on a memorial tablet on the execution wall. No one comes to shed a tear at their poor neglected gravesites. No one plants a tree or says kaddish. Only their black blood that has seeped into the cracks of the execution wall and the lead bullets that tore away their young lives—keep watch over their neglected graves, crying out from the unlucky wall: "Awake and call out for vengeance!"

[Page 248]

* * *

The only living witness who was present at this horrible act, the city councilman Gluchowski, had a heart attack and died several days later

* * *

As we wandered further around the desecrated cemetery, we encountered the first communal grave of several score of martyrs who had been thrown in different corners of the area—a number of Jews who had not long before emerged from the underground bunkers had gathered them up and brought them to the Jewish cemetery.

Not far from that spot we encountered a nest of ants. We stood there and watched enviously as the small, active creatures went around so freely, crawling here and there through the narrow tunnels in their underground quarters. Happy creatures! No fierce dogs and wild cannibals go after their poor lives, as they had gone after ours.

We arrive at that side of the cemetery that is near the neighboring Christian cemetery. Here, too, we look enviously at the symmetrically laid-out rows, at the monuments with crosses that stand by the graves, bedecked with greens and flowers. We see that each person who rests there left behind a heart that longs for him, a gentle hand that cares for his memory. Old women dressed in black kneel at the graves and whisper silent prayers for the soul of the person resting there. There are two young women at another grave, one planting flowers and the other with a watering can, and so on and so on…

We turn back to the rind cemetery, to the broken up monuments, to the desecrated and fouled graves, to the bones that are scattered around, to the mounds of ash that remains from our martyrs, to the blood that has soaked into the cemetery walls. And from our hearts arises a curse, a desolate curse on the evil world with its people, with its nature, and especially for the Earth, which has not place either for our living or for our dead.

Yontl Goldman with survivors bring exhumed Jews to the Jewish cemetery

Survivors at the memorial stone for the bones and skeletons that were brought for burial
Survivors say Kaddish

Monish Ridel delivers a eulogy

Simcha Lev commemorates the dead

[Page 249]

Our last, departing glance falls on the ruined and desecrated cemetery and I see how near a large pile of bricks and stones workers are busy—hired by the Jewish Committee—restoring the collapsed wall; in another spot, people are busy cleaning off other parts of the ruin—filling in the overturned graves, setting up collapsed tombstones, gathering the scattered bones. Resentment arises against the committee and its workers. I want to yell, "Stop! Don't erase our misfortune with your little good deeds! Restore nothing! The ruined cemetery, just as it is, is the most appropriate memorial of the destroyed, demolished community; we must preserve for coming generations this broken memorial—the work of Christian civilization and ethics. These dry, white human bones that fill the valleys along with the overturned, open graves should always remain thus, and like open mouths they should proclaim the destruction until the end of generations!"

* * *

Broken, with heavy hearts, we leave the destruction and the desecrated cemetery. I pull up some grass and throw it behind me, thus saying: "So should those be plucked up who plucked up my people!"

A spring breeze blew lightly and caressed the trees that stood by the entrance to the destroyed cemetery—the only witnesses who saw our destruction and shame. From the soft rustling of their leaves comes to us tune of the orphan, saying "Yisgadal v'yiskadash shemei raba…"

From Stories about the Shoah in Siedlce
> A Christian guarding the cemetery
> Showed me the place of sacrifice.
> His eyes flowed with tears like water
> At the memory of the awful robbery and massacre.

There I found a young woman
Sobbing on her parents' grave,
A bitter eulogy carried on high—
Her parents were strangled here before her eyes.

The Christian Told Me

Young boys and girls, infants and children,
Wise men and gentle women
Were taken together to the cemetery,
Tortured and killed in strange ways.

A forsaken and bitter woman,
Her delicate daughter hugs her children.
A Nazi dragged her to the slime
And with his stick he poked her eyes.

The girl groaned and called out,
"Mother, Mother, sweet Mother."
The Nazi went by and stopped her mouth.
The girl died, groaning, strangled.

I will not cover things over.
In most things evil will not cease.
But who knows the answer to the question
Why infants were killed who were innocent of
sin?

Hidden are the ways of God. The answer to all
the questions
To teach them, to make them understand, it is
impossible to ascend to the heights.

Monish Ridel

[Page 250]

Dates of the Jewish Martyrology in Siedlce

Translated by Theodore Steinberg

September 7, 1939 (23 Elul 5699), early Thursday: The Germans began their air attack on Siedlce, particularly on the Jewish streets. The bombardment lasted, with short pauses, until Monday (9/11/39) at night. During those days, about 2,000 people were killed, mostly Jews.

September 9 1939: Wanting to escape from the openness of the barbaric air attack, almost all of the civilian population left the city, abandoning their dwellings and all their possessions. The city is in flames. During the confusion, groups of peasants from surrounding villages come to steal from Jewish homes and businesses.

September 11, 1939 (27 Elul 5699), Monday nighty, the German hordes arrive in Siedlce.

September 14, 1939 (first day of Rosh Hashanah). A group of Germans surrounded the shul where a small group of Jews were praying. The Germans entered and beat them murderously, ripping off their taleisim. They shot at those who jumped out of the windows. Yosef Rubin was shot. Throughout the night, bands of Germans stole from Jewish homes and businesses. They seized people in their homes and forced them to go to to the concentration camp in Wengrow.

September 18, 1939: The Germans closed off the city, made a raid on all the streets and houses. All men aged 14 and over are taken and put in prison. They are held there for two days.

September 20, 1939: All the men who are being held, Jews and some Christians, numbering about ten thousand, are force-marched, with bare heads, to the concentration camp in Wengrow.

[Page 251]

October, 1939: A. The Germans order the creation of a Jewish Council of 25 people. B. The Jewish Council that has been formed is ordered by the Germans to pay an indemnity of 10,000 zlotys.

End of October, 1939: A group of Germans break into the shul and the beis-medresh, throw the Torah scrolls from the Holy Ark, rip them up and stomp on them.

December, 1939: The Jewish Council receives an order to pay another 20,000 zlotys.

December 24, 1939: In the middle of the night, the Germans set fire to the shul and the beis-medresh. Many Jews suffer burns and wounds. One Jew is burned to death.

November, 1940: The Jewish Council receives and other for payment, this time for 100,000 zlotys.

June 12 (first day of Shavuos): A band of fired-up Germans conducts a raid against Jews in the city. The iron merchant Binyamin Hertz is shot.

March, 1941: The Jewish Council receives yet another demand for payment of 100,000 zlotys.

March 23, 1941: The German army in Siedlce carries out a pogrom against the Jews that lasts for three days. They robbed and plundered. Six Jews are shot and hundreds are wounded. This was the result of a provocation: in Stari Rynek, people heard a shot, and the Germans claimed that it was a Jew who shot.

End of June, 1941: With the German invasion of Russia, the repression of the Jews increases. They are thrown out of their homes in large numbers.

Page 252]

August 1, 1941 (the eve of Tisha b'Av 5701): An order is issued to confine the Jews of Siedlce in a ghetto.

October 1, 1941 (Yom Kippur 5702): The large ghetto is enclosed, comprising these streets, beginning on the right: Kochanowskiena (Shpitalna), Stari Rynek, Berek Joselewicz, Mala, First of May, up to Sandowa. On the left: Pusta, Aslonowicz (Prospektowa), Targowa (Yatkowa), Browana, Okopowa, Blonia. After this enclosure, epidemic illnesses increase. The mortality rate goes up.

December, 1941: The Germans order the Jewish Council to turn over all furs and fur products that belong to Jews.

January, 1942: The Germans impose an indemnity on the Jews of 100,000 zlotys per month.

March 3, 1942 (Purim, 5702): The Germans seize ten Jews, take them to Stak-Lacki (a village near Siedlce). According to an order from the head of the governing council at the labor office, they are shot because they declined to work. The Jewish Council is forced to issue a declaration that the Germans were correct and that their judgment to kill the ten Jews—was justified.

June, 1942: The Germans requisition from the Jewish Council various workmen along with their machinery and tools. The selected Jews are sent away somewhere. Later on, people learned that they were sent to their deaths in Maidanek.

July, 1942: The Germans arrest thirteen Jews on the pretext that they refused to go to work. For several days the Jews were tortured. They were returned to the ghetto and, as they went through the ghetto gate, they were shot.

[Page 253]

August 22, 1942 (Shabbos, 9 Elul 5702)—Liquidation of the large ghetto. In the middle of the night, the large ghetto was surrounded by Germans, Ukrainians, and Polish police. Early in the morning, all Jews were driven out to the old cemetery. That day, the selection was conducted. The so-called "small ghetto" was created in the triangle formed by Kokolow, Aslanowicz,, and Targowa Streets.

August 23, 1942: Victims are taken to the train station.

August 24, 1942: Loading of victims onto the train cars begins. This continued into the next day, August 25 (Monday and Tuesday), until all the Jews had been taken to Treblinka.

August 24, 1942: Liquidation of the ghetto hospital. A group of Germans and Ukrainians, under the leadership of the city commander Fabish, laid siege to the ghetto hospital on Dluga Street, shot all the patients (about a hundred people) in their beds, as well as ten or so newborn infants. The doctors, aides, nurses, and all the hospital personnel are taken to the courtyard—and shot.

August 26, 1942 (13 Elul 5702): The Germans took thirty young women for work in the emptied ghetto: to sort and pack the goods that were stolen from Jews. In the evening, when the work was done, the women were taken to the cemetery where they were lined up against a wall—and shot.

November 25, 1942 (16 Kislev 5703): Liquidation of the small ghetto. The remaining Jews are taken to Gensze-Barki (about 2,000 souls).

November 28, 1942: In the middle of the night, Gensze-Barki is surrounded by a chain of Germans, Ukrainians, and Polish police.

[Page 254]

November 30, 1942 (21 Kislev 5703): The last 3,000 Jews of Sideline and vicinity are taken from Gensze-Barki to the train station, where they are packed into wagons and transported to Treblinka.

January 1, 1943: The new year finds Siedlce—free of Jews.

[Pages 255-260]

Name Index from
"On the ruins of my home; the destruction of Siedlce"

Transliterated by Yocheved Klausner

Please note: Page numbers refer to original book pages

Surname	First name(s)	Page(s)
א Alef		
ABARBANEL	Shlomo Shmuel	27, 57, 115, 124, 138
ADLER	Heniek	34, 162
EICHENSTEIN	Shlomo, rabbi	172
EIBESCHITZ	Yonatan	66
EISENBERG	Hershel	67, 71, 128, 135
EISENBERG	Y. Ch.	13
EISENBERG	Chana'le	99
EISENSTADT-LEVIN		76
EISENSTADT	Moshe Abe	85, 227, 233

בּ Bet

ד **Dalet**

ה **Hey**

HALBERSTAT	Motl	233
HALBERSTAT-YOM-TOV	Sara	75
HALBER	Avraham	98, 164, 186
HALBER	Itche	186
HALBER	Melech	186
HALBER	Hanke	164
HANDLASH	Yakov	151
HONIKWACHS	Meir	237
HUBERMAN	Motl	163
HUBERMAN	Bunim	66
HELLER	Rachel	228
HERZ	Binyamin	179
HERSHELE	rabbi	244

ו Vav

WOLAGOVITCH	Meir	169
WASSERBURG	Yehuda	135
WASSERZUG	Avraham	48
WASSERZUG	Yehuda	135
WASSERSTEIN	Ben-Zion	151
WACKSTEIN	Sara	247
WARSCHAWSKI	Asher	193
WEINTRAUB	Yitzhak Nachum	27, 65, 71, 85, 115, 124, 137, 219, 227, 232
WEINTRAUB	Minie	218
WEINAPEL	Avraham	13, 22, 89
WEINSTEIN	Leibush	23
WEINGARTEN		84
WEISSBERG	Getzl	199
WUNDERBAUM	Yidl	154
WUNDERBAUM	Yosef	212
WUNDERBAUM	Berl	154
WILK	Yakov	162

TENNENBAUM	Yakov	13, 76, 226
TENNENBAUM	Chaia	13
TENNENBAUM	Rozhe	226
TENNENBAUM	Hershl	67, 71, 179, 235, 239
TENNENBAUM	Yudel	227
TENNENBAUM-YOM-TOV	Ida	128
TUCHMINTZ	Dvora	165, 211
TUCHKLAPPER	Wolf	218, 227, 229
TEMKIN	Tzeshe	76
TEMKIN	Moshe	219, 232
TEMPELDIENER	Shmilke	162
TCHARNOBRODE	Berl	13, 76, 226
TCHARNOBRODE	Menashe	13, 65
TCHARNOBRODE	Hersh Yosef	85
TCHACH	Pintche	32
TCHIBUTZKA	Dintche	99
TCHIBUTZKI	Berl	66

׳

Yod

YABLON	Chaim Shlomo	53
YABLON	Israel	66
YABLON	Lila	99
YABLON	Salek	99
YABLON	Bronke	99
YABLON	Feigele	99
YABELKOVITCH	Yosef	177
YABELKOVITCH	Sara	247
YABKOVSKI	Hershl	151
YOM-TOV	Yakov	13
YOM-TOV	Eliezer Lipe, rabbi	53
YOM-TOV	Berish	53, 174
YOM-TOV	Israel'tche	43

LEVIN	Yakov	72
LEVIN-ADLER	Fele	193
LEVIN	Eliezer	235
LEVIN	Yoel	66
LAVIN	Notke	162, 164, 193
LEVITA	Shmuel	49
LOEWENSTEIN	Ester	13

מ Mem

MALIN	Nechemia	227, 229
MANDELMAN	Moshe	13
MANDELBAUM	Leib	51, 139
MANDELZWEIG	Leibl	44
MONTZIARSH	Gedalia	199
MORGENSTERN	David	227
MARECHBEIN		84
MILLER		162
MINTZ	Berl	218
MORDCHE'LE	[Mordechai], rabbi	244

נ Nun

NADWORNE	Avraham	189
NEIGOLDBERG	Naftali	80, 83
NEIYEDZHWIEDZH		218
NATAN	David, rabbi	244

ס Samech

SODOWNIK	Yosef	135
SARNOTZKI	Yankel [Yakov]	65
SICHODOLSKI		247
SUKENNIK		10
STOLOWE		247
SLUSCHNE	Avraham	13, 90

צ Tzadik

ק Kof

ר **Resh**

[Page 261]

Street Map

Translated by Theodore Steinberg

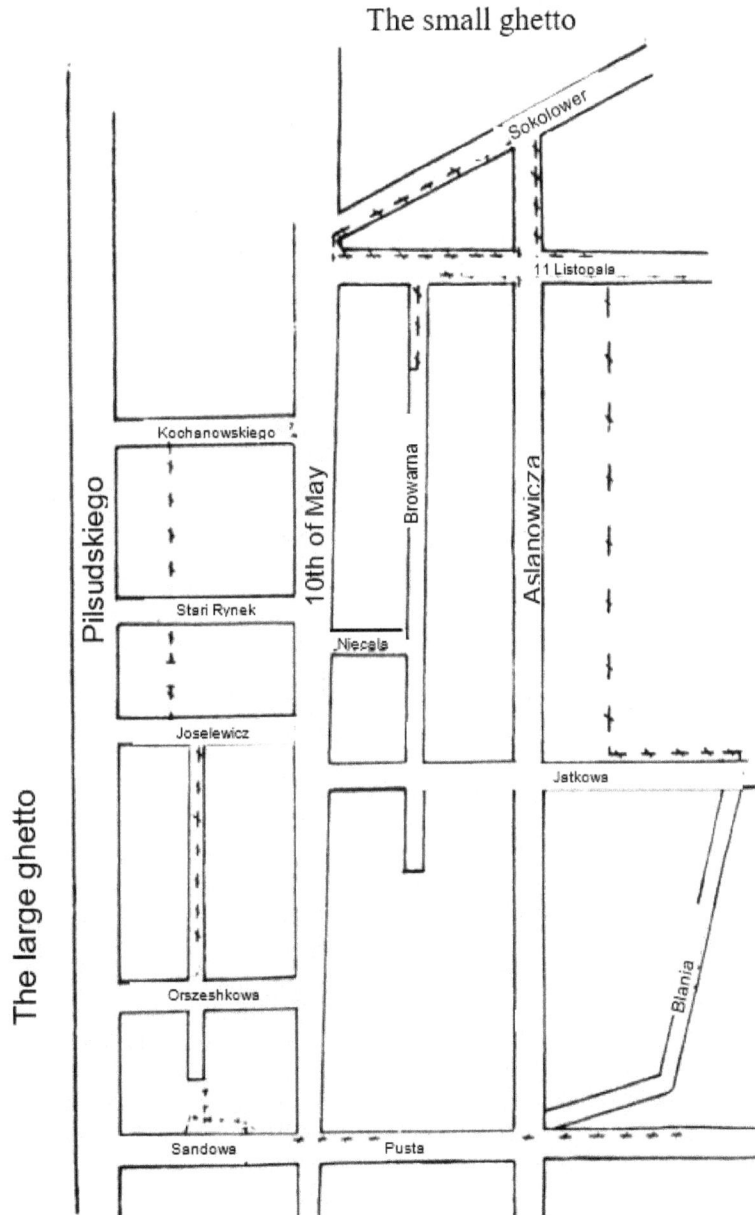

The small ghetto

Sokolower

11 Listopala

Kochanowskiego

Pilsudskiego

10th of May

Browarna

Aslanowicza

Stari Rynek

Niecala

Joselewicz

Jatkowa

The large ghetto

Orszeshkowa

Blania

Sandowa

Pusta

Translator's Note: I tried checking spellings against a modern map, but I found two obstacles: one is that some of the streets seem to have disappeared, and the other is that some of the names have been changed.

NAME INDEX

This is the Name Index for the English Translation

H

I

J

K

www.ingramcontent.com/pod-product-compliance
Lightning Source LLC
Chambersburg PA
CBHW050413110426
42812CB00006BA/1879